BENEFITS MANAGEMENT

BENEFITS MANAGEMENT

HOW TO INCREASE THE BUSINESS VALUE

OF YOUR IT PROJECTS

SECOND EDITION

By John Ward and Elizabeth Daniel

A John Wiley & Sons, Ltd., Publication

Library of Congress Cataloging-in-Publication Data
Ward, John, 1947–
    Benefits management : how to increase the business value of your IT projects /
by John Ward and Elizabeth Daniel. – 2nd ed.
        p. cm.
    Rev. ed. of: Benefits management : delivering value from IS & IT investments. c2006.
    Includes bibliographical references and index.
    ISBN 978-1-119-99326-1 (cloth : alk. paper)   1. Information technology–
Management.   2. Information storage and retrieval systems–Business.   I. Daniel, Elizabeth,
1962–   II. Title.
    HD30.2.W368 2012
    658.4'038011–dc23

                                            2012022586

A catalogue record for this book is available from the British Library.

ISBN 978-1-119-99326-1 (hbk) ISBN 978-1-118-38158-8(ebk)
ISBN 978-1-118-38160-1 (ebk) ISBN 978-1-118-38159-5(ebk)

Set in 11/13 pt New Baskerville by Toppan Best-set Premedia Limited
Printed in Great Britain by TJ International Ltd, Padstow, Cornwall, UK

Contents

About the authors

John Ward is Emeritus Professor at Cranfield University, School of Management. He was previously Professor of Strategic Information Systems and Director of the Information Systems Research Centre. Prior to joining Cranfield, he worked in industry for 15 years and continues to be a consultant to a number of major organizations. As well as publishing many papers and articles, he is co-author of the book *Strategic Planning for Information Systems*. He is a Fellow of the Chartered Institute of Management Accountants and has served two terms as President of the UK Academy for Information Systems.

Elizabeth Daniel is Professor of Information Management and Associate Dean Research and Scholarship at the Open University Business School (OUBS). Prior to joining OUBS in 2005, she worked in the IS Research Centre at Cranfield School of Management. Elizabeth's research has addressed a number of areas including benefits management and IS in marketing and supply chains. Recent work has included studies of home-based online businesses and the uses of consumer and employee data. She has published many papers in leading academic journals and a number of management reports.

Preface

Since the first edition of this book was published in 2006, interest in benefits management has grown, as demonstrated by the number of other publications on the subject and the increased adoption of benefits management approaches by organizations in public and private sectors in a number of countries. In the last six years some professonal bodies have also established benefits management Special Interest Groups.

The difficult financial situation since 2008 has also caused organizations to evaluate their projects more carefully to ensure that they produce worthwhile benefits. This applies to both IS/IT projects and other business change projects and programmes, and the benefits management approach is now being used effectively on non-IS/IT projects in many organizations.

However, our research studies since 2006 have identified that only about 30% of IS/IT projects are completely successful. But what they have also shown is that organizations which have management processes and practices closely aligned with the activities involved with the benefits management process described in this book are more successful than the others. Those studies also show that the issues affecting success are not changing over time: both poor investment decision making and ineffective implementation are still commonplace. It seems that, in many organizations, there is still a limited understanding of the nature of the benefits that can be achieved from IS/IT projects, what needs to be done to deliver them and the key role business managers play in the identification and realization of the benefits.

This book describes a proven process, frameworks and practical tools and techniques that organizations can and do employ to improve the realization of business value from their projects. The single most important tenet of the approach is the dependency of business benefits, not only on the implementation of IS and IT, but also on changing organizational processes and relationships and the roles and working practices of people inside and, in some cases, outside the organization. This inherent interdependency of *benefits* realization and change *management* is the reason why we refer to the approach as *benefits management*.

The process and the underlying tools and frameworks presented in this book are derived from extensive research undertaken by the Information Systems Research Centre (ISRC) at Cranfield School of Management over the last 20 years. In that period, the tools and frameworks have been continually developed and refined, based on their use in many organizations. The key elements of the benefits management approach have been adopted by several hundred organizations worldwide. The widespread application has also provided us with significant real-world insights into the use of the approach, much of which is captured in this book. Our further research, carried out in the last five years, also confirms that adopting a benefits-driven approach to managing IS/IT and other projects increases the business value that can be realized. The findings and management implications from those international studies are included in this edition.

Structure of the book

In order to help the reader navigate the book, its structure is illustrated in Figure 0.1. This shows how we consider activities needed to effectively manage benefits at two levels: the organizational level and the level of the individual project.

Chapter 1 considers the issues and challenges organizations have to address if they are to select the most appropriate projects and then manage them successfully. The problems and limitations of current project management approaches and the effects they have on the levels of success are discussed. That evidence also suggests that existing methods are insufficient to ensure that the benefits which could be achieved from IS/IT projects are adequately understood or managed effectively.

To be able to identify and manage the benefits, organizations need a clear understanding of the strategic rationale or business reasons for IS and IT investments and the context in which the benefits have to be realized. Chapter 2, therefore, presents tools, frameworks and ways of

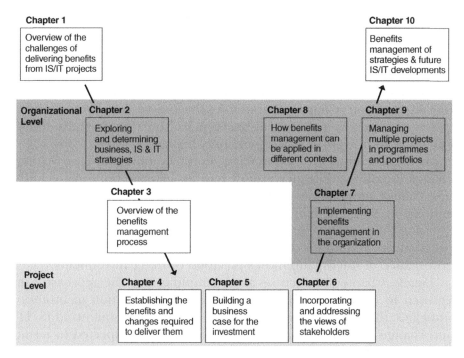

Figure 0.1: Structure of the book

thinking that are useful in exploring and determining business, IS and IT strategies.

Chapter 3 discusses how benefits management both differs from, but also complements, other proven ways of managing IS/IT projects. The chapter then presents an overview of the whole benefits management process, from initiation, through planning and implementation to final review.

Chapters 4, 5 and 6 consider use of the process at the level of individual projects. The tools and frameworks that underpin the approach are presented and their use discussed and exemplified, including an extended example of their use in a major enterprise-wide IS/IT project in a food processing company. This example is begun in Chapter 4 and is built on in the subsequent two chapters, such that a complete benefits plan is developed and presented.

Chapter 7 considers how organizations can introduce the benefits management approach, the practicalities of adopting the process, tools and frameworks and how they can be used in conjunction with other established investment and project management methodologies and best practices. It also reviews the factors that make some organizations more successful than others in delivering benefits in terms of a benefits management maturity model, developed from our recent research.

A premise of the benefits management approach is that the nature of the benefits that can be realized depends on the specific context of the organization. Chapter 8 considers the use of the approach in a variety of contexts, including distinct types of organization and different application types that are commonly being deployed.

As organizations are undertaking more complex and far-reaching change initiatives, they increasingly have to manage both major business change programmes that are often, at least in part, enabled by IT and also a range of individual IS/IT and other projects. Chapter 9 discusses the use of the benefits management approach in large change programmes and how it can be used to improve the management and governance of the organization's portfolio of IS/IT investments.

Finally, Chapter 10 discusses and exemplifies how the approach can be used to help in the formulation and implementation of business strategies, thereby providing closer links between investments in IS/IT and change programmes and the benefits that are expected to result from the business strategy. It also considers recent and expected future developments in IS and IT and how the benefits management approach can help with the new challenges these present.

Chapter 1

The challenges of IS/IT projects

Information systems and technology (IS/IT) are now essential components of the majority of businesses, allowing them to achieve greater efficiency of operations, increased agility in responding to changing market demands and the ability to develop innovative products and services. Equally, almost all public sector organizations could not deliver their services effectively and economically without the extensive use of IS/IT or ICT, as it is generally called in the public sector. However, despite the consensus about the strategic importance of IS and IT and the considerable investments that organizations continue to make in their purchase and implementation, the realization of benefits remains challenging. Our own research discussed in Chapter 5 (Ward and Daniel, 2008) has found that, in the majority of organizations we surveyed (57%), less than half of the projects they undertook delivered the expected benefits. This is consistent with earlier studies that show the majority of IS/IT projects are judged to be unsuccessful in terms of the benefits achieved.

> 'Companies currently spend about 5% of their revenues on IT. While there is a large variation in that number, there is an even greater variance in the benefit that companies get out of their IT.'
> *Upton and Staats (2008)*

We would suggest that the bald statistics hide a number of more subtle issues:

- Organizations are implementing more complex and sophisticated information systems and other IT applications, which require increasing levels of managerial and employee skill to deliver and use effectively.

- Expectations created by the IT industry are not realistic in terms of proven benefits or the time it takes to realize them. Despite this, many senior executives tend to believe the promises of instant success they read about in business magazines or hear being promoted by suppliers and consultants.
- The applications are often enterprise-wide and impact more people inside the organization and also relationships with external trading partners and customers. One organization cannot prescribe how others will conduct their business, and achieving benefits relies on the active cooperation of a wide range of stakeholders.
- The types of benefit that IS/IT can deliver are increasingly diverse and less easy to identify, describe, measure and quantify. Uses of IS/IT have increased the volume and quality of information available, but it is still difficult to explicitly value the contribution many of its uses make to organizational success.
- In many cases, it is difficult to relate business performance improvements to specific IS/IT projects, as they usually result from a combination of improved technology and other changes in the ways of working.
- The prevailing focus of many organizations on achieving a short-term financial return from their investments prevents many of the longer-term benefits of a coherent and sustained IS/IT investment strategy from being achieved.
- As will be discussed in various parts of this book, organizations do not consistently undertake benefit reviews at the end of projects and transfer lessons learned to future projects. Our research has found that this is the key differentiator between organizations that are more successful in delivering benefits from IS/IT projects and organizations that are less successful.

At the same time the commercial and social contexts in which those investments are made are changing rapidly, both in terms of globalizing industries and the extensive use of IT in individuals' lives. Organizations not only have to align and synchronize their IS/IT projects with evolving business strategies, but also meet the expectations of ever-more sophisticated customers and, in the public sector, citizens. The volume of information now held electronically, in combination with legislation, has increased the need for greater security of the data stored to counter the threats from fraud and 'leaks', as well as to protect organizations' assets and individuals' rights.

While these challenges largely result from the rapidly evolving use of technology and the complex problems associated with the scale and scope of deployment, there are a number of management issues that are critical to successful investment.

Strategic intent and actions required

Employees often report that their organizations are continually under-going change, and that the rate of change is increasing. This is often a result of senior managers developing strategies in order to respond to internal pressures on the organization. However, whilst managers are aware of the pressures and can decide on apparently appropriate responses, they are often unaware of the implications of those responses for the staff, ways of working and systems within the organization. Expressed another way, it could be argued that 'the devil is often in the detail'.

The public sector, in particular, often suffers from disconnects between strategic intentions and the actions that must be undertaken to achieve them. Politicians make announcements on policy or service changes, which often include significant IS/IT projects, without under-standing the implications of implementing those systems at the local level. For example, new healthcare systems in the National Health Service (NHS) in the UK usually require implementation across a large number of providers, either Hospital Trusts or Local Health Econo-mies, all of which are at different levels of experience and sophistica-tion with their current systems. The realization of benefits when many separate parties are involved, all of which are at different starting points, is highly challenging.

Recognition of organizational factors

The promises made by the vendors of information technology suggest that all an organization needs to do to improve its performance is to implement a given application or set of hardware – often termed the 'silver bullet' approach to IT deployment. However, considerable research has shown that such implementations should not simply be exercises in technology deployment, but, to be successful, should also be accompanied by complementary changes in processes, the working practices of individuals and groups, the roles of individuals and even the culture of the organization. It is the investment in these organizational factors that is often missing, and this is why benefits are not being realized.

Finding a fair balance of benefits

The increased adoption of enterprise-wide systems, as noted above, means that a wider range of users will have access to or be required to use information systems. The investment in such systems is often predicated on the benefits that will be realized by the organization; however, as noted by Jurison (1996), realizing those benefits depends on achieving:

> 'a fair balance of benefits between the organization and its stakeholders. The issue of gain sharing is of critical importance . . . with no apparent benefits to them, stakeholders are likely to resist the changes.' *Jurison (1996)*

A common understanding

The different stakeholders associated with many new system projects result in a variety of perspectives on what the system is expected to achieve and how changes could be made to deliver these benefits. Unless all the stakeholders understand why change is needed and can agree an approach to achieving the necessary changes, it is likely that individuals and groups will pursue multiple different, potentially conflicting, approaches that can waste time and resources, resulting in difficulty in realizing the expected benefits.

Dissatisfaction with current approaches to benefits delivery

In 2006–2008, we undertook two surveys (one in collaboration with Vlerick Leuven Ghent Management School in Belgium and the other with Cutter Benchmarking Consortium) of senior business and IT managers, in order to explore the activities involved in the delivery of benefits and satisfaction with those activities. In total over 200 responses were received from organizations in over 30 countries. The overall results were almost identical from the two surveys and showed few differences when analysed by geography, type of organization or

Table 1.1: Satisfaction with benefits management activities

	Not satisfied with their current approach
Identification of project costs	43%
Project prioritization	59%
Identifying benefits	68%
Development of business cases	69%
Planning the delivery of benefits	75%
Evaluation and review of benefits realized	81%

respondent. The findings relating to satisfaction are summarized in Table 1.1 and show that, in most areas, the managers surveyed were not satisfied with their current practices.

Table 1.1 shows that respondents were most satisfied with their identification of project costs. However, whilst some organizations take a comprehensive approach to identifying costs, the survey found that this is not always the case, with many organizations failing to include internal costs associated with achieving business changes, with the implementation of systems and with new ways of working once the system is operational. Without an understanding of the full costs involved in an IS/IT project, it is impossible to be clear on the overall financial value of undertaking the project.

The resources available for new projects are finite within any organization and, in difficult trading conditions, can become very limited. This results in organizations needing to be able to compare projects and identify those that they wish to undertake or, if they are not willing or able to refuse projects, to be able to identify their optimal order and timing. For those undertaking some form of project prioritization, the most frequently cited reasons given were:

- to align the objectives of each project with the strategy of the organization (92%);
- to avoid over-commitment of limited resources (87%);
- to set priorities across different types of investment (82%).

However, despite having clear intentions for the prioritization of projects, as shown in Table 1.1, the majority of respondents were not satisfied with their organization's approach.

Respondents were also dissatisfied with their approach to identifying the benefits from IS/IT projects. Only 35% felt that they were successful in identifying all the benefits arising from a project and only 31% believed that they quantified the benefits adequately. As discussed earlier, the success of projects often relies on a fair share of benefits being realized by all the stakeholders involved. Without such a distribution of the benefits, it is likely that some of the stakeholders will have little interest in the success of the project. Worse still, if they are going to be disadvantaged by the project, often described as receiving *disbenefits*, then they may actually resist the implementation.

The vast majority of respondents (96%) to the survey said they were required to develop a business case in order to justify investment in IS or IT projects. But, as can be seen from Table 1.1, the majority of respondents (69%) were not satisfied with their approach to business cases. While there is a recognition that information system investments are made to yield benefits to the organization, traditionally business cases have not been explicitly stated in these terms. In many organizations, the business case that is required is essentially a financial assessment. This emphasis is likely to make projects where the benefits are difficult, if not impossible, to express financially hard to justify. However, they may be projects that contribute directly to those areas of the business that are most important to the organization's future, for example customer care or employee satisfaction. The dominance of a financial mindset within business cases will tend to favour cost-cutting or efficiency projects, which, although worthwhile, may be less beneficial investments than those that improve effectiveness or enable innovation within the organization.

> 'Benefits are typically delivered through extensive changes to business practices and decision making. There is a growing consensus that organizational factors are far more critical to successful IS implementation than technical considerations.' *Markus et al. (2000)*

The surveys showed a clear correlation between higher levels of IS investment success and a wide range of benefit types included in the business cases. In particular, benefits associated with sharing knowledge, collaborative working, team effectiveness and individual job satisfaction were far more common in those organizations' business cases. The less successful tended to focus on efficiencies from process improvements and cost savings.

Delivery or implementation planning involves identifying and planning the activities needed to ensure benefit delivery from the IS/IT project. Whilst most organizations (64%) indicated that they planned technology implementation, far fewer (31%) had clear plans for the organizational changes necessary to realize benefits, for example how staff were organized and how they carried out their work. Again, as discussed earlier, considerable research has shown that, to be successful, technology deployment must be accompanied by complementary changes in processes, the working practices of individuals and groups, the roles of individuals and even the culture of the organization. These changes require as much, if not more, planning and effort in executing the plans as the technical and system elements of projects.

Finally, the area where there is the least satisfaction with current practices is in the evaluation and review of benefits realized. The vast majority of respondents said their organization reviewed the cost of projects (90%), on time delivery (89%) and technical quality (73%). However, only 49% reviewed the delivery of benefits. In addition to not setting aside sufficient time for such reviews, respondents indicated that they felt it was difficult to undertake reviews if the expected benefits had not been clearly set out in the business case at the start of the project. Another reason that organizations may be reluctant to carry out post-implementation benefit reviews is that, perhaps surprisingly, 38% of respondents were honest enough to say that when benefits are identified at the start of a project, they are routinely overstated in order to ensure that the project is approved.

As will be discussed later, further analysis of the survey findings, and subsequent research, has shown that undertaking benefit reviews is directly associated with organizations that are more successful with realizing benefits from their IS/IT projects. This is for a number of reasons. First, reviews allow them to identify unrealized benefits and to instigate further actions to realize those benefits. Reviews also allow the organization to pass learning from one project to another. Finally, if staff know that there will be a review of benefits, they are likely to be more realistic and robust in their identification and quantification of the expected benefits when preparing a business case at the start of a project. Consistent with this, the research found that routine benefit reviews resulted in the preparation of better business cases, resulting in projects that yielded few benefits being identified earlier and not pursued, allowing even greater focus on the worthwhile projects.

The need for a fresh approach: benefits management

The expressed lack of satisfaction with current approaches to the management of benefits suggests the need for a better way. As with any project, it is important to get things right from the outset or considerable time and cost can be wasted in reworking activities already undertaken. A new approach should therefore commence with improved project identification and planning. It should also address the other limitations already described, such as the lack of inclusion of planning and costing for the business change elements of information system projects and the lack of review mechanisms after implementation.

Starting in the mid-1990s, an extended research programme was undertaken by the Information Systems Research Centre (ISRC) at Cranfield School of Management to address the limitations of existing approaches. The research programme, which originally lasted three years but has since been the focus of further research and development activity, was undertaken in conjunction with a number of major private and public sector organizations. The process and tools resulting from this work have been extended and refined from experience gained from the many organizations that have adopted the approach in the last seven to ten years. Key elements of the approach are now in regular use by well over 100 organizations across the world including the UK, Europe, USA, Australia, India and the Far East.

The overall approach developed, called *benefits management*, can be described as:

> ### Definition: Benefits management
>
> The process of organizing and managing such that the potential benefits arising from the use of IS/IT are actually realized.

The approach is based on a life-cycle process: a set of linked steps to guide the identification, scoping, justification, planning and implementation of IS projects, such that the available benefits from those projects are achieved. The key steps of the process are formulated as interrelated tools or frameworks that can be used to guide and structure the activities and actions needed to implement a project successfully.

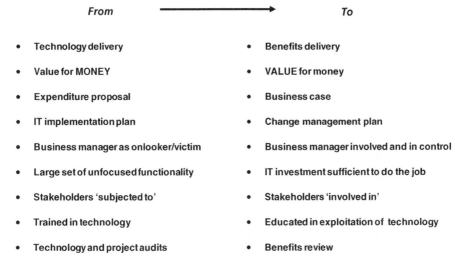

From	→	*To*

- Technology delivery
- Value for MONEY
- Expenditure proposal
- IT implementation plan
- Business manager as onlooker/victim
- Large set of unfocused functionality
- Stakeholders 'subjected to'
- Trained in technology
- Technology and project audits

- Benefits delivery
- VALUE for money
- Business case
- Change management plan
- Business manager involved and in control
- IT investment sufficient to do the job
- Stakeholders 'involved in'
- Educated in exploitation of technology
- Benefits review

Figure 1.1: Comparison of benefits management with traditional IS project approaches

The subsequent chapters in this book explain and illustrate, with practical examples, the benefits management process and its underlying tools and frameworks. Before addressing the detailed stages of the process, it is worthwhile considering how the benefits management approach compares with traditional approaches to IS projects and the improvements that it has been shown to yield. This comparison and the improvements resulting from the benefits management approach are shown in Figure 1.1. While we would not argue that the activities on the left-hand side of this diagram are wrong or unnecessary, experience from the use of the benefits management approach shows that on their own they are insufficient to deliver many of the anticipated benefits.

Benefits delivery

Central to the benefits management approach is the identification of and focus on the potential benefits that can arise from the investment, a focus that is continuous throughout the project, from the initial planning stage, through appraisal and implementation, to the final review of the project. Technology delivery remains a key part of the project and, as described later, robust project and systems development methodologies should be adopted to ensure that this part of the project is successful. However, too often technology delivery becomes the *raison d'être* of the project at the expense of the benefits the system will deliver to the users and the organization. Many implementations of customer relationship management (CRM), enterprise resource planning (ERP) and e-business systems have been driven as much by the promise of vendors and a fear of being left behind by competitors, as by a clear statement of the benefits they will yield to the organization. Too often, project managers find themselves required to implement the chosen application without a clear understanding of the expected benefits and the organizational changes that will be required.

A focus on value

Money is the language of business and translating all projects, not just IT projects, into a financial case allows senior business managers to believe that they understand the 'value' of the project. While they do not need a detailed understanding of technology or the workings of a system, the continued reduction of business cases to financial numbers and ratios reduces those managers' understanding of the role IS or IT can play in their organization and the types of benefits it can provide. Given also that the financial approach is unlikely to give a full picture, since more qualitative benefits are likely to be excluded from the case, this lack of understanding is likely to be exacerbated.

It is often easier to identify the costs associated with a project than the benefits or value that it will yield. This leads to statements commonly used to describe projects that focus on their cost, rather than their value, to the organization:

- 'we are investing £2.5 m in our new online purchasing system';
- 'our £36 m global HR database';
- 'the IT development budget for 2012 is £10 m'.

The emphasis on financial value to justify investments also results in the use of financial measures to monitor the progress of projects. This has obvious appeal since it is relatively easy to monitor the expenditure incurred on a project as it progresses, but it gives no information on the progress towards achieving the benefits required from the project, the real reason for the investment.

This use of financial measures to track progress also extends to measuring the success of projects, which are often judged to have been successful if they were delivered on time and on budget, regardless of the impact of the system on the performance of the organization. While overruns in either of these would not be encouraged, a project that takes longer or costs more but delivers the intended improvements to the organization should not necessarily be judged a failure.

When asked how they judged the success of an IS/IT project, senior management said it was the 'value delivered to the organization', whereas the project managers put delivery to time, cost and quality above value (Nelson, 2005). Although these were considered important by senior management, delivery of the expected benefits was their primary concern.

A business case linked to organizational strategy

This focus on the financial case for IS investments, and the relative ease of assessing the cost of a project compared to the value of the benefits it will generate, results in the investment cases often being effectively an expenditure proposal, rather than a true business case – a rigorous argument for a worthwhile investment. To be comprehensive, the business case should state clearly how the intended project will contribute to the strategy and performance of the organization. An investment could be justified on the basis of cost savings alone, but others will provide new capabilities, such as additional channels to market. If the business strategy stated a need for significant cost reductions or to increase the customer base, these projects would be clearly aligned with the strategy; if not, then,

'Nothing seems more obvious than anticipating business-based risks and focusing on managing the needed business changes in IT-enabled projects. Yet nothing has been more difficult, more misunderstood and more neglected in practice.' *Gibson (2003)*

although the projects sound attractive, other investments may be more important, especially when funds and resources are limited.

In the benefits management approach described in this book, the planning for a project and the subsequent development of the business case commences with an understanding of the current and expected strategic drivers acting on the organization and hence ensures that projects and benefits are tightly linked to organizational strategy.

The importance of change management

The lack of recognition of the importance of the social element to IS and IT deployment often results in the need for many of the changes to ways of working being overlooked. In particular, the tendency for such projects to be led by IS staff, rather than business staff, exacerbates this lack of recognition of the impact the system will have on individuals and groups. This may well not be intentional, but is often driven by inadequate understanding of how the business operates by those in the IT department. Many organizations are trying to address this issue by having individuals from within the business participate in IS/IT projects and even lead them. However, they may fail to release those individuals from their day-to-day responsibilities, whereby involvement in the project becomes an additional burden for which they have little time. This can result in participation in the early stages of a project, and then leaving it with the IT team until it is ready for delivery. Figure 1.2 shows an example of an organization that implemented its ERP system twice: the first time unsuccessfully for the reasons above, and, courageously, the second time having learned from the earlier failure.

If the project is more than six to twelve months in duration, it can be expected that many factors, both within the organization and in the wider business context, will change. Continued involvement of the business managers is required to identify the implications for the project and address the resulting issues as they emerge.

FIRST ATTEMPT - FAILURE	SECOND ATTEMPT - SUCCESS
IS led, with insufficient knowledge of the business function concerned	Business function led, by a newly recruited manager, experienced in the function, supported by IS
Belief that the requirements were simple and already known - just use the package to automate the current process	Site visits and reviews of other companies' procedures to establish best practice and system requirements
Belief that this was a low-risk and straightforward implementation	Knowledge that this would require some major changes
Lack of business buy-in led to both the new and old (mainly manual) systems remaining in place, and little move by the business to adopt the new system	New procedures completely replaced the previous system and all staff were required to use them; facilities for the old system withdrawn
Little business change	Organizational and business process changes
Bespoke amendment of package. Longer and more complex system build, and difficulty applying upgrades	Minimal changes to the package, and innovative use of built-in facilities. Shorter delivery timescale and easy future upgrade paths
Costs, no benefits	Benefits have exceeded expectations

From: Achieving the Benefits from Software Package Enabled Business Improvement Programmes Best Practice Guidelines (IMPACT 1998)

Figure 1.2: 'Before and after' – how adopting a benefits management approach turned failure into success

Commitment from business managers

The rapid pace of change of IT, coupled with the technical language of IT staff, frequently causes business managers to feel that they do not understand IT in the same way that they believe they are familiar with, for example, marketing or other functions of the business. They therefore feel vulnerable when involved in appraising IS/IT projects, contributing to their preference to have such projects expressed in 'hard' financial terms. This feeling of vulnerability was expressed by business staff in those organizations which took part in the original research project as a feeling of being *'an onlooker or victim where IT is concerned.'*

The benefits management process addresses this issue by proposing tools and frameworks that both the business and IT staff use together, in order to ensure both communities contribute their knowledge and that the combined knowledge produces something neither group could have developed alone. The tools and frameworks are all intended to be used in workshop settings, to encourage participation from multiple individuals from both the business and IT groups. It has been found, through the extensive experience of using the process, that it encourages collaboration, more than the exchange of large, complex documents. Those involved also often actually enjoy the experience, something many of them say has not happened in previous IS/IT projects!

IS/IT sufficient to do the job

IS and IT vendors are keen to promote the many features of their products and, all too often, organizations believe that the list of features equates to a list of benefits that the systems will provide to their organizations. However, this is seldom the case and can result in organizations buying and installing systems that either do not meet their needs or are overly complex. As a result, those systems tend to be under-utilized and hence fail to deliver the expected benefits.

The benefits management approach looks at this issue from the other direction. Rather than starting with the features and functions of the technology or system, benefits management elicits what is causing the organization to consider the investment and hence the improvements the project is expected to deliver. It is only when this and any changes needed to make those improvements have been identified that the IS and IT required should be assessed, leading to a technology specification that is 'sufficient to do the job'.

> 'William Ockham, the medieval philosopher, said theories should be as simple as possible. The same principle applies to enterprise IT systems: they should be designed with as few standards (such as network protocols, operating systems and platforms) as possible – ideally one of each.' *Upton and Staats (2008)*

This does not imply that organizations should purchase under-specified hardware or software that would soon be insufficient to meet their needs. Rather it is to counter the emphasis of many vendors on the long list of features and functionality that they can provide, which can lead to incurring unnecessary cost. However, it is also often the case that vendors sell their products in packages or suites, so that it will cost little more to buy some additional functionality than the cost of the minimum requirements. The additional functionality should be evaluated to see if it contributes further benefits that would address the strategy or objectives of the organization. If it does not, it should not be purchased or, if bundled in, should not be implemented.

Involvement of stakeholders

Just as business managers may feel they are 'victims' in IS/IT projects, others who will be impacted by the system often believe that they are 'subjected to IS/IT', rather than feeling that they are contributing to and shaping the project. An important part of the benefits management approach is the consideration of the project from the perspective of a wide set of stakeholders, in part at least to address the *'what's in it for me?'* question most of them will be asking. At the heart of the benefits management approach is having 'benefit owners' who take responsibility for planning the actions needed to realize each benefit. If no one is willing to take ownership, this suggests that the benefit is either not wanted or not credible and hence will not be realized.

Ideally, many of those stakeholders or their representatives, if they are large groups, should be involved in scoping and planning the project, and in particular identifying the benefits and changes involved. They are then needed to be actively involved in making some of the changes and in tracking and realizing the benefits. In most projects, one group will have to make changes to deliver benefits to another group, and the two will need to work together. In addition to encouraging participation in planning and implementation activities from a wide range of stakeholder groups, the approach includes a particular set of tools that specifically uncovers the views and concerns of each stake-holder group and identifies actions that may be needed to encourage or sustain their cooperation.

Educated in the use of technology

Surveys continue to show that firms invest little time and money in training their staff to use IT and IS. This problem tends to be particularly severe in the UK, with surveys showing that, compared to other European countries, organizations spend less per head of workforce on IT training, leading to reduced business effectiveness and personal productivity from IT use. Many projects are started with a defined training budget. However, this is often not sufficient to provide enough training for individuals to become familiar, let alone confident, with the new system (see Box 1.1). Even when a project does start with an adequate training budget, if it runs late or over-budget, it is often the training budget that is reduced to make up the shortfall elsewhere.

The iSociety report (2003) found that, all too often, training on new systems was left to informal, on-the-job training undertaken by colleagues. Even with formal training in place, such informal training is beneficial, since use of a system will depend on the details of a particular context. However, the existence of such informal mechanisms should not be taken as an opportunity for managers to abrogate their responsibility to provide basic systems, technology and even business skills training.

Box 1.1: The (in)adequacy of training budgets

The limited expenditure on staff training is highlighted by the activities of a major, worldwide professional services firm. The firm recently implemented a global financial system at a cost of tens of millions of pounds to improve the accounting, time recording and billing activities of the organization. All 15 000 staff in the organization are required to use the system to record their activities, if the expected benefits are to be realized. A significant budget was set aside for training staff to use the system. However, when the large number of staff and the average charge-out rate to clients of many of those staff are considered, the training budget equates to just 20 minutes per person!

While training staff in how to use technology and systems is important, this is often not sufficient in itself. To ensure projects deliver the full set of potential benefits, it is usually necessary not only to teach individuals which screens to access and which keys to press, but to demonstrate to them how the system can improve the role that they carry out for the organization. This training in the impact or exploitation of the technology should include an appreciation of how use of the system will impact others and other processes in the organization. Undertaking this education in exploitation will allow individuals to consider new ways of using the system or technology in their particular role, harnessing their experience and creativity.

Many systems today may not offer a net benefit to the individual. Rather, the major benefits accrue to the entire organization. This may include knowledge management and CRM systems, where individuals are expected to share their expertise or customer contacts. Without a clear understanding of how the use of these systems will benefit the organization, individuals will be reluctant to use them – particularly if it seems their role will be diminished. A lack of appreciation of the wider picture leads to individuals bypassing the new systems and continuing to store information on their local databases and personal devices.

Post-implementation benefits review

While many organizations have been keen to describe themselves as learning organizations, as shown in Table 1.1 few carry out post-implementation reviews, seriously limiting their ability to learn collectively from the experience gained from projects.

The benefits management process includes a post-implementation benefits review as an integral component of the project. This review should not concentrate on the use of technology or on the project management; rather, technology and project audits should be carried out separately. Instead, the benefits review should explore which of the planned benefits have been realized, whether there were any unexpected benefits arising and which planned benefits are still expected but may need additional attention to ensure that they are realized. Actions should then be put in place to enable these benefits to be realized.

The benefits review should also consider if, given what has been achieved so far, there is an opportunity for further benefits to be realized. It is often not possible at the outset of a large project to foresee all the benefits that can be achieved when the system is in operation, and new or emergent benefits are often identified as business changes are implemented. Many of the current large-scale enterprise-wide system deployments are initially intended to overcome problems resulting from the use of a range of existing, often incompatible, systems. Once the organization becomes used to operating without these problems, it can then consider how the system can be used to improve overall performance across the organization and also how it could enable new, innovative ways of working.

The importance of a common language

Before undertaking an exploration of how the benefits from information systems might better be realized, it is worthwhile considering and clarifying the terms that are used in this field. The following section discusses major terms in common use and defines how they will be used throughout this book.

Information technology (IT) refers to the technology on which information systems operate or run. It refers specifically to the hardware, software and telecommunications networks that underpin information systems. Some commentators and organizations, particularly in the government and public sectors, use the term *information and communication technologies* (ICT), rather than simply IT, in order to stress the convergence of traditional hardware and software with the networks that characterize communications technologies.

Our definition of information systems (IS) is adopted from the UK Academy for Information Systems (UKAIS):

Definition: Information systems

Information systems are the means by which people and organizations, utilizing technology, gather, process, store, use and disseminate information.

The UKAIS notes that the use and study of these systems includes both the underlying technological and social aspects. Within the business sphere, this social dimension is concerned with how individuals, teams and even whole organizations adopt and use information systems and how this use, in turn, shapes those information systems. This means that a consideration of information systems must take into account not only the technologies that enable them but also the inherent social implications. It can therefore be seen how the interchangeable use of these terms can lead to misunderstandings: with over-reliance on the term 'information technology' devaluing the importance of the social dimension, which, as has already been stressed, is critical to the realization of benefits.

Two other terms now in common usage are electronic commerce (*e-commerce*) and electronic business (*e-business*). Kalakota and Whinston (1997) define e-commerce as *'the buying and selling of information, products and services via computer networks'*, the computer networks primarily being the Internet. Hence, e-commerce refers to information systems carrying out trading activities focused outside the organization itself, for example with customers and suppliers. E-business, in contrast, refers to more general automation of information exchanges and organizations' business processes and transactions, both within organizations and with trading partners.

Another term that is often used when discussing information systems is *applications*. Applications are information systems that are used to accomplish a specific business activity or automate a particular process. Examples of simple applications are the word processing and spreadsheets found on virtually every PC. More sophisticated applications are used to carry out activities such as general accounting, production scheduling or warehouse management. Such applications are often now sold as *packages* or *suites*, comprising a number of separate applications. Recently there has been a trend to develop very large suites of applications that, when implemented, impact the activities of many processes or functions within an organization. These enterprise systems, which include ERP and CRM systems and enterprise portals, pose significant challenges for the realization of benefits, which will be considered throughout this book.

Organizations still face the difficult decision of whether to develop applications in-house to meet their specific needs, often termed *bespoke* or *customized* applications, or to buy a standard package from a software vendor. Prior to the 1990s, there was a tendency to develop bespoke applications, with the logic that little or no competitive advantage could be gained if a number of organizations in an industry used the same software package. More recently, the pendulum of opinion has swung in the direction of advising organizations to buy standardized packages, in which the vendors can embed best practices gained from their exposure to multiple organizations. As argued by both Carr

(2003) and Mata *et al.* (1995), it is not the software itself that will confer competitive advantage to any organization, but the skill that the management of the organization has in putting that software to work to address the objectives of their business and create changes to improve performance.

Summary

Given the continued reality of many IS/IT projects failing to deliver the expected benefits, there is a need for a fresh approach to how projects are undertaken. We suggest this should be a process approach that encompasses the entire life-cycle of the investment: commencing with the early exploration of the idea and planning the project, continuing throughout implementation and including a review when it has been completed. The focus throughout the project should be on the realization of benefits, since that, after all, is the reason the organization is making the investment.

A major feature of the benefits management process described in the following chapters is the recognition of the importance of the need for organizational and business changes to accompany the deployment of technology and how the realization of benefits is dependent on the successful achievement of these changes. Since a wide variety of stakeholders are likely to be affected by these changes, this suggests the need for a range of individuals to be involved throughout the project life-cycle in the benefits management activities, something that does not always happen with more traditional project management approaches.

As will be described, the starting point for the development of a benefits plan for a project is an understanding of the strategic drivers acting on the organization and its planned responses to these. An understanding of these drivers can show whether the investment being considered addresses areas that are important to the organization. It can also help in prioritization. As financial and management resources are finite in all organizations, deciding which projects not to do is often critical to being able to resource the ones that really matter. A number of tools and frameworks have been developed in the strategic and general management domain to help with the process of identifying and analysing possible strategies and making appropriate choices.

The importance of a well-thought-out and clearly stated strategy as the starting point for the realization of benefits from individual projects is underlined by the presentation and discussion of a key set of these strategy tools and frameworks in Chapter 2. Once the business strategy for the organization has been determined, it is necessary to develop an IS and IT strategy. While the IS strategy should support the business strategy, there is also a recognition that IS can shape the business strategy. This dynamic interrelationship between these two activities is termed *strategic alignment*. The nature and role of IS and IT strategies is also discussed in Chapter 2.

Chapter 2

Understanding the strategic context

When considering the implementation of a new technology or information system, it is necessary to understand the relevance of the investment to the three interrelated strategies that should have been defined by the organization – the business, the IS and the IT strategies – to ensure that the investment contributes to agreed business aims and objectives. Some investments that do not directly contribute to particular aspects of identified strategies may well generate worthwhile benefits, but priority should be given to those that enable the organization to achieve its chosen business strategy.

This chapter first discusses two different perspectives of business strategy formulation that consider the external or internal environment of the organization and how these can be reconciled. A number of tools or frameworks that can be used to help determine and develop business strategies are then described.

A discussion of the distinctions between business, IS and IT strategies and how these are interrelated is presented. How organizations can categorize, compare and assess the implications of the portfolio of IS and IT investments currently underway and planned is then considered. Issues in achieving the IS strategy are then explored further, by considering the key competences required for effective IS development and deployment and how these affect the value actually delivered from the investments.

> 'There may be a major disconnect between the strategic intent of a decision to implement a major change and the resulting actions that must be completed.' *Bancroft et al. (1998)*

The range of tools and frameworks discussed here are particularly appropriate for use in the context of the benefits management process.

However, there are many others that can also be used; for those, and also a fuller discussion of the ones presented here, the reader is referred to the many comprehensive texts on the subjects of business strategy (see, for example, Hill and Jones, 1998; Johnson and Scholes, 1999) or IS strategy (for example, Galliers and Leidner, 2003; Ward and Peppard, 2002).

It should be noted that industries and/or markets are not static and will change over time, sometimes quickly and unpredictably. Some changes may be outside the control of the firms competing in an industry, such as economic, political and legal changes, whereas others will be caused by the strategies being pursued by other players in the industry, such as mergers and acquisitions, the introduction of new products, new distribution channels or changes in pricing. Analysis of an industry or market and the development of a business strategy are therefore both dynamic and interrelated. Strategies need to evolve in response to changes in the business environment or as new opportunities emerge and therefore must be reviewed regularly.

Public sector and not-for-profit organizations must also constantly scan the external environment and take account of their internal resources and capabilities, in order to develop strategies that best meet the needs of their various constituents or stakeholders. Indeed, such organizations often have a large number of stakeholders, whose expectations and needs may at times be conflicting. This creates the additional challenge of balancing the needs of these different stakeholders in an acceptable and achievable way. The tools and frameworks presented throughout this book are suitable for use by both private and public sector organizations. However, it may be appropriate in some cases to change the terms used in the latter case; for example, rather than use the term 'customer', substitution of the word 'citizen' or 'client' may be more appropriate.

The external and internal perspectives of business strategy: the competitive forces and resource-based views

All organizations are interested in finding ways in which they can ensure their long-term viability, whether they are companies looking to maximize their shareholder value or public sector and not-for-profit organizations seeking to maximize their effectiveness. In that context, a business strategy can be described as *'an integrated set of actions aimed at increasing the long-term well being and strength of an enterprise'* (Porter, 1980).

A number of tools and techniques to guide and structure the formal development of corporate strategies were developed during the 1960s and 1970s. Some of these, such as the Boston Consulting Group's grid or matrix, are still proving useful today. These approaches encouraged the analysis of factors affecting the attractiveness of the markets in which the company operated or was considering entering. This emphasis on the external environment was continued by Porter (1980; 1985), who suggested that there were structural factors and forces acting within industries and markets that resulted in some offering a greater potential for profitability or growth (see the later discussions of five forces and value chain analysis). Organizations should therefore identify these more attractive industries and markets and the factors affecting profitability and then select appropriate strategies, such as 'low cost' or 'differentiation' in order to outperform competitors. This approach to strategy development is referred to as the 'competitive forces' view of strategy.

In the 1990s, some strategic thinkers (e.g. Barney, 1991; Grant, 1996) began to suggest an alternative view of strategy development. This was in part driven by the observation that the greatest variation in profitability was not between firms in different industries, but between firms in the same industry. This suggests that it is not so much differences in the structural factors within an industry that determine the profitability of firms, but what is inside an organization and the idiosyncratic ways this allows them to compete. It was suggested that an organization should consider the assets or resources it has at its disposal and what it is able to do, and particularly do well; that is, its competences and capabilities. If these resources, competences and capabilities are valuable, rare, inimitable (difficult to imitate) and non-substitutable – the so-called VRIN attributes – they can be used to implement value-creating strategies that provide sustainable competitive advantage. This consideration of the internal context of the organization in strategy formulation is called the 'resource-based view'.

Resources, competences and capabilities

In considering the resource-based view of strategy, the terms 'resources', 'competences' and 'capabilities' are often used interchangeably. A discussion of the terms, and how they are related, is given in Box 2.1 and shown in Figure 2.1.

Box 2.1: Resources, competences and capabilities

Resources are the assets, both tangible and intangible, that an organization owns or can access in order to pursue its chosen strategy. They may be physical, such as buildings and technology, people and finance, or intangible, such as know-how, brands, patents and customer loyalty. Resources may be categorized into two types: those that are similar to those available to competitors or easy to imitate and those that are unique to the organization.

Competences describe how resources are deployed through processes and structures in order to carry out the activities of the organization, such as product design, marketing, production, distribution and customer services. Managerial competences are also required in order to achieve effective linkages among these activities. It is the competences, rather than the underlying resources themselves, that are often the key to organizational performance. Competences can also be categorized into two types: those that

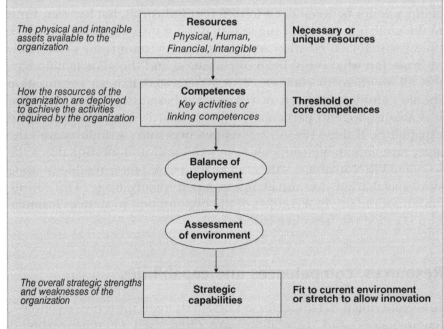

Figure 2.1: Resources, competences and capabilities (after Johnson and Scholes, 1999)

are similar to others in the industry and those that allow the organization to outperform the competitors. The latter are often called *core competences*.

The strategic *capabilities* of the organization describe the ability of the organization to meet the opportunities and threats of the external environment and are determined by the resources and competences available to the organization and how these are developed, combined and deployed. Benefits management can be considered a competence that enables organizations to have the capability to exploit IS/IT as an integral component of their business strategies.

Others have argued that strategic thinking has to accommodate and balance both the competitive forces and resource-based views of strategy (Collis and Montgomery, 1995). Long-term success, it is suggested, will result for organizations that can align their resources and capabilities in ways that match the demands of the environment. One approach which considers the balance of the external and internal attributes of the organization is the dimensions of competence framework presented later in this chapter.

Meeting the demands of the external environment suggests a need for the capabilities to *fit* the current environment, but there is also a requirement to *stretch* the capabilities in order to create new opportunities or counter potential threats.

Further studies, which recognize that many markets are becoming increasingly turbulent and volatile, have suggested that in such environments competitive advantage is transient, rather than sustainable (Teece *et al.*, 1997; Eisenhardt and Martin, 2000; Helfat and Peteraf, 2009). Managers must therefore concentrate on *renewing* rather than just *protecting* their sources of competitive advantage. No longer can they rely on the assets, staff, products, brands and other resources that they have assembled to provide their present competitive position. They must also be able to combine these resources in new ways and gain additional resources, and to do this repeatedly, if they are to compete successfully – so-called 'dynamic capabilities'. Such capabilities are viewed as critical to the future success of firms; they are somewhat akin to the processes of adaptation and selection witnessed in the natural world.

Ends, ways and means

Our discussion of the competitive forces and resource-based views of strategy can be summarized by considering three major elements of strategy formulation and implementation available to organizations: the *ends* they wish to achieve, the *ways* in which they can operate and the *means* they can draw on. Different strategic philosophies advocate starting the process of strategy development at different points, as shown in Figure 2.2.

The competitive forces approach to strategy development stresses the objective assessment of the external environment and encourages an organization to determine which industry it wishes to participate in and, within that industry, what market segments to address. As such, this approach focuses on the *ends* that the organization wishes to achieve, which, in turn, results in a concentration on targets and objectives. Having determined the intended ends, it is assumed that the organization can find the required ways and means of realizing these. Difficulties will often arise when it is found that no satisfactory ways and means are available. The example of the demise of Marconi (previously GEC), which restructured itself to pursue opportunities in the communications industry rather than its traditional industries, demonstrates the need to have the resources and capabilities as well as the ambition.

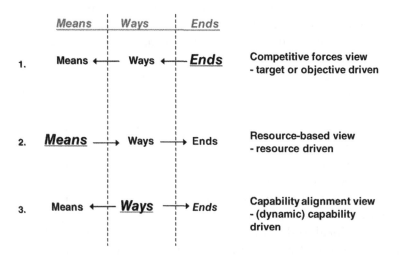

Figure 2.2: Different strategic paradigms

The focus on the ends to be achieved from strategy is typical of many US and UK organizations, due in large part to the origins of the competitive forces paradigm. A reliance on target setting in order to guide the actions of organizations was adopted on a large scale by UK central government in the management of public services in the 1990s. A decade later, this approach in isolation was seen largely to have failed and many of the imposed targets have been dropped, since, in many cases, both productivity and service quality declined rather than improved.

The resource-based view adopts the opposite starting point. Rather than commence with a top-down view of the desired objectives or ends for the organization, it first considers the range of *means* that are available to the organization, including the financial, people, product, technology and knowledge resources the organization has or can draw on. Such approaches tend to be reactive and while they can often work well in the short term, particularly in being able to respond quickly and effectively to market changes or copy competitors' actions, they may well founder over time due to the lack of a coherent long-term vision and limited creative capabilities. Once again, while not universally adopted, this approach is typical of many Japanese firms, particularly in the 1970s and 1980s.

The third approach is to concentrate on the *ways* available to an organization; that is, how it can operate in order to create a strategy that generates customer or user value. As we have seen already, as most markets are becoming increasingly dynamic, organizations cannot rely on an analytical approach to understanding their industry or market, since that market is changing in rapid and unexpected ways. Instead they must learn to develop capabilities that allow them to '*integrate, reconfigure, gain and release resources – to match and even create market change*' (Eisenhardt and Martin, 2000). Studies have shown that these capabilities are often tacit, take considerable time to develop, are composed of many hundreds of lower level skills and have a strong social or cultural element to them. This means that they are difficult for competitors to imitate and hence can, if developed, provide a sustained competitive advantage. This 'third way' of considering strategy can be found in the approaches adopted by a number of major firms within continental Europe.

Rather than being considered as an end in itself, IT should be considered a means or resource that is available to the firm. Most IT is now available to all organizations and therefore cannot provide an advantage to one single firm for long (Carr, 2003). Instead, the generation of sustained advantage is likely to come from the ways in which it is deployed or implemented and used by the enterprise. As described already, the complex and often tacit nature of the capabilities required for effective IT implementation and use by an enterprise means that they cannot be quickly or easily acquired, but require long-term development within the organization.

PEST analysis

All businesses operate within the broad economic and social environment. The particular attributes and workings of that environment are, in large part, determined by the country or countries in which the organization is based or in which it sells its products and services. However, as events such as 9/11 and the financial crisis of 2008 have shown, societies and economies around the world are becoming increasingly interconnected and events in one country can have serious ramifications on the operation of industries and markets in others.

As a precursor to more detailed strategy development, organizations need to understand the broader external environment in which they will operate by techniques such as political, economic, social and technical (PEST) analysis, as outlined in Table 2.1. The analysis should focus on a given product or service in a particular geographic market, since the impact of the four factors will vary for different products and different countries. The analysis should then be repeated for other products or services and across other geographic territories. This can help to identify new opportunities for the organization, for example, due to changes in the social behaviour of consumers. Equally, the analysis can highlight potential threats, such as the introduction of new legislation that requires changes to products or production methods.

Industry attractiveness and competitive forces analysis

An industry is deemed attractive when it offers the opportunity for those competing in it to generate above average returns for their owners or investors. Although different firms competing in the same industry will generate different levels of profitability, since they all compete in different ways, the competitive forces view considers the structure and attractiveness of an industry to be essential ingredients in the profitability of a firm.

Table 2.1: PEST analysis

PEST analysis factor	Issues to consider in analysis	Typical questions
Political (should also include legal and often environmental)	The impact of the political, legal and regulatory environment on the organization, its suppliers and customers. This increasingly includes international environmental and sustainability legislation and accords.	• Is the political regime conducive to the type of business I wish to undertake – and how stable is this regime? • Are the legal and regulatory frameworks sufficient to allow a well functioning organization to flourish? • How does environmental legislation affect our business plans: either limiting options or creating opportunities?
Economic	The impact of the local macro- and micro-economy on the operation of the organization, its suppliers and its customers. Also consider how the economy is related to other economies.	• What is the impact of the local interest, tax, exchange and inflation rate on the operation of my organization – and those of my suppliers and customers? • Are these stable enough to allow a reasonable planning horizon? • Is there a pool of suitable staff to draw from? Are local wage rates and the skills of available staff acceptable?
Social	The impact of social changes on the operation of the organization, its suppliers and particularly the needs and wants of its customers.	• What social changes are occurring that may affect the demand for our products or services, e.g. changing demographics in many Western economies resulting in declining birth rates and increased 'greying' of the population due to people living longer. • Public preferences for products produced from sustainable sources or less harmful environmentally.
Technical	The impact of new technological developments (including IS/IT) on the products and services offered by the organization and the processes by which they are produced and delivered.	• Are new technologies being developed that will allow us to improve the products and services we offer to our customers or production methods? Or will new technologies make our current offerings obsolete? • Can we adopt these new technologies? What are the benefits/risks?

As mentioned earlier, Porter (1985) proposed one of the best-known analytical frameworks for strategy development with his *Five Forces Model*. This model states that in any industry, whether it is domestic or international and whether it is product- or service-based, the nature of competition is embodied in five forces:

Porter's Five Forces

- **threat of new entrants:** the threat of entry into the market of new competitors;
- **power of suppliers:** the bargaining power of suppliers to the industry;
- **power of buyers:** the bargaining power of customers in the market;
- **industry rivalry:** the intensity of the rivalry among the existing competitors;
- **threat of substitutes:** the threat of substitute products and services replacing the demand for existing products and services.

These five forces in combination determine industry profitability, since they influence the prices firms can charge for their goods, the costs of the raw materials and the investment they need to make in R&D, plant, marketing and sales. Generally, as any one or a combination of the forces increases, the profitability expected from that industry is reduced. Companies should therefore consider developing strategies that shift the market forces in their favour. The forces, together with factors that tend to reduce the profitability of an industry, are shown in Figure 2.3.

New entrants

New entrants in a market may result in an over supply of the product or service, which can force price reductions throughout that market. They may also cause the resources necessary to make the product, such as raw materials or skilled staff, to be in high demand and therefore scarce and more expensive. New entrants are dissuaded from entering a market by barriers to entry. These are factors that make it difficult for a new player to compete with the incumbent players. Such barriers include factors such as: capital requirements, access to the necessary input goods and services, routes to market and the requirement for

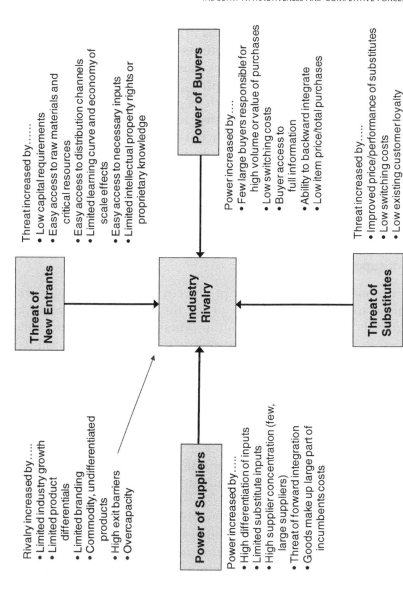

Figure 2.3: Porter's five forces

specialist knowledge. Restricted access to the advantages gained from experience, such as learning curve effects and proprietary knowledge, particularly when this is protected by patents or intellectual property rights can increase the barriers to entry.

Information-based industries, such as publishing, and those where products can be digitized, such as music and films, have been particularly vulnerable to new entrants in the last decade due to developments in IT, as can be seen from the rapid expansion of Amazon and iTunes. The economics of the industries have been changed dramatically, prices have fallen and the distribution channels transformed to the detriment of traditional retailers. This, in turn, has led to lower barriers to entry for new music artists and authors.

Power of suppliers

Suppliers control the inputs to the product or service being considered. In some sectors, such as manufacturing, this may mean access to key raw materials and components, but in others this may include skilled staff, specialist knowledge or the supply of capital. Suppliers will have increased power over a buyer if the cost of switching to another source of supply is high. This may be because the supplier is the sole supplier of the items in question, they are the only one in a given geographic area or they have specialist parts or specialist knowledge. The size of a supplier relative to the company will influence its power, with larger suppliers tending to have greater power. Also, if the items purchased from a supplier represent a high proportion of the value of the finished goods or services of a company, then that supplier will tend to have increased power.

Dominant suppliers are also vulnerable to technology innovations and capacity constraints, as exemplified by Intel's loss of share in the microchip market in recent years due to the exponential growth in demand for products such as smartphones and tablet computers. This has forced the manufacturers to find alternative suppliers, to the benefit of companies such as Advanced Micro Devices (AMD) and ARM Holdings.

Power of buyers

Factors that increase the power of buyers in an industry and hence are likely to reduce industry profitability include the size of the buyer relative to the producing firm. The larger the buyer, and the more it accounts for the output of the firm being considered, the more power it will have in negotiations about price and other terms. Buyers will also have increased power if they have low switching costs; that is, they can easily buy the same or similar goods or services from another source. This has had a significant effect in the travel industry as consumers can buy the components of most holidays easily, and sometimes more cheaply, online, either directly or through price comparison websites.

Industry rivalry

The nature and intensity of the rivalry among existing players in a market can be determined by a number of factors, as shown in Figure 2.3. These include stagnating markets, in which there is limited opportunity for growth and hence the existing incumbents must battle for market share, which inevitably means reducing costs wherever possible to be competitive on price. In such situations there is a tendency for takeovers or mergers in order to achieve greater economies of scale, as has been seen in a number of industries over the last ten to twenty years, including brewing and pharmaceuticals.

A limited ability to differentiate products and services also increases competition among existing players. Branding, the provision of additional complementary services, such as after-sales service, and additional distribution channels to access more segments of the market can all help to increase perceived product and service differentiation and hence reduce this force within an industry.

Exit barriers, such as the cost of decommissioning a plant or the cost of redundancy payments, may make companies reluctant to leave an industry, even if their profits are below the level desired. This is likely to lead to overcapacity in the industry, which results in downward price pressure and hence further reductions in profits. The automotive industry has been in this situation for many years, during which overcapacity and the high costs of closing plants have made competition intense. With the rising prosperity in newly developed economies such as China, India, Russia and Brazil, demand for cars is increasing rapidly, providing a return to profitability for companies such as General Motors – which, in 2010, sold more cars in China than in the USA.

Threat of substitutes

The threat of substitutes describes the likelihood of customers seeking alternative products and services, either as a replacement or as an alternative use of the expenditure available. These may allow the customer to carry out the same activity as current products, either at lower cost or in a better way, or may completely obviate the need for the current products or services.

Digital imaging has not only affected traditional film and photographic paper producers, but has also all but eliminated film-processing companies. More recently, the high resolution now available on many mobile phones has even reduced the need for a camera. Downloading of music from websites has dramatically reduced CD sales, leading to many record stores and some distributors closing down.

External value chain analysis

Having identified an industry that appears to be attractive or having understood the forces within their current industry, a firm should next consider in more detail how to work with other firms in order to develop, produce, market and distribute the goods and services required by their customers. In most industries it is very rare that a single organization undertakes all of the value-adding activities from raw material production to the delivery of the final product or service to the customer. The firm is usually one in a number of firms linked in a chain or system, with each firm specializing in one or more of the value-adding activities involved. The analysis of such systems of interconnected firms was proposed by Porter (1985) and is referred to as external or industry value chain analysis.

The intention of external value chain analysis is to understand the ways in which the organizations within an industry contribute to the value that is eventually delivered to the customer or consumer. A generic value chain is shown in Figure 2.4. The diagrams should focus on the value-adding activities undertaken at each stage in the chain. For example, in the case of the automotive value chain, the distributors operate showrooms, hold stock, arrange test drives and provide financing, usually via a third party finance house. The value chain should also show the flow of physical goods, both parts and finished goods, and the flow of information between the parties involved. It can then be examined to see how the performance of the value chain can be improved.

One activity that can often be improved in a value chain is the flow of information between organizations. As shown in Figure 2.4, information on the demand for goods should flow from right to left, from the

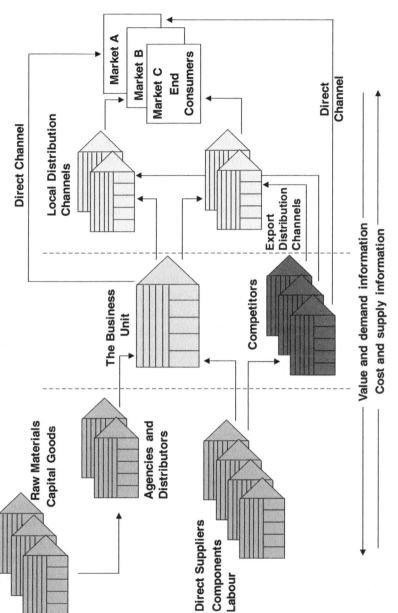

Figure 2.4: External value chain

end consumers to the firms upstream in the supply chain. Equally, information from the suppliers on the availability of materials and parts can be shared with those downstream. How well demand and supply information can be matched at all points in the chain will make a major contribution to the efficiency of the industry, by removing the need for excess capacity and stock holding; it will also affect how responsive it is to changing customer or market demands. Such improvements in the performance of the value chain are, in turn, likely to result in increased profitability of the individual firms within the chain. Opportunities to improve the flow of information to all parties in the chain, in terms of comprehensiveness, accuracy or timeliness, should be actively examined. This will increasingly depend on the level of integration achievable between the information systems of the participating organizations.

Value chain analysis initially proved valuable in developing IS strategies with the advent of Electronic Data Interchange (EDI) systems and Value Added Networks (VANs) in the 1980s and again in understanding the potential benefits and implications of e-commerce as the Internet became commercialized in the 1990s. It is now also a component technique within many business improvement methodologies such as Business Process Modelling and Six Sigma and is being used to help develop business-based information architectures.

It is recognized that many firms do not interact in a linear way and the terms 'value streams', 'networks' and 'constellations', among others, have been coined to describe the nonlinear relationships between some firms. While the case of a linear value chain has been considered here, the basic principles discussed can be applied to other forms of networks among firms.

Traditional IS/IT, and particularly e-commerce, has had a significant impact on the external value chain in a number of industries. In many industries, e-commerce is being used to enable companies to 'go direct' to the end customer or parties further down the value chain, cutting out existing intermediaries. This is termed *disintermediation* and can be seen in, for example, the travel market, where airlines, car rental companies, holiday companies and train operators are allowing consumers to buy directly from their websites, bypassing traditional travel agents.

While in certain cases intermediaries have been removed from the value chain, in others new intermediaries have been introduced. New online intermediaries are often based on information processing and are termed *infomediaries*. Examples include Internet search engines, online auctions and price comparison websites.

Internal value chain analysis

Internal value chain analysis considers an enterprise as a set of separate, but linked, activities by which the organization transforms inputs into outputs that customers value.

Figure 2.5 shows a simplified internal value chain for a car manufacturer. It can be seen that the activities of the company are divided into primary and support activities (which include many management activities). Primary activities are those directly concerned with creating value through the production and delivery of the organization's goods or services. These are typically divided into five categories:

- **Inbound logistics:** activities concerned with the replenishment, receipt, storage and distribution of the materials needed to produce the finished goods or services. In the case of the car manufacturer, this includes the ordering of components and subassemblies required to meet production plans and the receiving and routing of them to the correct part of the production process at exactly the time when they will be used.
- **Production:** activities involved in producing the final goods and services from the inputs. For an automotive manufacturer, this obviously

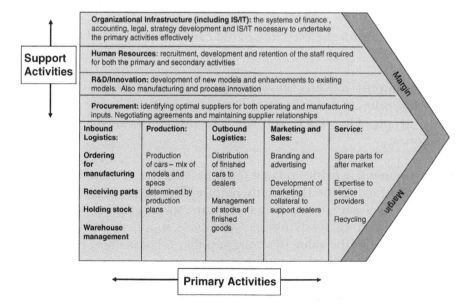

Figure 2.5: An example of an internal value chain

consists of all of the activities required to produce the final car, from building assemblies through to testing and quality control.

- **Outbound logistics:** activities required to store and distribute the final products and services to customers. In the case of services, this may require the organization to provide facilities where the customer can receive the service, as is the case with hospitals or restaurants. For a car manufacturer, outbound logistics entails the transportation of cars to the dealers, either to meet particular customer orders or to hold for display purposes.

- **Marketing and sales:** these provide the ability to take and process orders for the items produced as well as seeking to understand the needs of customers and to make them aware of the products and services of the organization. In the case of the car manufacturer, these activities would include international advertising campaigns as well as generating demand and attracting customers by local advertising and promotions by dealers.

- **Service:** includes operations such as installation, repair and training. Car manufacturers such as Mercedes and others provide 'collect and delivery' options for car servicing, including courtesy car provision to reduce customer inconvenience while the car is being serviced or repaired. Increasingly, environmental legislation requires that such operations must also take responsibility for decommissioning or retiring the original product. For example, in Europe, the End-of-Life Vehicle (ELV) Directive requires automotive manufacturers to take responsibility for the recycling of old cars at no additional cost to the final owner.

The support activities shown in the internal chain are those that allow the primary activities to be undertaken as efficiently and effectively as possible. They are typically divided into the following categories:

- **Procurement:** activities related to identifying the optimum suppliers and contracting for the inputs required for production and other services necessary for the firm to operate, such as capital equipment, and maintaining relationships with these suppliers. With growing recognition of the value of strong supplier relationships, this activity is receiving increased attention.

- **R&D/innovation:** activities associated with developing new products and services. R&D and innovation activity can also be focused on improving production processes and other activities, both within the organization and with trading partners. In the automotive industry, effort is being made by all the major manufacturers to design a standard or 'global' car that can be produced at any of their plants around the world and sold to customers in different countries with only minor modifications. Most major manufacturers are also investing in the development of electric or hybrid cars to meet the increasing demand for low or zero emission vehicles, as well as the legislative requirements to reduce carbon emissions.

- **Human resources:** recruitment, development, reward and retention of staff in all areas of the organization. In the case of the large car manufacturers, this activity will span operations around the globe and will require attention to many cultural differences. In many organizations this will include relationships with trade unions and other representative groups and ensuring compliance with employment legislation.
- **Firm infrastructure:** this includes strategic planning, finance, accountancy and other activities and management tasks needed to support the primary activities and to operate as an enterprise. This also includes the physical infrastructure of buildings and facilities, including the IT infrastructure, plus the management of the organizational structure, its control systems and culture. It will also normally address managing the relationships with the main external stakeholders, such as shareholders and the communities within which it operates. Since top management exerts considerable influence on shaping these parts of the organization, they should also be viewed as part of the firm's infrastructure.

Organizations undertaking internal value chain analysis should first consider how each primary activity adds value to the final customer offering and then how these and the support activities help it to sustain and develop its chosen strategy. If an activity cannot be shown to be adding sufficient value or contributing to achieving the strategy, it should be improved or, in some cases, discontinued.

While the value-adding activities that make up a firm's value chain may provide competitive advantage, it is likely that, over time, these will be copied by competitors. The performance of a firm is likely to be more robust and difficult to imitate if value is added in the linkages between the activities. IS/IT can enable a company both to improve the performance of individual activities and to coordinate and synchronize linkages between activities, hence helping to sustain its competitive advantage.

For example, the sales department could share up-to-date sales data with others in the firm via a company intranet or portal. This could allow the marketing department to tailor promotional activity to where it would be most effective; it could also enable production to tune their output to the actual demands of customers. Information collected by the field service operation could be shared with R&D to allow issues with existing products to be addressed quickly or for new products to be developed. Linkages can also be developed between the support activities of the firm and other organizations. The automotive industry is pursuing 'supplier-led innovation', in which the car manufacturers work with their suppliers to identify potential innovations to the core components and major assemblies. The success of this development activity depends on the organization sustaining effective relationships with its suppliers and R&D working closely with colleagues in procurement, who are responsible for supplier relationships.

The ultimate aim of IS/IT use in many companies is to allow information to flow seamlessly through the organization to wherever it is needed. Microsoft's CEO, Bill Gates, refers to the IS and IT linking the activities of the internal value chain as 'the digital nervous system of the firm' (Gates, 1999). He asserts that how companies gather, manage and share information internally, throughout the activities in the internal value chain, will increasingly determine which firms succeed or fail.

An example of an attempt to create a significant variant on the very well-established automotive value chain is described in Box 2.2.

Alternative internal value chain configurations

The 'linear value chain' is well suited to describing and understanding the value-adding activities of traditional manufacturing and retailing companies. However, it is less suitable for the analysis of many service and network businesses. Stabell and Fjeldstad (1998) consider an insurance firm and ask: what is received, what is produced and what is shipped? They observe that few insurance executives would consider 'uninsured people' as the raw material from which they produce 'insured people'. Clearly, such a firm's value-adding activities include the assessment of risk via actuarial calculations, developing policies, reinsurance of that risk, claims handling and customer relationship management. However, these activities are difficult to depict as a linear value chain. These authors therefore propose two alternative configurations of

Box 2.2: Revolutionizing the automotive value chain – a bold experiment

The Smart Car, launched in 1998, was produced by Micro Compact Car AG (MCC), a wholly owned subsidiary of Daimler-Benz, but managed as an independent entity, completely outside of the structure of Daimler-Benz. This meant that MCC had license and funds to create new products and services which could be delivered through innovative business models and processes.

The remarkable design of the two-seater 'Smart City Coupe' car attracted attention and interest in the new individual mobility concept developed by Nicolas Hayek (inventor of the Swatch watch) and others. The concept was used to promote the car's credentials as a solution to congestion and environmental pollution in urban areas. In addition, the intention of MCC was to revolutionize the value chain of car production, logistics and marketing.

A new production site had been constructed and a new dealer network and marketing organization had been developed. Cooperation was a primary feature of the business model for the company, in order to share the risks and costs of such an innovative product concept but also to motivate partners by sharing the profits. As such, the business model and highly integrated supply-chain concept went beyond existing practices in the automotive industry in a number of ways:

(Continued)

- customers could configure the car online to their preferences, yet order-to-delivery lead times were counted in weeks;
- suppliers co-invested in the production location and took a greater share in the final assembly process;
- dealers had to invest in 'Smart Car Towers' to stock and display 24 cars.

Dealerships – Smart Centres – were located in highly frequented places in urban areas, such as shopping centres on the outskirts of cities. Cars were mainly built to customer orders and a single-stage sales concept allowed Smart Centres to procure their cars directly from the plant, instead of through a dealer or import organization. Through this concept, Smart aimed to minimize ordering and delivery times, reduce costs and allow production planning to be based on point-of-sale data.

The initial target market segment for the product of 'DINKies' (double income, no kids) turned out to be too narrow, as Smart proved attractive to a wider range of customers, especially senior citizens and students – 'low-cost' segments. The target markets were redefined to include customers that were 'young or young in mind' and fashion-conscious. However, it was never clear how big that market was, whether the new concept would be a practical proposition or whether the business model could work to the satisfaction of all the parties involved.

Unfortunately, in all cases the 'forecasts' proved over-optimistic. Sales were lower than expected and manufacture proved more complex and costly than anticipated, leading to lower profit shares for all involved. As a result, the alliances and partnerships on which the success of the venture depended were put at risk.

In the more difficult and less optimistic economic climate following the dot.com 'bust' after 2001, it became increasingly apparent that the Smart 'experiment' was not a viable business proposition for the long term. Costs were out of control and the losses were no longer sustainable. Over the period 2002–2005 the Smart Car business model was abandoned and the supply chain reorganized and re-integrated with Daimler-Benz: a more traditional, proven model which resulted in increased sales and produced profits.

internal activities that can be used to analyse the value-adding steps within an organization.

The value shop. Value shops are organizations that solve specialist problems for customers or clients by applying their expertise. Firms that can be considered value shops vary their activities and their sequence of application depending on the nature of the customer or client problem. Examples of value shops are professional service firms such as those in the fields of law, architecture and consultancy. Certain functions or parts of firms that are themselves more conventional value chains can operate as value shops; for example, the research and development activity within a pharmaceutical company is problem solving in nature, and hence best characterized as a value shop.

Value shops are typically populated by experts in the particular domain in which the organization specializes. Although the activities of a particular firm vary according to the nature of both its clients and its experts and specialists, a generic set of primary activities, shown in Figure 2.6, can be drawn from the field of problem solving and decision making. Many organizations in the public and not-for-profit sectors are actually examples of value shops, finding solutions to problems presented by particular groups of the population, for example the elderly, students or patients.

The value network. Firms that can be modelled as value networks are those that provide a connecting or mediating service that allows customers to be linked to other customers. Examples of such firms are

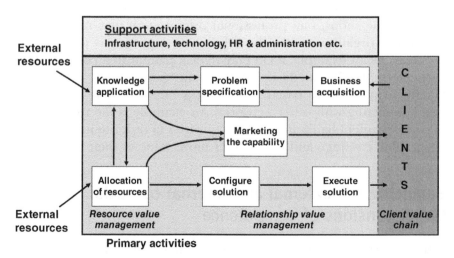

Figure 2.6: The value shop (after Stabell and Fjeldstad, 1998)

telephone companies, banks, postal services and online auctions and exchanges. The networking between customers can be direct, as in the case of telephone companies that provide communications infrastructure, or indirect, as in the case of banks that pool the money from depositors and in turn lend this to borrowers, without putting the two groups directly in contact.

The term 'network' is used to stress that the value these companies deliver to any particular customer is the population or network of other customers with whom they can interact or communicate. The value of the service provided by the firm increases with the number of other customers who use or can be accessed through the network, termed the 'network externality' effect. The last decade has seen the development and exponential growth of many Internet-based network organizations, including Facebook and the professional network service LinkedIn. These are now some of the largest organizations in the world in terms of both capital value and numbers of 'customers'.

The primary activities for value networks include the operation of the network infrastructure, the provision of services to users and the management of contracts, either with those users or for others providing support or services to the network. Support activities are similar to those found in other value configurations and include human resources, R&D, procurement and IS/IT.

A summary and comparison of the three alternative internal value configurations discussed is shown in Table 2.2.

As observed in the earlier discussion of the external value chain, most firms tend to operate in conjunction with other firms. In the case of value shops, one professional organization may refer a client to another organization for the solution to a particular part of their problem. As an example, a GP may refer a patient to a consultant for particular specialist medical tests that she cannot carry out herself. Finally, firms that are based on networks increase their coverage by interconnecting with other networks. An example is the use by banks of correspondent banks in overseas countries in order to increase their geographic coverage and hence offer more value to their customers.

Balancing the external and internal contexts: the dimensions of competence

A framework for strategy development which enables an organization to consider both the external world in which it operates and its internal

Table 2.2: Comparison of alternative value configurations

	Value chain	Value shop	Value network
Value creation logic	Transformation of inputs to products	Solving customer problems	Linking customers together
Primary activity categories	Inbound logistics Manufacturing Outbound logistics Marketing and sales Customer service	Problem/ customer qualification and acquisition Problem solving Relationship management Solution execution	Network promotion and contract management Service provisioning Infrastructure operation
Sequence of activities	Sequential	Cyclical and iterative	Simultaneous, parallel
Key cost drivers	Economies of scale Capacity utilization	Cost of experts Resource allocation	Scale Capacity
Key value drivers	Product cost Product specification	Expertise Reputation	Customer reach Capacity utilization
Industry structure	Interlinked chains	Referred shops	Layered and interconnected networks

capabilities was proposed by Treacy and Wiersma (1993). This model suggests that any organization, whether it is a for-profit or a not-for-profit organization, can find a route to industry leadership by excelling at one or more of three generic activities. These activities, termed the 'dimensions of competence' and shown in Figure 2.7, are:

- **operational excellence:** a focus on business processes to outperform others by delivering consistent quality to customers at acceptable costs;
- **customer intimacy:** tailoring products and services to the needs of particular customer groups, exceeding expectations and building loyalty;

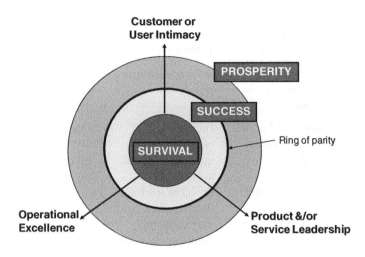

Figure 2.7: The dimensions of competence

- **product or service leadership:** continuing product innovation that meets or even anticipates customers' needs. This implies not only creativity in developing new products and enhancing existing ones, but also astute understanding of customer needs and preferences.

Organizations can use this framework by considering how well they perform on each of these dimensions compared to their competitors or similar organizations, if they are in a non-competitive market. If no actual benchmark measures of performance are available, then the comparison can be purely qualitative; that is, it can be undertaken by discussing the question: 'How do we think we compare with other organizations in our market or industry?' Those involved in these discussions should then mark their position and those they are comparing themselves with on each of the three axes accordingly. If their performance is similar to that of other organizations, they should mark themselves on the dark 'ring of parity' shown in Figure 2.7. If they are performing better than others on any or all of the three dimensions, they should mark themselves outside this ring on the relevant axis or axes. This is termed the *zone of prosperity*. If they are performing less well than competitors on any dimension, they should mark themselves inside the ring. Finally, if their performance in any one, or more than one, dimension falls a long way short of their competitors, they should mark themselves inside the central circle on the relevant axes.

The contention is that excellence in at least one of these dimensions of competence, matched by satisfactory or comparable performance in the others can lead to a strong competitive position. If an organization believes that its performance in two or more of the dimensions falls within the central circle, then it is likely to be struggling for survival.

It is most important for those involved in this analysis to consider and record what is causing the organization's performance to be as it is. The assessment of the organization's performance relative to others, together with discussion of the causes of this level of performance, allow the dimensions of competence framework to bring together the external, competitive forces view of strategy formulation and the internal, resource-based view.

Clearly, the dimensions are interdependent to some extent; for example, inadequate products will reduce the potential customers, and ineffective customer service could lead to poor perception of the organization's products. Hence, performance in one dimension will often be affected by the others and the strategy needs to identify the underlying causes of both excellent and unsatisfactory performance.

Based on the assessment, the organization can start to identify how it might capitalize on dimensions where performance is ahead of others to create further advantage or how it can make changes to overcome poor performance in any dimension which is creating a disadvantage compared with others. It must also recognize that, over time, many of the competing or comparable organizations will improve their products and services and become more efficient, causing the 'ring of parity' to slowly move farther out from the centre of the model.

An example of the use of the dimensions of competence model is given in Chapter 4.

Linking business, IS and IT strategies

As noted at the end of Chapter 1, once the business strategy for the organization has been determined it is necessary to develop IS and IT strategies. While IS should support the business strategy, there is also a recognition that IS can shape the business strategy. The dynamic relationship between the business and IS strategies is termed *strategic alignment* (Venkatraman *et al.*, 1993). Figure 2.8 depicts the relationship between the business, IS and IT strategies proposed by Ward and Peppard (2002), which draws on earlier work by Earl (1992).

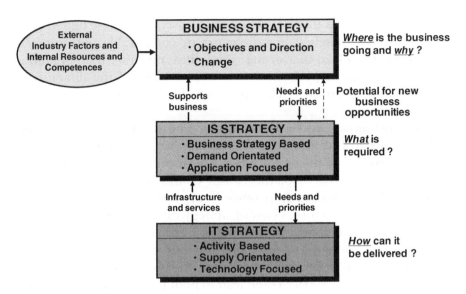

Figure 2.8: Linking the business, IS and IT strategies

The business strategy for the organization should answer the basic questions: *where* is the business going, *why* has this direction been chosen and *what* do we have to do to get there? The answers to these questions should be stated as clear objectives for the organization. Including objectives for both the short and medium term will ensure that they generate a sense of direction and purpose for the organization. They should also clearly encapsulate the nature and degree of change that will be required for the organization to move from where it currently is to where it wants to be.

IS should be considered as just one ingredient that enables the delivery of the identified business objectives alongside other business activities such as marketing, HR and R&D. The IS strategy should take the business strategy as its starting point and consider *what* information systems and processes are required to enable the identified objectives to be achieved: they should be driven primarily by the demands of the business and focused on applications of IT that can meet those demands.

Additionally, there will be some cases where IS developments or availability of new IT can create strategic opportunities. For example, with the advent of e-commerce, many new businesses were launched based on the ability to offer goods and services directly to consumers over the Web. Hence, the opportunities offered by e-commerce shaped the strategies pursued by these organizations as, over time, the new channel enabled them to extend their markets and even develop new types of products. Organizations should always include opportunities (and threats) resulting from the availability and capabilities of new technology as inputs to the business strategy as well as considering IS/IT a means of implementing their chosen strategy.

It is important to stress that the IT strategy should be distinct from the IS strategy, otherwise the latter tends to become dominated by technology issues, rather than showing how applications can meet the stated business needs. The IT strategy should address the technology, infrastructure, resources and specialist skills needed; that is, it should describe *how* the IS strategy will be delivered.

Managing the portfolio of IS/IT investments

Many IS managers face significant challenges in prioritizing the range of activities the organization is undertaking. This often results in spreading finite resources too thinly to be effective. Adopting a portfolio approach to projects can help organizations to balance new IS/IT requirements and opportunities with changes to existing systems and also to allow resources to be concentrated on those areas that are most important to the organization. These projects can then be finished more quickly and deliver business benefits earlier.

Ward and Peppard (2002) describe a framework – the applications portfolio – which managers can use to balance the IS requirements suggested by the business strategy, by enabling the contribution to the strategy of current, planned and potential systems or applications to be better understood. It allows managers to consider the different purposes or expected contributions when making decisions on which investments to pursue and which to ignore or postpone. It also highlights the different types of benefits that the investments will deliver and the complexity of the changes needed to fully realize them. In turn, this leads to the need for different approaches to justifying, resourcing, developing, implementing and managing the four different types of IS/IT applications indicated by the framework. In the context of this book, an adjusted version of that framework, focusing on new investments in IS/IT and changes needed to make more effective use of existing applications to achieve the strategy, is shown in Figure 2.9.

The portfolio classifies investments into four types, depending on their current or expected contribution to future business success.

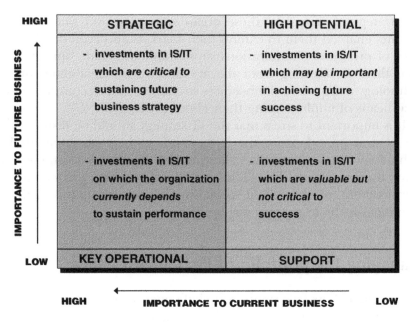

Figure 2.9: The IS/IT investment portfolio

High potential

High potential investments play a similar role to R&D activities by allowing an organization to experiment with new systems or technologies to understand the business opportunities and benefits they offer, together with the costs that are likely to be associated with such developments. Once these are better understood, managers are able to make informed decisions as to whether further investment is worthwhile now or may be worthwhile in the future, or, alternatively, whether the idea should be abandoned.

High potential investments have certain characteristics: they are, by their very nature, high risk and may fail to show a return on the investment made if, after evaluation, the idea has insufficient promise and has to be abandoned. They will often be championed by an individual who is highly committed to the idea and they lend themselves well to the development of prototypes, in order to demonstrate the value of the application to others. Despite the inherent risks, high potential investments are important to the future success of an organization, since it is through experimentation with new ideas and concepts that firms can identify and develop systems to create future competitive advantage.

Strategic

While high potential investments are uncertain, and may or may not provide tomorrow's competitive advantage, strategic applications are those that already provide advantage or are expected to do so in the near future. Strategic investments are therefore integral to the business strategy, particularly in enabling or creating new ways of doing business that differentiate the organization from its competitors. They may well have previously been successful high potential evaluations.

Since they are intended to deliver business advantages, it is hard to argue that new IS/IT applications which many of the incumbents in an industry already have are strategic. Advantage can only be derived from investments in IS/IT that are distinctive or are being used in different and innovative ways. This does not suggest that organizations need to invest in 'bleeding-edge' technology. Indeed, given that the future success of the organization is going to be dependent on such investments, it is better that they do not use leading-edge technologies, but ones that are tested and proven, at least in other contexts.

Key operational

Key operational systems are those that are critical to sustaining the current performance of the organization. They normally include the basic transaction processing and recording systems for most types of business, such as the point-of-sale systems in supermarkets and the transaction processing and reconcilement systems in banks.

While the effective operation of such systems is *key* to the performance of the organization, they are likely to be fairly consistent across an industry and can therefore give very little competitive advantage. Indeed, the effective operation of these systems is likely to be considered 'mandatory' for survival in an industry: they prevent disadvantage rather than provide advantage. However, as the industry develops and extends its use of IS/IT, many key operational systems will require further investment and even replacement to maintain the current level of business performance in critical activities.

Key operational systems may once have been the result of strategic investments, but are applications that have since become well established throughout an industry. An example would be the provision of ATMs (automatic teller machines) by the retail banks. When these were first introduced in the 1960s and 1970s, a network of ATMs provided a point of differentiation for a bank and could be considered as providing a strategic advantage. Now they provide no differentiation and are considered key operational systems, to the extent that many banks share networks of ATMs to reduce costs.

Support

These systems tend to be aimed mainly at improving business efficiency and individual productivity, resulting in lower operational and administrative costs. They are valuable to the business but not critical to the operation of the business, since, while they increase the efficiency of individual staff, for most businesses they do not contribute directly to delivery of the goods and services produced. Examples of such systems are routine accounting and record keeping plus the provision of personal applications such as word processing and spreadsheets on the PCs of individual staff.

Due to their widespread use throughout the organization, maintaining support applications can often consume a large part of an organization's IS and IT resources, detracting from its ability to make new, more important investments. Organizations need to resist this tendency to consume resources at the expense of other types of investment, and many do this by the extensive use of packaged software or by outsourcing the support activities.

Using the applications portfolio in practice

By identifying the resources, either staff time or funds required for the development, operation and maintenance by the applications in each of the four categories, the portfolio can help us to understand and adjust inappropriate spending, enabling more beneficial investment of those resources. While organizations would expect to have a range of current and planned investments that are spread across the four different types shown in the portfolio, there is no ideal distribution. An appropriate spread for a given organization would depend on the context of the organization, the prevailing industry conditions and, in particular, its current performance relative to competitors or comparable organizations.

Considering the dimensions of competence model shown in Figure 2.7, if an organization considers itself outside the ring of parity on any of the three axes, then it can make strategic and high potential investments which build on its success in that dimension. Where the organization considers it is less successful than competitors, particularly if its performance is significantly worse, then it should concentrate resources on improving the effectiveness and contribution of its key operational systems, or even replacing them, to enable it to regain parity with its competitors in the area of weakness.

In our surveys of current benefits-related practices, mentioned in Chapter 1, we asked questions about managing the IS/IT investment portfolio. It would seem logical that if around 75% of IS/IT projects fail to deliver the expected benefits, then one way to improve success rates is to stop doing those that are in the 75%. Portfolio management is aimed at selecting the right investments to make and then prioritizing them, so that maximum business value is achieved from the resources available. Our surveys showed how important this was seen to be: 90% of the organizations do some form of portfolio management, but the majority of respondents (60%) were not satisfied with how well they did it.

How taking a strategy-driven approach to managing the investment portfolio can increase the business contribution of IS/IT through more effective planning, decision making, project management and resource allocation is discussed, along with the key findings from our recent studies of portfolio management in practice, in Chapter 9.

An example of the use of the portfolio for a supermarket chain is shown in Box 2.3.

Working with the investment portfolio: the why, what and how of IS/IT investments

In order to position a new IS/IT project in the appropriate quadrant of the portfolio, it is often helpful to pose three questions:

Why is the investment being made – why does the organization need to change and how critical to its future is the successful management of the changes?

What types of benefit is the organization expecting to achieve by making the changes – reduced costs, improved operational performance, new customers, a new capability, etc.?

How can a combination of IS/IT and business changes deliver those benefits at an acceptable level of risk?

The answers to these questions, including instances where the answers are not known, will suggest where the investment belongs in the portfolio. If the answer to the first question is primarily about

Box 2.3: Applying the investment portfolio – a supermarket chain

An example of part of the IS/IT investment portfolio for a supermarket chain is shown in Figure 2.10. It also includes existing applications that use significant amounts of IS/IT resource to support and enhance them.

Like a number of the leading supermarket chains, this organization is exploring the use of radio-frequency identification (RFID) of goods. As well as improving the tracking of goods during distribution and in warehouses, this technology allows the items in shopping trolleys to be recorded without needing to pass each item separately over a scanner. Shoppers could simply pass their entire trolley through the reader, reducing queuing time at the till and increasing customer satisfaction. However, the reliability of such systems and the cost of the tags are still uncertain, resulting in this investment still being considered *high potential.*

The organization has a number of current systems that it considers to be providing advantages relative to its competitors. The organization offers a shared loyalty card that gives shoppers the

Figure 2.10: Applications portfolio for a supermarket chain

opportunity to collect rewards on purchases from a range of retailers in different sectors, which makes the scheme more attractive to customers than a single retailer scheme, resulting in greater participation. Equally, the wider range of information collected about customer purchases provides a more complete picture of the customers' preferences, enabling improved targeting of offers. Cooperating with other retailers also allows joint promotions to be developed.

Other systems that are considered *strategic* are: a system to improve the effectiveness of the merchandizing of goods, particularly those on promotion; one to improve new product development (working with suppliers); and another to manage the purchasing, stocking and sale of the increasing variety of non-food items now sold. Due to limited growth, there is intense competition in the supermarket sector, so winning market share from competitors is the route to success. Price cutting, through the effective operation of promotions, innovation through the introduction of new products and diversification into non-food items are the current major weapons.

The supermarket operates a number of *key operational* systems, which include electronic point of sale (EPOS) systems and the warehouse, distribution and replenishment systems that control the flow of goods from suppliers to the individual stores. While these systems do not provide advantages, ineffective use will result in goods being out of stock, one of the major contributors to customer dissatisfaction and lost sales. As it has become harder to acquire new sites, the basis of competition has moved away from expansion to fighting for market share, so systems to identify the optimal new sites, which would, in the past, have been considered strategic, are now less important and hence considered key operational. Similarly, online shopping, which was once considered highly strategic, now offers little differential advantage since it is offered by all the major players.

The supermarket also operates many *support* applications, including those to manage its HR function, payroll and its property portfolio, such as the payment of rates and utility bills. Such systems are common to all types of business and while the effective operation of such systems is important, the key focus should be on efficiency.

improving efficiency, resulting in reduced costs, it is likely to be *support.* As new or replacement support systems normally address activities the organization is currently doing, and they are similar to many other organizations, it is likely that there will be a number of alternative answers to the third question.

When the answer to the first question is mainly concerned with improving the performance of current activities or processes, then the investment is probably *key operational.* Although there may be less certainty about what specific benefits can be achieved than for support systems, it should be possible to answer the 'what the organization hopes to achieve' question by considering which processes will be impacted and by how much they need to, or could, improve. But it may be less clear how this can be achieved in terms of the best combination of business and IS/IT changes.

If the answer to the first question is about gaining significant advantage compared to competitors, then the investment is *strategic.* However, it is likely that the organization may not have well-defined answers to the last two questions and the early stages of the project will focus on finding those answers. The greatest area of uncertainty will be with *high potential* investments, which may be recognized by the ability to answer any of the three questions in more than the broadest terms. This is because such projects are often undertaken in order to understand the benefits a new technology or business model might offer the organization; it is about evaluating a new opportunity, rather than finding a solution to an identified problem.

The relevance of these three questions to the benefits management process is discussed in Chapter 3 and explored in detail in Chapter 4.

Organizational information competences

In an extended study undertaken with several major organizations to examine the specific competences organizations need to effectively develop and exploit new information systems, Ward and Peppard (2002) developed the model shown in Figure 2.11. This model links business strategy with IS demand and exploitation by the business and IT supply and can therefore be considered an extension of the model shown in Figure 2.8.

The six major competence areas identified in the model are defined as follows:

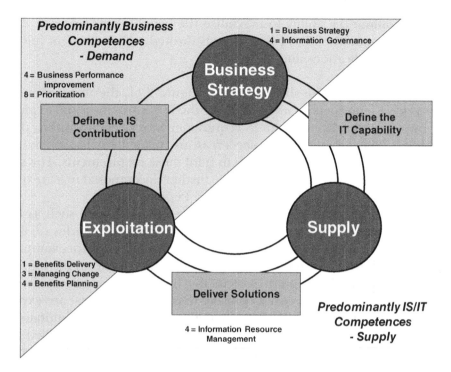

Figure 2.11: Information competences (after Ward and Peppard, 2002)

- **Business strategy:** the ability to identify and communicate an effective strategy for the organization, including an evaluation of the implications of IT-based opportunities as an integral part of this strategy.
- **Define the IS contribution:** the ability to translate the business strategy into processes, information and systems investments and change plans that match the business priorities identified. This should be the basis of the IS strategy.
- **Define the IT capability:** the ability to translate the business strategy into long-term information architectures, technology infrastructures and resourcing plans that enable the implementation of that strategy. This should be captured in the IT strategy.
- **Supply:** the ability to create and maintain an appropriate and adaptable information, technology and application supply chain and resource capacity.
- **Deliver solutions:** the ability to deploy resources to develop, implement and operate IS/IT business solutions that exploit the capabilities of the technology.

- **Exploitation:** the ability to maximize the benefits realized from the implementation of IS/IT investments through effective use of information, applications and IT services.

As indicated by the shaded area in Figure 2.11, the three competence areas – business strategy, defining the IS contribution and exploitation – are all related to the IS requirements or demands within the business. The other competence areas are related to the supply of applications, technology and skills to fulfil those requirements. The six areas of competence identified can be further decomposed to a greater level of detail, as described in Ward and Peppard (2002).

While some of the competences are largely functional, such as IT supply, others extend well beyond the traditional boundaries of the IS/IT domain and include organization-wide competences: for example, exploitation, which includes the realization of benefits from the implementation of IS/IT, should exist in the business areas where those systems and technologies are deployed. In organizations that are experiencing difficulties with deriving benefits from IS/IT, the limitation may not be within the IS/IT function, which may be very skilled at designing technical solutions and developing systems. The limitation may well be that they are not supplying the systems the business really needs, due to this not being communicated to them accurately or the inability of the business to effectively deploy and exploit the systems that are supplied.

The model, particularly at the level of the detailed competences, can be used by organizations in a diagnostic mode. Managers, usually in a workshop, can consider their current performance in each of the competence areas relative to their required performance. The managers participating in the assessment must be drawn from various business functions, in addition to IS/IT managers, to provide a comprehensive and balanced analysis. The identified gaps in performance should lead to actions to develop or improve the areas of weakness.

Workshops undertaken with mixed groups of managers from a wide range of organizations have shown that there are some detailed competences that most organizations find challenging. These are also shown in rank order in Figure 2.11. The two areas that organizations tend to find the most difficult are the development of an effective *business strategy* and the *delivery of benefits* from IS investments.

Managing the business and organizational changes associated with the exploitation of new IS was identified as the area where organizations felt they had the next greatest problem. To realize benefits, new systems and technologies must, almost always, be accompanied by changes in how the organization's processes work and, within those, how individuals are expected to work. As explored throughout this book, these changes may well be more difficult and time consuming than the purchase and deployment of the underlying technology.

Four competences were judged equally to be the next most challenging: *benefits planning, information governance, information resource management* and *business performance improvement*. *Benefits planning* is the ability to explicitly identify and plan how to realize all the benefits from an IS investment. *Information governance* is concerned with the development of information management policies and the roles and responsibilities of individuals within those policies, whereas *information resource management* deals with the development and operation of processes that ensure that data, information and knowledge management activities meet organizational needs and satisfy corporate policies. *Business performance improvement* relates to the ability to identify the knowledge and information needed to deliver the business objectives through improved management processes.

Prioritization of the applications and technologies identified as beneficial to the organization was also an area in which organizations believed they were underperforming. The investment portfolio, discussed earlier in this chapter, can help organizations understand the varied contributions of the IS/IT investments as the basis for agreeing priorities. This is discussed in more detail in Chapter 9.

Overall, Figure 2.11 shows that the majority of the detailed competences that are problematic in many organizations are those related to IS demand, as opposed to IT supply-side issues. The increased adoption of proven packaged software and the improved reliability of hardware, mean that it is becoming easier to develop and implement technology and systems to a high standard. However, determining which investments to make and ensuring the maximum business benefits are obtained are still problematic for many organizations.

Summary

This chapter described approaches and tools that can assist organizations in developing business strategy, assessing IS/IT investment opportunities and determining priorities. Ways of understanding the potential contribution of different IS/IT investments were introduced and the main challenges organizations face in delivering the maximum impact and benefits from those investments were discussed.

The next few chapters of the book describe a benefits management process that organizations can adopt to develop and improve the three specific competences discussed earlier: benefits identification and planning, the associated management of business changes and benefits delivery. Chapter 3 presents an overview of the process and its relationship to well-known project management and system development methodologies. Chapters 4 to 6 then cover, in detail, a set of tools and techniques that enables organizations to develop sound business cases and comprehensive benefits plans for their investments, thereby increasing the benefits actually realized.

Chapter 3

The foundations of benefits management

As discussed in the previous chapter, our research has found that many organizations consider themselves weak at maximizing the benefits realized from the implementation of IS/IT projects. IT exploitation involves three component competences – benefits planning, change management and benefits realization. These are intrinsically business-based competences, therefore improving them will mean changing how IT specialists and business managers and users work together.

This situation is not new, but effective management of IT implementation and adept use of its capabilities are becoming increasingly integral to improving business performance. It is therefore essential that business managers are not only responsible for deciding on IS/IT projects and priorities, but also for the delivery of the benefits.

Figure 3.1 suggests that an inability to realize the benefits of particular IT investments has significant implications beyond each of the investments. The lack of ability to deliver benefits reduces the organizational understanding of the business value that IT can provide, which leads to an inability to make consistent or appropriate investment choices or set priorities. This, in turn, limits an organization's ability to identify how IT can best be used to improve performance or support new strategic developments. As a result, business strategy formulation often does not adequately include the consideration of opportunities available from new IT-based options or threats arising from the deployment of IT by others in the industry. It could be argued that the money many organizations wasted in the period 2000–2001 on ill-thought-out 'ventures' in e-business was, at least in part, due to business managers' lack of knowledge about the benefits that IT might deliver and the changes in business practices that were needed to cause the benefits to flow.

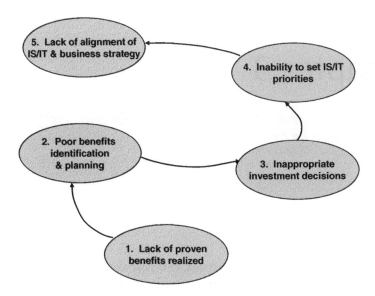

Figure 3.1: The implications of poor benefits management

This chapter first considers the reasons for the continuing poor record of organizations in realizing the intended benefits from IS/IT projects due to the incompleteness of existing methods and processes. It then describes how that gap can be filled by an approach that specifically addresses benefit identification and realization, but also enables the integration of other methods to increase investment success. The stages in a proven benefits management process are then outlined and the key differences from other existing approaches and practices are discussed.

Subsequent chapters explain in depth how tools and techniques used within the process framework can enable organizations to identify and deliver the benefits available from different types of IS/IT project.

The gaps in existing methods and the implications

Over the last 30 years a range of processes and methodologies has been developed to improve the success rate of IS/IT developments and implementations. However, the overall success in terms of investments that deliver the expected benefits seems stuck at around 30%. This is not to imply that nothing has been learned or that the processes and methodologies do not work. The investments being made today are more varied, more complex and more pervasive than in the past and often have a more significant impact on the business and organizational performance. But the conclusion can be drawn from the lack of improvement that existing methodologies and processes are insufficient and new thinking and approaches are needed if the success rate is to improve.

Existing methodologies have tended to be developed to address the 'supply-side' issues that affect organizations' abilities to specify or deliver an appropriate IT solution, to manage the project that is being conducted or to assess whether or not to make the investment. Given general agreement that the weakest area of competence is *exploitation*, none of these, other than some change management methodologies, deals explicitly with the set of issues that affects benefits realization. The change management methodologies were not normally devised for IT-enabled change and need to be adapted to fit with the IT supply-side methods, which still tend to dominate the 'way things are done' in many IT projects.

It is not the purpose of this book to critique existing methodologies either collectively or individually, but their purpose and scope need to be understood to differentiate the benefits management approach described in detail here and also to show, later in the book, how this approach is complementary to and can be integrated with the 'best practices' from other processes and methods. Each of the types of methodology is briefly outlined below and references are included to further sources of information about them.

IS/IT strategic planning

Modern approaches to strategic IS/IT planning tend to be frameworks which are used to achieve the following objectives (see Ward and Peppard, 2002):

- identifying IS/IT-enabled business opportunities;
- aligning IS/IT projects with business strategies and priorities;
- sourcing and implementing IT architectures, infrastructure, applications and services;
- developing organizational resources, competences and capabilities to deploy and utilize the technology effectively.

Most approaches recognize that the formulation of comprehensive long-term strategies is not feasible in the context of increasingly rapid business and technological change. Rather, strategies have to be adapted frequently to deal with emergent issues and opportunities. However, the elements of the IS/IT project plan should either be derived from conscious strategic analysis or be validated against the organization's business imperatives and objectives.

Systems development

Traditional methodologies such as SSADM (Structured Systems Analysis and Design Methodology) and newer 'agile' development methods are processes and methods designed to ensure that the right system is developed in the most appropriate way to meet agreed functionality, quality and performance requirements. Other methodologies such as SSM (Soft Systems Methodology) (Checkland and Scholes, 1999) address the organizational and people issues to ensure that the right problem is being solved in a feasible and effective way. Others, such as ETHICS (Effective Technical and Human Implementation of Computer-based Systems) (Mumford, 2003) and MULTIVIEW (Bell and Wood-Harper, 1998), balance the technological and organizational viewpoints. Avison and Fitzgerald (2002) provide comprehensive descriptions and a comparison of different methodologies.

Project and programme management

Methodologies such as PRINCE2 (Projects In Controlled Environments 2) are essential for managing activities and resources associated with a project to deliver the system and complete the tasks to agreed times and costs; most organizations now recognize that this is a shared responsibility between business and IT management. Ultimately, it is the organization that suffers the real consequences of poor project management and business project managers are often appointed for major IS/IT projects, although their roles and responsibilities are not always clear. McManus and Wood-Harper (2002) discuss different project and programme management methodologies.

Investment appraisal and evaluation

These terms are often used interchangeably, but to provide some clarity, investment appraisal is used in this book to mean pre-investment assessment, whereas evaluation implies assessment during and after implementation. There are many methods, ranging from standard financial techniques for calculating the expected return from IS/IT projects from an economic perspective, to more organizational assessments that allow for less 'tangible' benefits (i.e. those that cannot legitimately be converted to financial values) to be included (see Farbey *et al.*, 1993; Renkema, 2000). Most project management methodologies include a post-implementation evaluation stage and processes have also been developed to enable more 'active' evaluation over the whole investment life-cycle, rather than at just the 'go/no go' decision (Remenyi *et al.*, 1997). Some companies have introduced formal 'health checks' during implementation to revalidate the business case, as discussed later in the chapter.

Change management

The term 'methodologies' is perhaps less appropriate in the area of change management than 'frameworks' or 'approaches', except in the sense of proprietary methods from consultancies. All approaches recognize that the nature of the changes (for example, process or organizational), the extent of change (how much of the business or organization is affected) and the degree of innovation (or how radical the changes are) should determine the way the changes are managed and by whom, both in terms of the activities involved and the style of management needed. Several frameworks have been developed to assess the overall type of change being undertaken, its characteristics and consequently the steps required both to accomplish it and for managing the project, programme or initiative that is established to deliver the change. Of particular relevance to 'IT-enabled' changes are the frameworks described by Benjamin and Levinson (1993), Kumar *et al.* (1998) and Simon (1995) – these are considered in more detail in Chapter 6. Discussions of different approaches to managing 'strategic' change can be found in Balogun and Hope Hailey (2004) and Pettigrew and Whipp (1991).

Risk assessment techniques and risk management processes

These are usually components of comprehensive systems development or project management methodologies or are included in investment appraisal methods, depending on the nature of the technical and financial risks involved. However, few of these techniques assess the risks from the perspective of how they affect the delivery of the available benefits. This aspect of risk assessment and management is considered in Chapter 5.

As already stated, few organizations have a process focusing specifically on identifying and managing the business benefits required from IT or other investments. All of the above methods include some components of relevance to managing the benefits, but as ancillary rather than primary activities. Even in many investment appraisal approaches, identifying benefits is largely done to enable a business case to be developed, to justify the IT costs and to obtain funding. Investment appraisal can be considered as an event, or 'one day' in the life of the investment (albeit an important one), within an overall process of benefits management, as defined in Chapter 1.

Since the purpose of any IS/IT project is to deliver improvements to organizational performance, it would seem logical that the key process around which others should fit is benefits management rather than the project management, investment appraisal or systems development approaches. These should be adapted to match the types of change involved in the investment and the nature and range of benefits expected to be achieved. How the benefits management process relates to the other processes and approaches is therefore as depicted in Figure 3.2. These relationships and their implications are considered in more detail in Chapter 7.

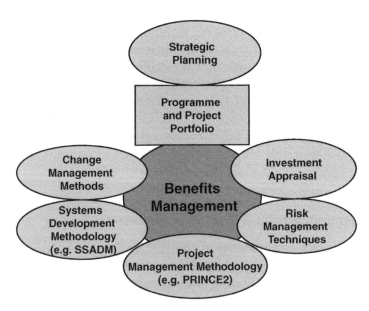

Figure 3.2: The context of benefits management

Figure 3.2 also demonstrates that most of the existing methods are the responsibility of specialists, such as project managers, finance or HR, rather than line managers. One enduring issue in IS/IT projects has been gaining and sustaining line manager involvement throughout the development and implementation processes. This is partly due to the lack of clarity of their role in the project in relation to the specialists. It would seem obvious that they should take primary responsibility for defining the benefits they expect and then ensuring they are realized – benefits management. People in other roles should contribute their specialist knowledge to ensure that the approaches adopted will enable that to happen.

The origins of the benefits management approach and process

The process described here was developed by studying what actually happened in a number of major information systems projects in large organizations across all sectors of industry, commerce and public bodies. Some were actively trying to manage the benefits, others were not. By studying the projects and particularly by conducting in-depth post-implementation reviews, it was possible to understand why some projects were more successful than others in delivering benefits. A new approach, which consisted of the process described here and a set of new and adapted tools and techniques, was developed. By applying the approach to subsequent, new projects it was possible both to avoid the 'loss' of benefits that were clearly achievable and in most cases to identify and realize more extensive benefits than from previous, similar investments.

Another outcome of applying the approach was that IT costs were actually reduced for some investments. In extreme cases, projects were cancelled because no benefits could be delivered, but more commonly the essential IT functionality required could be identified more explicitly in relation to the benefits an organization wanted, thus eliminating IT costs that delivered nothing of value. It was also possible to reduce the amount of IT functionality deployed, by making more changes in business practices to utilize package software 'off the shelf' or to reduce procedural complexity rather than automate it.

Since the completion of the original research and development programme, the approach, process and the tools and techniques have been refined, extended and improved as a result of the feedback from the organizations that have used them. Experience from many of those organizations is reflected in this book – some as explicit examples and some more generically. Many organizations have realized that this approach is not only applicable to IS/IT projects but can also be used to improve the success of other change programmes, business developments and strategic initiatives. Of course, in more and more of these, IT is one of the enablers of change and many organizations have taken the stance that, apart from infrastructure projects, there are now really no IS/IT projects *per se* – there are only change projects that have significant IS/IT components.

An overview of the benefits management process

In considering the activities required to manage the delivery of benefits, it is assumed that the technical implementation is achieved successfully. However, as the process proceeds and the changes needed to gain the benefits become clearer, the technical specification will undoubtedly have to be revised. It is assumed that the change control processes in the development methodology can deal with this. The other related activities are the organizational and business changes of many types that have to be made to deliver the benefits. The benefits management process should be the driving mechanism for managing these change activities.

The benefits management process draws on the model for managing strategic change developed by Pettigrew and Whipp (1991), by recognizing that the process by which a major change is managed needs to be relevant to the content of the change involved – in this case primarily IT-enabled change – and must be appropriate to the prevailing organizational context – both internal and external. The process also recognizes and includes some of the best practices developed in Total Quality Management (TQM) and business improvement and process excellence approaches and methods (such as Six Sigma). As well as creating a number of new techniques specific to benefit identification, definition and realization, it incorporates a number of tools and techniques from different sources to address particular aspects. It also enables organizations to utilize their existing methodologies in conjunction with the benefits management process and toolkit.

The five stages in the iterative process and the links between the stages are shown in Figure 3.3 and are described in outline in the following sections.

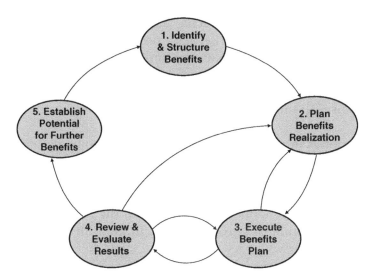

Figure 3.3: A process model for benefits management

Step 1: Identifying and structuring the benefits

Based on the outcome of the IS/IT strategic analysis and planning activities, the overall business rationale for a new or improved use of IS/IT will have been identified and the overall nature of the business contribution expected from the investment can be determined, i.e. whether it is strategic, key operational or support, as described in Chapter 2. If the nature of the contribution is uncertain, then the investment should first be put through an R&D stage (as per the high potential segment of the portfolio) to understand what the possible benefits are and if they are relevant and achievable. While the entirety of the benefits management process does not really apply to R&D investments, a simplified version and some of the techniques can be used to enable the benefits to be identified and assessed.

The purposes of the first stage of the process are to:

- establish agreed objectives for the investment and ensure that these relate to one or more of the drivers for change in the organization;
- identify all the potential benefits that could be obtained by achievement of the investment objectives;
- understand how a combination of IS/IT functionality and business changes can cause the benefits to be realized;

- establish ownership of the benefits and determine whether they can be measured to prove that they have occurred;
- identify any organizational issues or implications for particular stakeholder groups that could hinder the project or even cause it to fail;
- produce an outline business case to decide whether to proceed further or stop the investment now.

These points introduce a few terms that need to be defined clearly and explicitly, so that there is consistency in the language used by everyone involved and misunderstandings are avoided. The definitions and their implications are explained in more depth during the discussion of the use of the tools and techniques in the next three chapters. However, it is helpful to introduce the definitions of the most important concepts here.

Definition: Business drivers

Issues which executive and senior managers agree mean the organization needs to make changes – and the timescales for those changes. Drivers can be both external and internal but are specific to the context in which the organization operates.

Definition: Investment objectives

A set of statements that describe what the organization is seeking to achieve from the investment. They should be a description of what the situation would be on successful completion of the investment.

Definition: Business benefit

An advantage on behalf of a particular stakeholder or group of stakeholders.
    This implies that the benefits are 'owned' by the individuals or groups who want to obtain value from the investment.

Definition: Benefit owner

An individual who will take responsibility for ensuring that a particular benefit is achieved. This usually involves ensuring that the relevant business and enabling changes progress according to plan and are achieved. Due to the need to ensure that things get done, the benefit owner is usually a senior member of staff.

Definition: Stakeholder(s)

An individual or group of people who will receive the expected benefits or are either directly involved in making or are affected by the changes needed to realize the benefits.

Identifying the potential and achievable benefits involves an iterative process of interpreting the investment objectives and considering the improvements that implementing the technology and associated changes could deliver. Achieving each objective could deliver a variety of different benefits across the organization and also to trading partners and customers. The process is inevitably iterative since objectives may be modified and new benefits identified as ideas and options are considered.

For each potential benefit it is important to be as precise as possible about *where* in the business, or in trading partners, it will occur, in order to determine how it can be measured and who in the organization should be responsible for its delivery. As will later be explained in more detail, if the benefit cannot be measured or no one owns it, it does not really exist.

All business performance improvements are measurable in some way and so are all of the benefits delivered by information systems. Some can be measured directly, for example, staff reductions due to automation or a decrease in product rejects due to improved production control. Many of these can also be converted into financial values. Where this can be done, it should be, to enable an economic appraisal to be made. In other cases the benefit and its measurement may be less direct. Better timing and control of deliveries could lead to more satisfied customers, an improvement that may lead to increased sales or at least fewer lost sales due to delivery problems. The level of customer satisfaction will need to be measured and some estimate made of the sales implications of improved delivery. In essence, every benefit should be expressed in ways that can, in due course, be measured, even if the measure will be subjective, for example, customer or staff opinion. If there is no possible way of measuring the benefit, it should be discarded.

Next, the feasibility of achieving each of the benefits needs to be considered. The first step, as already mentioned, is to determine owner-ship of the benefit and hence responsibility for its delivery. This is easy to identify if the system is mainly within one function or area of the business, but it is more difficult when the system crosses functions, especially when reorganization and rationalization of tasks across functions are integral to the delivery of benefits. Responsibility may have to be shared, but then this must be made explicit. Again, any benefits lacking ownership should be removed from the list.

The interdependence of benefits and change

Having identified and allocated responsibility for benefits to stakehold-ers, the next step is to determine the changes required for the delivery of each benefit and how the IS/IT development will enable these to occur.

A key output from this activity is described as a *benefits dependency network*, which relates the IS/IT functionality via the business and organizational changes to the benefits identified. Developing such net-works is also an iterative process, since, as required changes are identi-fied, a network of interrelating changes and benefits will evolve, and the feasibility of achieving some of the benefits will be questioned. Equally, further benefits may well be identified. Creating the network requires knowledge to be shared among business managers and key stakeholders, including the IT specialists, so that they all understand what the benefits are and how realizing each of the benefits depends on specific changes being made.

There are essentially two types of change, in addition to introducing new technology.

Definition: Business changes

The new ways of working that are required to ensure that the desired benefits are realized. These will be the new ongoing ways of working in the organization – at least until the next change initiative.

Business changes cannot normally be made until the new system is available for use and the necessary enabling changes have been made.

> **Definition: Enabling changes**
>
> Changes that are prerequisites for achieving the business changes or that are essential to bring the system into effective operation within the organization. Enabling changes are usually 'one-off' activities rather than ongoing ways of working.

Examples of enabling changes are agreeing new working practices, redesigning processes, changes to job roles and responsibilities, new incentive or performance management schemes and training in new business skills (as well as the more obvious training and education in the new system). They can often be made, and sometimes have to be made, before the new system is introduced.

As with the benefits, ownership and responsibility for each change should be identified and agreement reached on the evidence needed to determine whether or not the change has been achieved successfully.

Before embarking on the significant amount of work involved in the development of a comprehensive benefits plan, a 'first-cut' analysis should be prepared to assess whether there are sufficient potential benefits to justify the approximate expected cost and to define the further work needed to produce the full benefits plan and business case. If the achievable benefits are clearly insufficient, the project should be stopped.

It is also advisable to carry out an initial stakeholder analysis to identify all the relevant parties involved and assess whether, based on the balance of benefits and changes that affect each stakeholder group, the necessary commitment of resources and knowledge will be made to the project. In this step, potential negative impacts on particular stakeholders need to be identified, so that actions can be considered to mitigate these 'disbenefits'. Stakeholder analysis is considered in more detail in the next stage of the process, but for some projects much of the assessment can be made in the first stage.

Step 2: Planning benefits realization

The main purposes of this stage are to develop a full benefits plan and a business case for the investment, which will be submitted to management for approval. In order to do this, the following also have to be achieved:

- A full description of each of the benefits and changes, with responsibility for delivery clearly defined and agreed.
- Measures for all the benefits and, where appropriate, estimates of the expected 'values' of each benefit at the end of the investment. This assumes that many of the improvements can be quantified in advance and, for some, financial values calculated. The basis and rationale for such estimates must also be made clear.
- Measurements to establish the current 'baseline' at the start of the investment, which may require new measurements to be introduced to ensure that the benefits resulting from the project are accurately attributed to it.
- Agreed ownership of all the changes and actions in place to address all the stakeholder issues that may affect the achievement of the changes.
- The evidence or criteria to be used to assess whether each change has been carried out successfully.
- A complete and fully documented benefits dependency network to show all the benefit and change relationships.

A full description of the contents of a benefits plan and business case (including risk assessment) and how to carry out the activities involved is provided in Chapter 5. Like any plan it includes activities, responsibilities, timescales, resources and deliverables, but perhaps most importantly a clear description of the relationships and dependencies that are critical to achieving the benefits and investment objectives.

Benefits realization: the stakeholder perspective

Before the dependency network and resulting benefits plan can be finalized and a sound business case proposed, a thorough stakeholder analysis should be completed. The purpose of stakeholder analysis is to understand organizational and people factors that will affect the organization's ability to implement the required changes and achieve the expected benefits. This is effectively an aspect of risk analysis, which considers the implications for the project in terms of how different stakeholder perceptions can impact particular components of the benefits plan. Some stakeholders will be mainly beneficiaries of the investment, others will largely be involved in the changes and some may be both beneficiaries and responsible for significant changes.

The main objective is to address the 'what's in it for me?' problem of IS/IT projects. Projects often fail due to the lack of cooperation of parties who are not considered central to their success, but whose ability or willingness to accept change is essential to delivering the business improvements required. The purpose of assessment is to obtain ownership and buy-in of relevant individuals and groups and to identify organizational factors that will enable or frustrate the achievement of the benefits. Some stakeholder groups may have genuine concerns that cannot be addressed during the project and the investment scope or implementation plans may have to be modified to avoid serious conflict and possible investment failure. Some of the 'disbenefits' that have been identified may be deemed unacceptable and, again, the objectives or scope of the system may need to be revised.

Another reason for the analysis of stakeholder interests is to consider aspects of business change outside the particular project and the possible implications on achieving the benefits. For instance, other business initiatives, reorganization and possible changes in key stakeholders may have a significant impact on the project. A number of techniques for carrying out a stakeholder analysis are discussed in Chapter 6. Only when this assessment has been completed and the feasibility of achieving the target benefits thoroughly tested should a business case requesting funding for the IS/IT project be developed.

The stages involved in steps 1 and 2 of the process can be summarized as a set of questions that have to be answered to produce a benefits plan. These are shown in Figure 3.4.

Step 3: Executing the benefits plan

As with any plan, the next stage is to carry it out and adjust it as necessary as issues and events affecting its viability occur. Monitoring progress against the activities and deliverables of the benefits plan is just as important as for the IS/IT development plan, and the two plans are components of the overall project plan. It may be necessary to establish interim targets and measures to evaluate progress towards key milestones or the final implementation.

Normally a business project manager is appointed to ensure that the project is delivered to meet the business needs without undue disruption or risk. The role that a business project manager can and

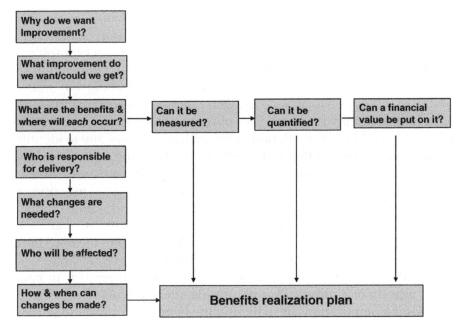

Figure 3.4: Key questions in developing a benefits plan

should fulfil is considered in detail later in the book, but one aspect of that role is to be the 'custodian' of the benefits plan on behalf of other business stakeholders and to ensure that each stakeholder carries out his or her responsibilities as defined in the plan.

As the project evolves, inevitably the plans will have to change, due to changes in resources and personnel plus unexpected events or problems that have to be assessed and dealt with. It is the business project manager's responsibility to decide, in consultation with the other relevant business managers, what action to take in terms of reviewing the scope and specification of the system or the business and enabling changes. In some instances, the investment justification may need complete reappraisal to decide whether the project should continue. The starting point for any interim review should be 'what is the effect on the benefits and our ability to achieve them?' both to ensure that actions are appropriate to the overall project objectives, rather than just the immediate problem, and that all the relevant stakeholders are involved in decisions to change the plan. An example of an investment interim review or 'health check' is described in Box 3.1.

Box 3.1: Project health checks at a pharmaceutical company

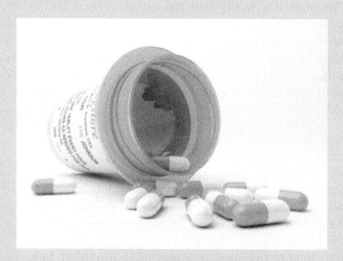

As economic conditions worsened in 2008, a major pharmaceutical company looked to increase the return on investment it achieved from its IS/IT projects. The IT department, working within R&D, was set targets for financial and productivity benefits to be delivered across the portfolio of IS/IT projects. To improve both project performance and investment decision making, they decided to introduce project 'health checks' on all major investments. These were in addition to normal project progress reviews and focused specifically on the benefits that would actually be delivered in relation to the original business case. It was realized that approvals were often based on relatively unreliable estimates, that benefits could change as the project evolved and post-implementation reviews were often too late to influence the outcome.

The health checks were normally carried out about three months into implementation and involved the project manager and sponsor. The independent review team consisted of experienced project managers from other parts of the organization – the review process was formalized and recommendations passed to the IT investment board.

(Continued)

As a result of the reviews, a few projects were cancelled to avoid wasting further resources on what had become less than worthwhile investments, many had the scope revised to improve the project return and in others, further benefits were discovered. In combination, these results ensured that the benefit targets were exceeded by a significant margin in the first year. This, in turn, led to more ambitious targets for year two but also improved the quality of business cases so that benefit estimates became more realistic.

During implementation, further benefits may also be identified and, again, the business project manager should obtain agreement on appropriate action to revise the plan to accommodate the benefit or defer any action until step 5.

Equally, it may become apparent that intended benefits are no longer feasible or relevant and the benefits plan should be modified accordingly, along with any consequent reduction in the IS/IT functionality or business changes. Factors outside the benefits plan itself, such as changes in the organization or problems in meeting the requirements at the intended cost will, of course, initiate reviews of the project deliverables and plan and, in turn, cause a reassessment of the benefits plan and even the business case.

Step 4: Reviewing and evaluating the results

The purpose of a benefit review is twofold: to assess the investment itself and to gain organizational learning:

- to determine and confirm which planned benefits have been achieved;
- to identify which expected benefits have not been achieved and to decide if remedial action can be taken to still obtain them or if they have to be foregone;

'The major differentiator between organizations that are successful with their IT projects and those that are not is that the successful ones undertake a review of the benefits achieved at the end of projects.' *Ward and Daniel (2008)*

- to identify any unexpected benefits that have been achieved and any unexpected 'disbenefits' that have resulted;
- to understand the reasons why certain types of benefits were or were not achieved and provide lessons for future projects;
- to understand how to improve the organization's benefits management process for all projects.

Once the new technology, system and business changes have been implemented, there should be a formal review of what has and has not been achieved. This is a business review aimed at maximizing the benefits gained from the particular investment *and* increasing the benefits from future investments. All comprehensive project management, systems development and change management methodologies include a review process following implementation and they should be carried out prior to the benefit review. The results of those assessments may provide explanations for the non-delivery of intended benefits, as well as knowledge to improve the management of future projects or systems design and implementation.

The evaluation should involve all key stakeholders and focus on what has been achieved, what has not (or not yet) been achieved and why, and identify further action needed to deliver outstanding benefits, if possible. The reasons for lack of benefit delivery may be due to misjudgements or lack of knowledge in preparing the benefits plan or problems during its execution. Another aspect of this review is to identify any unexpected benefits that have arisen and understand how they came about. This, again, may prove valuable input to improve the first stage of future projects. Equally, any 'disbenefits' that resulted should be understood in order to try and avoid them recurring in future projects.

It is worth stating that any post-implementation review should not become a 'witchhunt'; it must be an objective process with future improvements in mind, not a way of allocating blame for past failures. If it is seen as a negative process, honest appraisal and a constructive critique of what has happened become impossible and the whole process falls into disrepute or is not carried out.

Step 5: Establishing the potential for further benefits

Having reviewed what has happened, it is equally important to consider what further improvement is now possible following the implementation of the system and associated changes and in the light of the new levels of business performance that have been achieved. This should be a creative process similar to step 1, involving the main stakeholders and any others who may be able to contribute, using the increased knowledge now available to identify new opportunities and the benefits they offer. These benefits may be achievable through further business changes alone or may require more IS/IT projects. In the latter case, these potential benefits should be the starting point for investment consideration via the stages in step 1 of the process.

If this is not done, many available benefits may be overlooked. If maximum value is to be gained from the overall investment in IT, benefit identification should be a continuing process from which IS/IT and business change projects are defined. This 'benefit-driven' approach to determining the investment portfolio, as well as maximizing the return from each investment, is considered in Chapter 9.

Table 3.1 summarizes the main activities involved in each of the process stages.

What is different about this approach?

The purpose of the benefits management process is to improve the identification of achievable benefits and to ensure that decisions and actions taken over the life of the investment lead to realizing all the feasible benefits. This approach recognizes the criticality of business manager involvement in achieving organizational value from IS/IT and is complementary to the methodologies and processes that address other aspects of the project shown in Figure 3.2. Improving existing methodologies, which largely deal with the complexity of the 'supply side' of investments, will not address the gap on the 'demand side'. The benefits management process was developed to fill this gap. Each element of the process can be aligned with steps or deliverables in other methodologies and, as depicted in Figure 3.2, the benefits management process can be the means of integrating the other approaches, since it maintains a focus on the purposes of the investment, rather than the means of delivery.

The majority of value from IT comes from the business changes that it enables the organization to make. The achievement of benefits obviously depends on effective

> 'Organizations that coupled investments in IT with organizational learning and change achieved increased value from IT.'
> Gregor et al. (2006)

Table 3.1: Stages and main activities of the benefits management process

Stage	Activities
1 Identifying and structuring the benefits	• Analyse the drivers to determine the investment objectives. • Identify the benefits that will result by achieving the objectives and how they will be measured. • Establish ownership of the benefits. • Identify the changes required and stakeholder implications. • Produce first-cut business case.
2 Planning benefits realization	• Finalize measurements of benefits and changes. • Obtain agreement of all stakeholders to responsibilities and accountabilities. • Produce benefits plan and investment case.
3 Executing the benefits plan	• Manage the change programmes. • Review progress against the benefits plan.
4 Reviewing and evaluating the results	• Formally assess the benefits achieved or otherwise. • Initiate action to gain outstanding benefits where feasible. • Identify lessons for other projects.
5 Establishing potential for further benefits	• Identify additional improvements through business changes and initiate action. • Identify additional benefits from further IT investment.

implementation of technology, but evidence from project success and failure suggests that it is organizations' inability to accommodate and exploit the capabilities of the technology that causes the poor return from many IT investments (Markus *et al.*, 2000). This has been recognized and addressed in the socio-technical approaches to systems development, but these methods do not specifically consider the links between the technology and business changes and the way they are brought together to deliver particular benefits. The 'benefits plan', which is the main deliverable of the first two steps of the process, and the benefits dependency network, which underpins the plan, are means of ensuring that these links are made. The benefits plan is also the basis for the business case, not only for obtaining funding but also for managing the project, since it includes not only *what* benefits are intended but also *how* each one can be achieved.

In essence, the most obvious difference in this approach is the benefits plan and its role in 'governing' the investment process. But, perhaps more importantly, the approach and the associated tools and techniques change the nature of the involvement of business managers and other stakeholders in the management of the investment through-out its life-cycle. In particular, the first step in the process is designed to encourage the stakeholders to share their collective knowledge to reach agreement on the overall outcome they expect and to determine whether they are able and willing to undertake the changes needed to reach the objectives. That will, to a large extent, depend on the benefits each stakeholder perceives and hence the emphasis on the ownership of benefits.

Gaining business ownership of the benefits and the change pro-gramme requires more than a new process, better tools and another plan. The mode of engagement between the IS/IT specialists and busi-ness stakeholders also has to change. The process and tools are designed to enable business managers to become more effectively involved in IT developments and in control of the parts of the project only they can make successful, while respecting the fact that they are inevitably busy people with many competing priorities for their time. However, this is difficult to achieve by asking the stakeholders to fit in with the meth-odologies of the IS/IT specialists, which are not an intuitive or conven-ient way of working for most business managers.

Inevitably this approach is more demanding of manage-ment time, especially at the start of projects, but experi-ence has shown that clarity and agreement about what the project should deliver, as early as possible, prevents signifi-

'The participation of users and other stakeholder groups in the design and development process can be considered essential.'
Walsham (1993)

cant and expensive corrective action later – assuming that corrective action is actually possible. It does, however, make more effective use of the time managers can devote to the project, by improving the com-munication about those aspects of the investment that are most critical to its success.

The other key difference in this approach is the emphasis on post-implementation evaluation of the extent to which benefits have been achieved, and the assessment of the further benefits that are now avail-able having completed the investment and achieved some or all of the objectives. Exploiting the learning that has been gained from previous

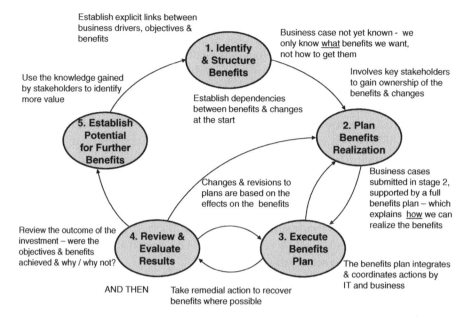

Figure 3.5: Key areas of difference in the benefits management approach compared with others

IT investments is essential to increasing the value from future investments. That will not happen without formalizing the reviews as integral parts of the process and ensuring that they are carried out.

Some of the key differences of this approach are shown in Figure 3.5.

Summary

This chapter began by reporting that many organizations consider themselves weak in the ability to realize the benefits from IS/IT projects. The benefits management process described in this chapter has been used successfully in many organizations to change the way in which IS/IT projects (and other change programmes) are managed, resulting in improved benefit delivery. This is because it not only recognizes the inextricable link between change and benefit, but also provides a way of maintaining that link by more appropriate involvement of business stakeholders at the inception and throughout the life-cycle of the investment. In turn, this changes the working relationships between business managers and IT specialists, based on a clearer understanding of how investment success depends on the collective knowledge and abilities of everyone involved in the project.

Using the *ends–ways–means* logic of strategic management, the *ends* in this case are the realization of more value from IS/IT projects. The *means* normally imply the functionality or capability of the technology, available technical resources and the abilities of those designing and implementing the new system. This view often neglects the knowledge and skills of business managers and other stakeholders, which are essential to understanding how, in the particular organizational context, the new IT capabilities can actually be used to improve performance. Realizing value from IS/IT projects depends on the *ways* in which an organization uses its collective technical, business and managerial knowledge and skills to identify what it can achieve through a combination of technology and other changes, and the *ways* it uses its resources to achieve the investment objectives.

The benefits management process provides the foundations of a new way of managing IS/IT projects that makes more effective use of the means that most organizations already have at their disposal, but which all too often are not being combined to create the organizational competences necessary to obtain all the benefits available from their IS/IT projects. The tools and techniques and how they can be used to bring about new ways of managing are discussed in the next three chapters.

Chapter 4

Establishing the why, what and how

This chapter describes some of the frameworks that enable the key questions posed in Chapters 2 and 3 to be answered for a particular investment. Those questions are:

- Why is the investment being made?
- What types of benefit is the organization expecting to achieve?
- How can a combination of business changes and IT deliver those benefits?

The frameworks are described in terms of their use in completing the first two steps of the benefit management process shown in Figure 3.3: identifying and structuring the benefits of a particular investment and the preparation of a benefits plan and business case. In the implementation phase of the project (step 3 in Figure 3.3), the outputs from the use of the frameworks guide the project management, systems development and change management activities, as described in Chapter 3. The progress of the project should be reviewed against the initial benefits plan and any variances should be addressed. This may either require additional effort applied to the business changes or revisiting the plan in the light of any unexpected or emergent constraints. The benefits plan will also provide the baseline against which to undertake a formal review at the end of the project – step 4 in the process – and also a means of identifying further benefits that may be realizable.

The chapter ends with an extended example of the use of the tools by a food processing company seeking to improve its profitability, operational performance and administrative processes. This example is further developed in Chapters 5 and 6, in order to generate a complete benefits plan.

Why: identifying business and organizational drivers

As described in Chapter 2, organizations should develop a strategy which describes the contribution IS and IT can make to the business, before doing a benefits analysis for a particular investment. However, all too frequently, such strategic planning is carried out at senior levels but not communicated or shared with others in the business. Staff lower down in the organization are therefore often unclear about the strategic direction and why and how an individual investment contributes to the strategy. To address this lack of shared understanding it is suggested that all benefits management work starts with discussions to clarify and confirm the strategic influences or forces acting on the organization. Even if there is a well-communicated business strategy, it is important to ensure that there is a common and consistent understanding of the rationale for the strategy and the implications of the organization's objectives.

Driver analysis

Driver analysis seeks to identify and understand the forces, or drivers, causing the organization to make changes either to what it produces or to how it conducts its business activities. The definition of business drivers is presented in Chapter 3, together with definitions of the other key elements of benefits management.

As per the definition, in establishing this list of organizational drivers, the perspective of the most senior managers, usually the executive management team, is taken. This ensures that the drivers are actually strategic to the future of the whole enterprise, rather than merely affecting the interests of certain departments or functions. Often, localized priorities are found to conflict with the best interests of the future of the whole organization. Also, as is described in Chapter 5, when developing a business case, the case will be stronger if it can be explicitly linked to what is important to the organization's executive and senior management.

The timescale over which these drivers should be considered will depend on the industry sector. For example, the utilities and transport sectors, which require significant investments in fixed infrastructure, may need to take a five- to ten-year horizon for their strategic analysis. In sectors such as the nuclear industry, mining or waste disposal, an appropriate horizon may be up to 20 years. In contrast, for those operating in very fast-moving or turbulent environments, such as fashion goods or information technology, a one- to two-year horizon would be more appropriate.

Sources of drivers

Many drivers will be external to an organization, due to the industry or marketplace in which it operates, or the general business or economic environment. For example, changing customer behaviours, increasing costs of key resources or the improved performance of competitors may result in drivers on the organization that require it to change its current products or modes of operation. Changes may also be a consequence of legislation or regulation, either of the organization's particular industry or of all businesses in a geographic market, for example, European environmental legislation regarding carbon emissions.

Drivers also arise from within the organization. For example, many organizations are concerned about their ability to share and reuse the business knowledge they have generated. They may describe themselves as 'reinventing the wheel' every time they undertake a new project and that it is imperative to improve knowledge sharing within the organization. Other organizations are concerned with their ability to attract and retain the best talent in their industry or sector. This may be due to a shortage of skilled individuals or the organization's poor reputation for developing its employees or the working environment is considered too stressful. For many organizations offering an acceptable work/life balance for staff may be critical to attracting and keeping the highly skilled or experienced people required to remain competitive.

Drivers should be described in enough detail to ensure that they are explicit to the organization's particular situation in the specified timescale. They should also make clear why change is needed and also the implications of not taking action to respond to the drivers.

For example, an external driver could be:

> 'We are losing too many customers due to our inconsistent service levels and increased consumer expectations which our main competitors can now achieve 90% of the time.'

An internal driver might be:

> 'Our rate of new product introductions is below the level required to replace the profits from obsolescent products in the next three years.'

Strategic drivers, dimensions of competence and the nature of change

One effective method of establishing the drivers and the degree of change required to address them, is to use the dimensions of competence framework, based on the work of Treacy and Wiersma (1993). This was introduced in Chapter 2 (see Figure 2.7). The framework brings together consideration of the external or competitive environment in which an organization operates and its internal resources or capabilities. The framework asks managers to assess where they are in relation to their competition or peer organizations according to three dimensions of competence: *product or service leadership, customer intimacy* and *operational excellence.*

Identification of performance 'behind' that of competitors on one or more dimensions will suggest the need for changes to address it. If performance is assessed to be a long way behind competitors or, in non-competitive markets, well below what is expected by stakeholders, there is probably a need for more radical or extensive change in order to 'catch up' or stop further deterioration in performance. This may also require the elimination of activities that are seriously hampering the performance of the organization, which may only be possible by restructuring the business, the replacement of many ineffective legacy systems or outsourcing a number of business processes.

The need for radical change is usually associated with performance well below competitors or expectations, but it may also be required by organizations currently performing at an acceptable level on all the dimensions, due to drivers affecting a combination of the dimensions. For example, Reuters, the information agency, had to change radically, by creating new products and services as well as dramatically reducing its costs, to maintain its leading position, as the sources of similar information expanded rapidly following the commercialization of the Internet.

Poor performance in just one of the three dimensions will imply drivers that can be addressed through more targeted change. Performance that is comparable to that of competitors in any or all of the three dimensions will suggest drivers that are related to maintaining this status quo and incremental changes to maintain 'business as usual'.

Although an organization that is performing better than its competitors or exceeding stakeholder expectations may have no perceived need for change, its external environment will continue to evolve, often driven by the activity of competitors or the rising expectations of key stakeholders. Being in a leading position implies that the organization should search for further innovations or performance improvements that will increase or at least maintain the gap between it and its main competitors. Innovations may require some radical changes, although this may not appear as critical or difficult as the radical change required by laggards in an industry. As the fate of many of the organizations described in Peters and Waterman's *In Search of Excellence* (1980) demonstrated, maintaining a leading position cannot be taken for granted and requires considerable creative skill and the ability to innovate or adapt to avoid being caught or overtaken by the competition.

The linkages between performance levels identified by the dimensions of competence framework and the associated nature of change are summarized in Table 4.1.

Table 4.1: Nature of changes suggested by competence analysis

Performance from dimensions of competence	Associated nature of change	
Performance well below that of competitors on one or more of the three dimensions of competence	Elimination of problems and constraints and potentially radical change	Improvements by removal of problems, constraints or inefficiencies
For organizations with, at least, parity on all axes and an advantage in one dimension, opportunities exist to move considerably ahead – outside the ring of parity – in one or more dimension	Innovation and potentially radical change	Performance improvements from doing something new or in a completely new way
Performance below that of competitors on one of the three dimensions	Targeted improvement	Level of change required to meet specific business objectives and/ or achieve more effective use of resources
Performance equal to or better than competitors on all axes	Business as usual or incremental improvement	Managing a stable situation to avoid disadvantage

Strategic drivers and application types

Figure 4.1 shows generic or typical drivers that tend to relate to the different types of IS/IT projects, as described in the applications portfolio discussed in Chapter 2.

High potential investments often result from a radical new business idea or new technology, or a combination of the two resulting in an opportunity to create change within the organization, its products or in the market in which it operates.

Strategic applications are often developed as a response to competitive pressures within the industry or to achieve a competitive advantage by satisfying a market need ahead of the competition.

Key operational investments often derive from a need to improve the effectiveness of current operations in order to overcome known causes of current competitive disadvantages or to avoid becoming disadvantaged in the future. This may result from unfavourable comparisons with other firms in the industry or from a level of performance that is no longer acceptable. Such improvements in effectiveness are often accompanied by cost savings, but this is not normally the main objective for the investment.

STRATEGIC	HIGH POTENTIAL
Perceived market requirements Competitive pressures Achieve business changes	Innovative business idea New technology opportunity Create change
Improved performance of existing activities (effectiveness) Integration/rationalization to speed up business processes Industry legislation	Cost reduction and efficiency improvements through automation General legislation
KEY OPERATIONAL	SUPPORT

Figure 4.1: Typical drivers for different application types

Finally, investments in *support* applications result from a need to increase the efficiency and reduce the costs of specific organizational activities. This is often achieved by removing time-consuming and error-prone steps in current processes or by the automation of information tasks and clerical activities.

Establishing investment objectives

The drivers exist independently of any decision by the organization to invest in a particular project. Indeed, external drivers will persist, even if the organization chooses to 'hide its head in the sand' and do nothing about them.

The next step is to establish an agreed set of objectives for the investment or project. Investment objectives are formally defined in Chapter 3. They can be thought of as a set of statements that define the 'finish line' for the project, or 'paint a picture' of the way things will be if the project is successful. Success criteria are therefore often included in the statement of the objective, although these tend to be high level statements, rather than detailed operational measures. As discussed later, detailed measures should be applied to the individual benefits that will be realized from the project. The identification and use of measures is an important ingredient of the benefits management process and is discussed further in Chapter 5.

While it is impossible to be prescriptive, projects should have a few clearly stated and compelling investment objectives, rather than a long list of incremental and overlapping ones. The longer the list, the harder it is to remember what the objectives are and the task of achieving them all becomes more complex and difficult. It also increases the probability of conflict and confusion over the relative priorities among the objectives. Experience of applying the benefits management process in a large number of organizations and with very different types of project has shown that the majority of projects can be described perfectly well with between three and six carefully worded objectives. There is often a tendency to think that a project's significance is dependent on the number of objectives rather than the importance of each of them.

It is important to note that each of the investment objectives should explicitly address one or more of the drivers, to ensure that the project will clearly contribute to achieving changes that are important to the organization's future. They should also 'tell a story' that the stakeholders will believe makes the investment worthwhile and therefore will gain their commitment. From experience, the sequence of expressing the objectives can also be important for the following reasons:

1. Positive, creative objectives about new or better things that will happen should come first, since they are more likely to encourage action than negative or reductionist objectives.
2. Externally facing objectives that will benefit customers will have broader organizational acceptance than objectives that suggest benefits to particular internal groups.
3. The sequence of objectives should flow logically such that it can be understood by stakeholders.

For example, in a local authority, the objectives of its new 'People System' were described in the following way:

- people's skills will be developed to meet the changing demands for public services;
- services will be better organized to make better use of the available skills, experience and resources and reduce the stresses due to resource shortages;
- new approaches to recruitment, outsourcing and contracting will reduce the skills and capabilities gaps as services evolve;
- cost savings will be achieved by introducing self-service personnel processes for employees to use and reduce numbers of administrative staff.

The objectives and their sequence helped to achieve more buy-in to the changes from the majority of staff, and also enabled more pragmatic and acceptable approaches to achieving the necessary changes to be identified.

SMART objectives

An increasingly popular means of creating compelling and manageable objectives for projects is to test each objective against the 'SMART' checklist shown in Table 4.2.

As is discussed further in Chapter 5, although it is important to review realization of the objectives and benefits at the end of the project, this does not mean that all objectives must be associated with

Table 4.2: SMART objectives (after Doran, 1981; OGC, 2004)

Objectives should be	
Specific	Precisely describe a well-defined accomplishment in a way that all stakeholders to the project can understand
Measurable	Be capable of being measured or have some means of knowing that the objective has been achieved
Achievable	Be realistic given the context in which the organization is operating and the constraints that it has
Relevant	Address issues that are important to the organization
Time bounded	Be associated with a particular timeframe in which the objective should be met

a quantitative measure. Subjective measures, such as those related to the customer perceptions of service improvement or product quality, or employees' views of the working environment are acceptable.

Linking the investment objectives to the drivers

Having identified the drivers and determined the objectives for the particular initiative or project, it is necessary to bring these together by specifically aligning each objective with the drivers it addresses, as shown in Figure 4.2. As indicated, not all drivers will be addressed by a particular project. Any project that claims to be able to address all the drivers is likely to be too large and complex to be successful, since the drivers will affect many parts of the organization in different ways and over different timescales.

Clearly, any projects that do not address at least one of the business drivers should not be considered further, since it will not be possible to develop a credible business case. If a project only addresses one or very few drivers, it does not imply it has a low priority. By definition, each driver is important and the project may be the only way that the organization can address the issue.

The project team and management should ensure that the project objectives are not simply a description of the IT system or do not effectively become that over time. As research into the implementation of enterprise systems has shown, many strategic investments to create

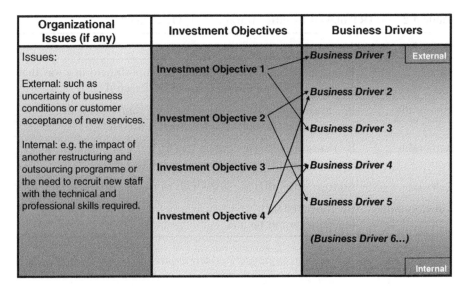

Figure 4.2: Bringing investment objectives and drivers together

new organizational capabilities become essentially software replacement projects over time (Ward *et al.*, 2005). Ensuring that the investment objectives are, and continue to be, linked explicitly to the organizational drivers should prevent this from happening.

Concerns may also arise over the project's relationships with other projects or programmes that may overlap with it or on which there are critical dependencies. Alternatively, discussion may identify either issues that may introduce risks to the investment or opportunities to increase the chances of success. As shown in Figure 4.2, a note should be made of these issues to ensure that they are dealt with, usually during the development of the benefits dependency network which is presented in a following section.

As with a number of the benefits management frameworks, the table shown in Figure 4.2 should be completed from right to left. An example of the use of the framework is given in the extended example at the end of this chapter.

What: the business benefits

Having agreed the investment objectives, the benefits can be identified by considering the improvements that will be realized if each of the objectives is achieved. As shown in Chapter 3, benefits are defined as advantages on behalf of particular stakeholders or stakeholder groups.

An important attribute of a benefit is that it should be specific to an individual or group. For example, many management information systems and 'business intelligence' investments are expected to yield the benefit 'improved decision making', but are often not specific about who would be able to make 'improved decisions', which decisions would be improved or even what is expected to result from the improved decisions! For example, if an organization wanted to realize increased revenues from its marketing campaigns and sales activity, then such benefits may be expressed as 'better design of promotions by marketing staff to ensure increased customer leads from campaigns' and 'prioritization by sales staff to follow up the leads with the highest potential value'.

Each investment objective is likely to give rise to a number of benefits for different stakeholders. For example, one of the objectives may have been agreed as 'to increase the loyalty of customers', which could follow from identifying a driver of increasing defection rates amongst high value customers. If the project could increase customer loyalty, then a variety of benefits could be expected in relation to the interests of different stakeholders. For example, increased customer loyalty might result in: 'greater satisfaction for customers', 'reduced spending of the promotions budget on customer (re)acquisition (by marketing)' or 'reduced administration costs in customer accounts'. If, as in many industries, loyal customers are found to spend more than new customers by trading up to higher value products and services, this might also lead to 'increased sales of high margin products (leading to increased bonuses for the sales staff)'.

How: the benefits dependency network

The earlier chapters of this book have stressed that the realization of benefits from IS/IT projects will, in most cases, depend on changes to business processes and relationships and the ways in which individuals or groups work within the organization. Such changes are often overlooked or underestimated.

The central framework in the benefits management process is designed to enable the

> 'Improvements . . . from IT . . . are conditional upon appropriate complementary investments in workplace practices and structures.'
> Melville et al. (2004)

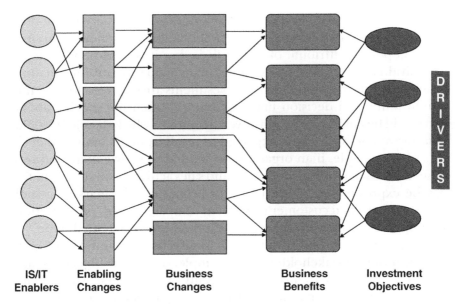

Figure 4.3: The benefits dependency network

investment objectives and their resulting benefits to be linked in a structured way to the business and IS/IT changes required to realize those benefits. The framework, called a *benefits dependency network (BDN)*, is shown in Figure 4.3.

The network should be created from right to left. The origins of the BDN and the reasons for right-to-left working are explained in Box 4.1.

Construction of the network starts with understanding the drivers, and agreement on the objectives for the particular investment should then be identified together with the business benefits that will result if the objectives are achieved. It is then necessary to consider the changes to business activities, structures and ways of working that are necessary to realize the potential benefits identified.

Each benefit should be considered in turn and the changes needed to realize it should be identified and described on the dependency network. Two distinct types of change need to be recognized. *Business changes* are new or different ways of working that will be required permanently in the future to achieve and sustain the benefit. In contrast, *enabling changes* are one-off changes that are necessary to allow the enduring business changes to be brought about or to introduce the new technology.

Business changes

Business changes can include a wide range of different types of change, particularly for large enterprise-wide systems. The types of change frequently identified include new or different:

- business processes or business models;
- sourcing options for some activities and functions;
- ways of dealing with and providing services or products to customers;
- roles and responsibilities for departments, groups and individuals;
- organization structures;
- relationships and ways of working with trading partners;
- reporting or governance arrangements;
- performance measures;
- appraisal and reward schemes;
- practices for collecting, managing and sharing information.

Changes may well be required in many different parts of the organization. In some cases, many individuals or groups will have to make similar sets of changes and in others, each group will have to undertake changes specific to their roles and activities.

While business changes may be considered the way the organization wishes to work in the future, the organization may well be undertaking other projects which cause the business changes to be altered again after a relatively short period. Such constant change now appears to be a standard part of the operation of many organizations.

Enabling changes

There is also a wide range of enabling changes that may be required in order to ensure the identified benefits can be realized. These may also involve many different groups or functions in the organization and they typically include:

- training in how to use the new system or technology;
- education in how the new systems can improve the performance of individuals, groups or the whole organization;
- definition of new measures and the information needed for them;

- collection of current performance data to provide a baseline for future comparison;
- mapping of current processes and the design of new processes;
- definition of new roles, job descriptions, responsibilities and organizational structures;
- establishment of rules and practices for the migration of data from legacy systems or collecting the new information required;
- business rules and standard practices for managing the information life-cycle (acquisition, renewal, retirement);
- decommissioning of legacy systems;
- definition of new application and information governance structures;
- reallocation of resources/budgets.

Enabling changes tend to be required either before or as the system goes live. For example, training in the use of a new system is often undertaken just before the system goes live so that staff, and perhaps customers and suppliers, are ready to use the system when it is available. The decommissioning of replaced or redundant systems and processes should ideally occur soon after the new system goes live. A short overlap ensures that a smooth changeover can occur both for business operations and technical support and allows the organization to have the 'backup' of the existing systems in case of teething or 'shakedown' problems. However, if the old systems remain operational for too long, users may not switch to the new system, leading to limited benefits being realized.

Enabling IS/IT

Once the major business and enabling changes have been identified, the IT systems need to be considered. This may result in the need for additional changes, particularly enabling changes, which should then be added to the network to show how they lead to the delivery of specific benefits.

Definition: Enabling IS/IT

The information systems and technology required to support the realization of identified benefits and to enable the necessary changes to be undertaken.

If the project requires technology other than IS/IT, or new facilities, then these can be included in the enabling IS/IT part of the network, as they will have the same characteristics and require the same approach to their planning and management.

IS/IT projects may require the purchase or development of new systems or changes to existing IS/IT applications and infrastructure. The reason for deferring consideration of technology until this stage is to ensure that the focus of the investment is on what the organization wishes to achieve and the related change management, rather than the technology solutions that are available. Technology vendors are keen to promote the features of their products and, all too often, organizations are persuaded that the list of features equates to a set of benefits that the technology will provide. This can result in buying and installing systems that either do not meet the organization's needs or are overly complex and unduly expensive. Having explored all other areas of the investment, it is possible to consider what IS/IT is 'sufficient to do the job'.

This is not meant to encourage organizations to purchase IT that has limited capabilities, but to enable them to clearly understand what is required and what is not, in terms of providing relevant, realizable benefits. The explicit linkages shown on the benefits dependency network should help to identify potential capacity and capability constraints as well as the new functionality leading to purchasing more appropriate technology and systems. For example, if benefits have been identified from having all an organization's customers in one system, then the assessment of alternative suppliers' products should be based on the costs of holding and accessing all types of customer information in a single database and whether it can accommodate expected growth in customer numbers.

Following the identification of the benefits and the required business and enabling changes, it may be apparent that the organization does not need to invest in new IS/IT. Indeed, it is often found that if the changes identified were made, many of the benefits could be realized with existing systems. The problems are sometimes due to the way people are working or using existing systems or the inability of the organization to establish the more effective and efficient practices enabled by the systems.

Concentration on the business benefits and the change management implication at the start of the process will also encourage business managers to become involved. Surveys show that effective engagement of business managers is often lacking and this is recognized as a key

Box 4.1: Origins of the benefits dependency network – right-to-left working

The format of the benefits dependency network is derived from a well-known technique in project management called the Precedence Diagramming Method (PDM) (Dobson, 2003). In PDM, the activities within a project are shown in nodes connected by arrows that denote dependencies between tasks. The approach, which is often incorrectly called PERT charting after the Program Evaluation and Review Technique for project management, can also be termed *activity on node* charting. This is in contrast to the other popular charting method of ADM (the Arrow Diagramming Method) or *activity on arrow*. In this method activities are indicated on the arrows between nodes.

PDM commences with a starting node on the left-hand side of the page and connects all the activities in the project in the sequence in which they must be undertaken and completed across the page to a finish node on the right-hand side. Each activity or node in the network, apart from the start node, therefore has one or more predecessors – that is, an arrow or arrows coming into it from activities that must be finished before it can be started. Similarly, each node, except for the finish node, has at least one successor – an arrow from it to the subsequent task or tasks. A number of methods for describing the links between changes and benefits, for example, 'results chains' (Thorp, 2003), are based on the PDM technique.

The *benefits dependency network*, as shown in Figure 4.4, has a similar form to a completed PDM network. The desired finish is the achievement of the investment objectives and associated benefits, which are therefore shown on the right-hand side of the diagram. The necessary steps required to achieve them are shown on the left-hand side. However, a significant difference between benefits dependency and PDM networks is the order in which the elements are identified. In the latter, having identified the desired outcome and key activities for a project, a network is usually built up from the start to the finish; that is, from left to right. In the benefits network, the network is built up from right to left: the investment objectives are agreed and used to identify the specific benefits that might be expected. Similarly, consideration of each benefit or benefit stream then leads to the identification of the necessary business and enabling changes.

Having derived the network from right to left, implementation will tend to occur from left to right, although some activities may be started before earlier ones are complete. The early stages will normally involve the development or introduction of the necessary IS/IT and undertaking the enabling changes that are the prerequisites to making the enduring business changes happen.

reason why organizations fail to realize benefits from IS/IT (Nelson, 2007). Discussions that are essentially about the functionality of IS/IT, or are dominated by it, are usually of little interest to business managers who can even feel threatened due to their limited understanding of technology. As has been stated before, one key aspect of the benefits management approach described in this book is to create an environment in which both business and IS/IT staff participate fully and willingly in the discussions, to contribute and share their knowledge and learn from their colleagues.

An example of a completed benefits dependency network is given in the extended example at the end of this chapter.

Joining up the network: highlighting dependencies

The dependency network diagram in Figure 4.4 shows each investment objective giving rise to one or more benefits. Hence, arrows are drawn from the objectives to the benefits. As discussed in Box 4.1, implementation will tend to occur from left to right, with the IS/IT, enabling and business changes required before benefits can be realized. These are therefore connected with arrows from left to right.

The network can be joined up as it is being produced: each objective can be considered in turn and the benefits that would arise from its achievement, the required business and enabling changes and the necessary IS/IT can be identified, before considering the next objective and its associated benefits and changes. Alternatively, the full benefits arising from all the investment objectives can be identified before moving on to consider the necessary changes to working practices. In either approach, the connecting-up process can be used as a sense or completeness check of the changes and benefits identified.

It should be noted that benefit dependency networks, particularly for large projects that span multiple functions of an enterprise, will tend to become large and complex. Connecting them up can be a challenge: often there will be dependencies between business changes, with some requiring other changes to occur before they can be implemented. In complex networks, it is helpful to group or organize the benefits and their associated changes into 'benefit streams': sets of related benefits associated with a particular activity, such as customer service, or arising from a related set of changes. Such sets of benefits and changes may be relatively independent of other aspects of the project and can offer the opportunity to break the project into phases.

Definition: Benefit streams

A set of related benefits and their associated business and enabling changes and enabling IS/IT.

The main purpose of joining up the network is to understand the *dependencies* between the identified changes and the achievement of benefits. The linkages show that a given benefit will only be realized if the connected changes are achieved successfully. Considering each benefit, it is worth asking 'is this benefit significant enough for us to make the associated changes?' Measuring and quantifying benefits and assessing their importance are discussed in Chapter 5, where the issue of building a business case is addressed. However, even at this early stage of exploring a project, it is often known which benefits are essential to realizing the maximum value from the investment.

Alternatively, consideration may begin with the nature of the changes identified on the network. A change may, for example, be something the organization has tried in the past but failed to achieve. If this is the case, what can be done to ensure it is successful this time? If any change is seen to be unachievable or highly problematic, then any dependent benefits should be removed from the network. The issue of investment risk for projects is considered more fully in Chapter 5, but the explicit recognition of the dependency between organizational changes and the realization of business benefits is an aspect of risk analysis for the project.

Box 4.2 describes the derivation of a benefits dependency network for a project to improve the booking of patient appointments in the healthcare sector.

Measurement and ownership

Having developed a first version of the benefits dependency network, it is necessary to add further information to each of the benefits and changes to test how feasible the project is and to ensure that the benefits can be realized.

Each benefit and change should be considered in turn and two important aspects identified for each.

Benefits

1. Can the benefit be measured?

Before undertaking the often significant work involved in producing a robust and well-founded business case, it is worthwhile at this stage to specify how individual benefits might be measured. This will also often improve the clarity or precision about what was meant by a particular benefit. For example, a benefit may have been expressed simply as 'increased sales'. However, in considering how this might be measured, it may become apparent that sales could increase for a number of reasons. Hence, the measure should be limited to the increase that can be attributed directly to this investment, for example, sales of a new service or to a new customer group or in a new geographic market. Consideration of measurement of the benefit would therefore lead to a more precise wording of the benefit, for example: 'increased sales of new products X and Y' or 'increased sales in specified overseas markets'.

2. Does anyone own the benefit?

As discussed in Chapter 3, each benefit should have an owner assigned to it. A benefit owner should be an individual who gains the advantage inherent in the stated benefit and therefore is willing to work with the project team, either personally or through the resources and influence that he or she has, to ensure that the benefit is realized.

Box 4.2: 'Choose and Book' in public healthcare

The National Health Service (NHS) in the UK is currently under-taking what has been estimated to be the largest civilian invest-ment in IT. 'Connecting for Health', as it is being called, has a number of strands of activity, one of which, 'Choose and Book', provides patients with the option to choose a date and time for appointments. With the new system, the doctor or surgery manager will book an appointment during the patient consultation, or the patient can do it from home. By allowing the patient to select the date and time of the appointment, the number of wasted slots, called 'DNAs' (did not attends) should also be significantly reduced.

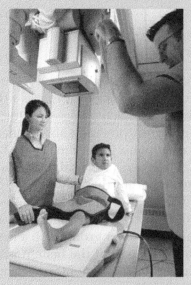

A simplified benefits dependency network for the project is shown in Figure 4.4. A number of benefits are indicated, including improved patient experience, a reduced unit cost per X-ray due to the reduction of DNAs and cost savings for both GPs and hos-pitals since there is no longer a requirement for referral and appointment letters. An associated system can also transmit the results of tests back to GPs, leading to additional benefits. For example, the doctor can know the results of the test sooner, and hence initiate treatment or follow-up tests more quickly. Also, by recording all of the test results, the system can prevent patients

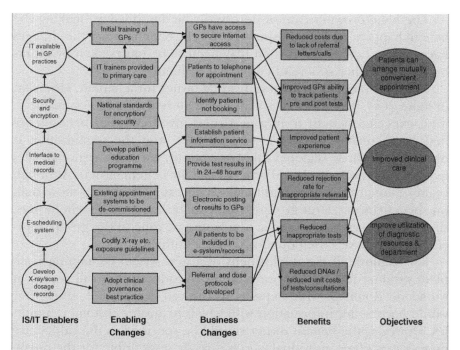

Figure 4.4: Benefits dependency for 'Choose and Book' project

having to have tests repeated due to the loss of information that happens with paper records. In the case of X-rays, this will also improve patient safety by ensuring radiological guidelines on exposure are not exceeded.

The network shows that the changes involve not only staff within the hospital, but external parties, such as GPs and patients. Unless these are also prepared to undertake the necessary changes, it can be seen that many of the benefits expected will not be realized. Certain benefits also rely on resources or capabilities outside the project. For example, with many tests, such as X-rays, it is not only having the test procedure completed that is important, but it is having those results interpreted by a relevant expert to generate a report. While electronic transmission back to the referring physician may reduce the delays associated with the handling of paper-based reports, these delays may be trivial compared to those introduced in the process if there is a shortage of experts to generate reports.

The benefit owner cannot necessarily be described as 'making the benefit happen' or 'being responsible for the benefit', since the changes necessary to deliver the benefit may need to be undertaken by others outside his or her sphere of control or influence.

It is preferable to have an individual owner for a benefit. However, in some cases, it may be necessary to have more than one. For example, if an expected benefit from a particular investment has been identified as 'increased sales of a new product' and the organization is divided into three regional sales operations, then the regional sales managers or directors should be named as the benefit owners. Although organizational structures might make it necessary to identify more than one benefit owner, large groups should not be named as benefit owners, since getting agreement and action from everyone in the group, especially if they have varied opinions, will be difficult.

For example, if the deployment of a new system containing complete product information were being considered in a call centre, it would no doubt provide benefits to the call centre staff, since they would have better information with which to answer customer enquiries. However, the benefit owner should be specified as the call centre manager or other individual who is directly responsible for the operation of the centre.

While large groups of staff should not be named as benefit owners, their views on the project, particularly concerning 'what is in it for them' and how they will be affected by the required changes, are critical to realizing the benefits and should be expressly addressed. How the views of such stakeholder groups can be considered is discussed in Chapter 6.

Business and enabling changes

1. How will we know the change has been successful?

Measures or 'evidence of achievement' that can demonstrate that the required business and enabling changes have been made successfully should also be established. Once again, this is likely to lead to more careful consideration of what is meant by the change and particularly how critical its successful completion is to realizing the dependent benefits. For example, one enabling change identified in many networks is that of 'training users on the new system'. In considering how the achievement of this should be measured, there is a range of alternatives, both in terms of measures and how the training is provided.

Is it sufficient to offer training courses such that people who require training can attend? Or is it important that everyone is trained in how to use the system and therefore attending the course is mandatory? It would then be important to measure the number of staff involved who did not attend the training. Better still would be to measure how effective the training was in terms of how well individuals use the full functionality of the new system. This would require some evaluation of the extent to which individuals have acquired the necessary skills and knowledge from the training, and perhaps how well this has been retained after a few months.

2. Who is responsible for making the change?

It is also necessary to identify change owners, named individuals or groups who will be responsible for making each of the identified changes happen successfully.

> **Definition: Change owner**
>
> An individual or group who will ensure that an identified business or enabling change is achieved successfully.

The change owner should be the named individual, or the person in a specific role, whose area of responsibility includes the identified change. The change owners may not be personally responsible for making the changes, but are accountable for the changes being effected successfully. They therefore must be willing to dedicate sufficient personal time and knowledge to planning and managing the changes and be influential enough to ensure the necessary resources are made available to carry out the changes. As with the benefit owners, it is preferable to have a single individual named as the change owner, otherwise, if problems arise, the responsibility for resolving them may become unclear.

The nature of benefit and change 'ownership'

Benefit owners' involvement in the project should be active rather than passive. In particular, the benefit owner is responsible for deciding how the benefit will be measured and how its value is included in the business case. This means carrying out any work required to quantify the benefit, including providing evidence for the quantity or size of the benefit that should be achievable. They should then work closely with those who are managing the changes to address any problems affecting achievement of the benefit and use their knowledge and resources to help resolve any issues. At the end of the project, the benefit owners are expected to report on the actual benefit achieved and, where necessary, explain the reasons for any underachievement.

In the case of change owners, they should be senior or influential enough to ensure that the change identified will be achieved successfully, as and when needed in the project plan. If the named owner is very senior, it can be reasonably assumed that he or she will not have day-to-day involvement in carrying out the change and this will be delegated to others. However, if difficulties are encountered in achieving the change, then the change owner will use his or her resources or influence to ensure that they are addressed.

A test that should be applied to all benefit and change owners is their interest in and perceived commitment to the project. The tools and frameworks discussed in this chapter should not be used by an individual or the project team working in isolation, but to facilitate knowledge sharing and gain agreement between the project team and project stakeholders, including those who are likely to benefit and change owners. Benefit and change owners should be roles that the appropriate individuals nominate themselves for and should not be responsibilities that are 'awarded' to someone who has not been involved. Lack of willingness to take on the responsibilities probably suggests a lack of interest in or commitment to the project, and if this is the situation with a number of the most appropriate change or benefit owners, especially for the more critical changes or most significant benefits, the organization should question whether the project is worth pursuing.

Project team and operational staff as owners

As the benefits identified in a network are expected improvements in the future operations of the organization, they should be owned by business managers and staff. Similarly, the business changes are those that are required to the processes and practices of the organization and therefore responsibility for achieving them must also lie with operational managers.

Organizations adopt essentially two different approaches to organizing and resourcing projects. Some assemble 'dedicated' project teams by assigning or seconding staff on a full-time basis for the duration of the project. This approach is often adopted for large or business-critical projects or where specialist knowledge or skills are required. It enables projects to be undertaken quickly, but can cause the project to become isolated from the practical issues affecting how the organization works. This approach can also leave operational staff feeling that the project is being 'done to them'. Projects involving a significant number of external consultants or contractors are particularly prone to developing a life of their own, leading to a lack of buy-in by operational managers and staff.

The alternative approach is to ask operational and specialist staff to undertake the project alongside, and in addition to, their existing responsibilities, supported by a number of dedicated staff, such as IT specialists and a project or programme manager. This has the advantage that the project should remain closely aligned with the operations of the organization. However, it may take longer and coordination of activities is more complex, as staff members have to balance the project priorities with the need to 'keep the shop open'.

These two different approaches will result in different patterns of ownership of benefits and changes on the dependency network. In the former case, where there is a dedicated project team, the individuals in that team should only feature on the network as owners of some of the enabling changes. In the latter case, those members of the project team who also have ongoing operational responsibilities can take responsibility for both enabling and business changes together with business benefits.

Recognizing where ownership by different individuals on the network is appropriate and, in particular, understanding the limited responsibilities of dedicated project staff is important. Some organizations wishing to ensure good performance from project teams try to incentivize the team by making them responsible for the delivery of benefits from the project. However, benefits from IT are only likely to be realized from changes to everyday operations and activities, and project staff can rarely be responsible for achieving such changes or the resulting benefits.

An appreciation of appropriate ownership of benefits and changes is also important for the structuring of agreements with software suppliers or consultancy firms, especially with the risk-sharing agreements that are sometimes adopted in the public sector. In large or complex projects, organizations may wish to incentivize or share risks with external suppliers or partners. They are therefore increasingly seeking to make these external organizations responsible for the benefits, invoking financial or other penalties if the required benefits are not delivered. However, as in the case of in-house projects, the realization of benefits from IT is dependent on the achievement of changes within the organization, which, again, can rarely be the responsibility of external parties. They can, of course, be held responsible for the on-time and on-budget delivery of the technology and other enabling activities, such as training or the redesign of business processes. However, they cannot, for example, ensure the effective ongoing operation of those new processes, which is the responsibility of the organization itself, unless those operations are outsourced. The use of benefits management tools in different contexts, including that of risk-sharing projects such as the private finance initiatives (PFI) in public sector projects, is discussed in Chapter 8.

A balance of benefit and change owners

Having identified owners for each benefit and change, it is then important to understand the balance and relationships between those responsible for the changes and those receiving benefits. If different names appear on all the changes compared with the names on the benefits, it should be considered whether they will be prepared to make the changes if they will gain little or no benefit from doing so. This can be a significant issue in some projects and it needs to be addressed as early as possible, otherwise it can lead to difficulties later. How this is best done will depend on how well the drivers and investment objectives are understood and accepted by all the stakeholders. If those responsible for actually undertaking the changes support what the organization is trying to achieve and have been consulted regarding how this can best be done, they are more likely to agree to make the necessary changes. Their cooperation may also be dependent on their involvement in other ongoing or planned projects: if they appreciate that while others will receive major benefits from this project, other projects being undertaken will, in turn, provide them with benefits, they can be expected to be more cooperative. The impact of the balance of changes required to benefits realized forms an important part of stakeholder analysis and is discussed in Chapter 6.

An alternative approach to dealing with an imbalance between the benefit and change owners is to consider whether the project can be restructured or rescoped. This should aim to provide those who have to undertake changes for the benefit of others with some benefits from the project. It may be necessary to forego some of the benefits if it is considered that those individuals or groups identified will not be willing or able to make the necessary changes. Obviously, this trade-off will depend on the significance of a particular benefit to the organization.

Benefit and change templates

While the benefits dependency network is an effective means of exploring the linkages between the realization of benefits and the need for change, the resulting networks can become very large and difficult to read. It is therefore advisable that, once a network has been agreed, the information and logic it contains is copied to benefit and change 'templates', where more detail can be added to begin to develop the benefits plan. Formats similar to those shown in Tables 4.4 and 4.5, in the worked example below, have been adopted by a number of organizations.

In the case of the *benefit template*, the intention is to set out, for each of the benefits, its owner and the changes on which it is dependent. Similarly, the *change template* identifies the required change, whether it is an enabling or business change, who is responsible for ensuring it occurs and any other changes on which it is dependent. It is advisable to develop a simple coding system to number the benefits and changes in order to retain the links defined on the network.

Additional information to complete the templates, such as the type of benefit, expected value, resourcing the changes and the timing of the realization of benefits, is discussed in Chapters 5 and 6. Examples of the use of the benefit and change templates are given in the worked example below.

Worked example: improved control within a food processing organization

This worked example is continued through the next two chapters to demonstrate the use of the tools and techniques.

The creation of a benefits dependency network

Background

FoodCo is a medium-sized business based in the UK that prepares fresh vegetables for sale in supermarkets and use in the catering and food service industry. In addition to its state-of-the-art food preparation facilities, it owns farms where it grows many of the raw materials that are included in its products. The firm is therefore a vertically integrated producer with control from the field to the consumer's plate, which is important in an industry where safety and traceability are essential. In addition to its own farms, vegetables are bought from other growers in the UK and Europe.

The firm sells its products to the leading supermarkets in the UK, particularly in the area of 'own-label' salads. It also sells via wholesalers to independent retailers, and sells raw ingredients to sandwich and ready meal manufacturers and to caterers. Sales are also increasingly being made in Europe. Innovation is a critical area for the food industry and FoodCo undertakes regular marketing and consumer research as part of its ongoing new product development activity.

The business challenge: rapid sales growth

In the early 2000s, the firm was undergoing unprecedented growth in sales revenues. Healthy eating and eating out were both growing in the UK and across Europe and the high quality and fresh products of FoodCo were ideally suited to take advantage of these trends. However, despite this growth in sales, the profitability of the organization was falling. The problem was seen to be lack of control of both direct and indirect costs.

The operating and administrative processes of the firm were inefficient and complex. Problems were exacerbated by delays in information availability and the difficulties in reconciling information from the piecemeal systems in the organization. As the scale of the operation grew, the effects of those inefficiencies and delays had grown disproportionately, reducing the profitability of the organization. A major project was initiated to review the operational and administrative processes and systems.

Driver analysis

The project began with directors and managers from key areas of the business, together with relevant IT staff and other specialists, attending a workshop to agree the objectives for the investment and derive an initial benefits dependency. As a first step, the 'dimensions of competence' model was used to assess and agree the drivers acting on the organization. The diagram shown in Figure 4.5 was generated. A fuller description of each of the identified drivers is given in Table 4.3.

It can be seen that there were both external and internal drivers. The demand by consumers for a continuous stream of new and exciting products, the pressures from regulators and public agencies for improved food handling and particularly the traceability of all ingredients and the power of the large supermarket chains were all external drivers that needed to be understood, interpreted and addressed.

However, the key area of weakness that required improvement immediately was agreed to be the lack of effectiveness of the company's internal operations. In particular, there were unacceptably high levels of wastage of materials and delays and errors in the administration and control processes.

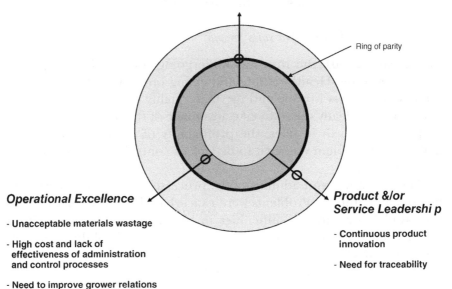

Customer Intimacy

- Price pressure due to power of large customers

Ring of parity

Operational Excellence

- Unacceptable materials wastage

- High cost and lack of effectiveness of administration and control processes

- Need to improve grower relations

Product &/or Service Leadershi p

- Continuous product innovation

- Need for traceability

Figure 4.5: The dimensions of competence for FoodCo

Although the firm grew many of its raw materials, an increasing proportion was being sourced from other growers and this trend would continue. The payment structure to these growers was very complicated, having a fixed price element but also a variable element that was calculated on the yield and the price obtained from the final customer. The complexity of these payments was adding to the administrative burden on the organization. Payments to growers were often late, and sometimes incorrect, causing a souring of relations with some growers. These problems were all contributing to increasing costs within the business.

The project: regaining control of the business

Recognition that the existing systems were no longer adequate led to the consideration of replacing them with an integrated enterprise resource planning (ERP) system. ERP systems provide an integrated set of applications for the core processes of an organization, including: order management, production planning and scheduling, inventory control, shipping and transport and after-sales service, together with

Table 4.3: Drivers acting on FoodCo

Drivers	
Customer intimacy	
Power of large customers – significant price pressure	Supermarket sector is highly consolidated, resulting in considerable power of key customers. Significant pressure on prices.
Product and service excellence	
Continuous product innovation	Continuous demand from customers (and end consumers) for new product introductions including new packaging formats.
Need for traceability	Regulation requires ability to trace product from consumer's fork back to the farmer's field.
Operational excellence	
Unacceptable materials wastage	Perishable nature of products requires accurate matching of orders to sourcing of raw materials.
High cost and lack of effectiveness of administration and control processes	Administration and control systems seen to be inefficient with many disparate systems causing delays, errors and reconciliation failures in key processes.
Improving grower relations	Keen to maintain good relationships with best growers. Access to high quality raw materials is a key contributor to quality of final product. Good relations with suppliers are key to maintaining supply in times of shortage.

modules for activities such as the general ledger, supplier and customer accounts and payroll. In addition, real-time management information can be extracted from the systems for decision making.

It was expected that part of the solution to their problems would be found in a new information system. However, it was recognized that this would not be sufficient in itself and that considerable change to how individuals and groups within

> 'Successful implementation of ERP involves probably the greatest technological change most organizations have ever undergone; even more difficult, and important, however, are the major changes in business that come with an ERP project.' *Davenport (2000)*

the organization were currently operating would be required if the desired improvements were to be realized. It should also be stressed that buying and implementing a complete ERP suite was not a foregone conclusion. Such suites contain many applications or modules, some of which may be of little relevance or benefit to a particular organization or require too much or risky organizational change to deliver the benefits. The approach adopted was to work back from the desired objectives and benefits, through the business changes, to the specific applications or modules required, to ensure the 'minimum IS/IT to do the job' was identified.

Identifying investment objectives

Based on the drivers, it was important to focus on a comprehensive but achievable set of improvements that would directly address the issues identified. After much discussion, three investment objectives for the ERP project were agreed:

- to simplify and automate all business transactions;
- to integrate key processes and systems;
- to improve the financial control of business assets and resources.

The linkages between the agreed investment objectives and the drivers are shown in Figure 4.6.

Organizational Issues (if any)	Investment Objectives	Business Drivers
External: Need to maintain growth with supermarkets to keep contracts. Customer determines contract details and varies them frequently. Internal: Pricing structures and options too complex to automate? Over customized to individual grower/customer situations.	1.Simplify and automate all business transactions 2.Integrate key processes and systems 3.Improve financial control of business assets and resources	*Continuous product* External *innovation* *Need for traceability* *Price pressure due to power of large customers* *High cost and lack of effectiveness of internal processes* *Improve grower relations* *Unacceptable materials wastage* Internal

Figure 4.6: Linking investment objectives and drivers at FoodCo

Simplifying and automating business processes would improve the effectiveness and reduce the costs per transaction of those processes. It would also provide more accurate information about activity costs and improve decision making for new product developments.

Integration of separate processes and systems would improve performance by creating streamlined, simpler processes and also reduce data collection and information reconciliation costs. Integration would also help provide the required traceability for all products and reduce the levels of wastage being experienced.

Finally, *improved financial control* would allow the organization to negotiate more effectively with its large customers to achieve an acceptable margin on its products. It would also impact positively on the payments made to growers. Being able to make these payments on time, with guaranteed accuracy, would improve relations with the independent growers.

A couple of example issues which had to be addressed or resolved during the project if the objectives were to be achieved are also shown in Figure 4.6.

Developing the benefits dependency network

The benefits dependency network developed is shown in Figure 4.7.

It can be seen that the first objective, to simplify and automate key processes, gave rise to a number of benefits. However, achieving the second objective, when processes were integrated across production, stock control and order fulfilment, would deliver the most significant benefits. Improved financial control would also give rise to a number of distinct benefits both to FoodCo and its key suppliers, the independent growers.

The changes needed to improve individual or discrete processes were fairly well contained and simple. For example, the physical scanning of goods currently utilized during manufacturing could be extended to dispatch in order to reduce dispatch and invoice errors. However, integration of the processes spanning the organization, from the sourcing of raw materials, through production to sales, required a more extensive and interrelated set of changes. At the centre of these changes was the need to develop and implement a new planning process, which could draw real-time information from all points in the organization to provide improved production scheduling, both in terms of resource use and changes in customer orders. An enabling change that was seen as essential was reducing the degree of local

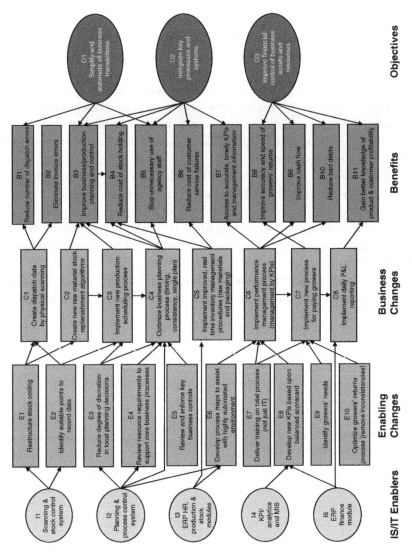

Figure 4.7: Benefits dependency network for FoodCo

discretion in production planning, thus ensuring decisions could be coordinated across all stages of production.

Another key area of change concerned the key performance indicators (KPIs) used to manage the business. The automation of the new processes would produce accurate and timely information that could be used to monitor the most critical and sensitive aspects of business performance; that is, those that had the most immediate or significant effects on sales or costs. However, merely being able to produce the figures quickly and frequently would not ensure that they were used effectively. To ensure that the benefits of having the information would be realized, a number of business and enabling changes had to be made. First, those indicators that most accurately reflected the level of performance and overall financial health of the organization, and which required management actions to control, had to be identified. Having done this, it was necessary to define and implement new processes to ensure that the identified KPI information was disseminated to the relevant managers. It was also necessary to ensure that they were able to understand the implications of the KPIs and take prompt action to address any unacceptable variances in performance.

Having identified the expected benefits and the necessary changes, the underlying IS and IT functionality was identified. This was specified as key modules or components, thus allowing flexibility in the choice of solutions, which were to purchase a complete ERP suite or to select independent systems in a 'best-of-breed' approach.

Adding benefit and change owners

Having developed the network, ownership of the benefits and changes was agreed, as shown in Figure 4.8. As discussed earlier in this chapter, rather than assign or delegate these to individuals who were not present at the workshop, the roles shown were those of the people who had participated in developing the network. This involvement not only helped to demonstrate their commitment to the project, but also ensured that the desired benefits and necessary changes were derived from a thorough and relevant understanding of actual business operations.

Figure 4.8 shows a good balance of responsibilities across the benefit and change parts of the network. Those who were responsible for making significant changes, in most cases, also received benefits. Although this suggests that the people involved should be willing to actively engage in the project, it was necessary to carry out a full stakeholder analysis. This ensured that the views of the production and

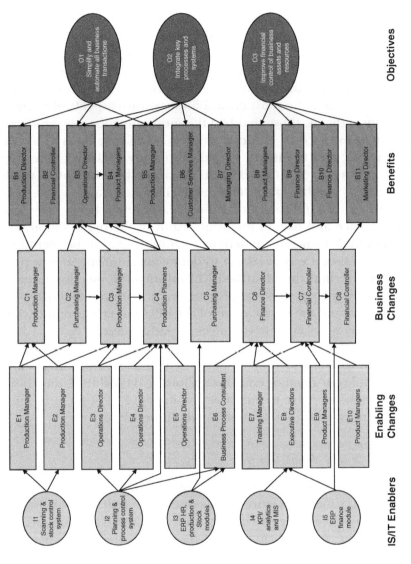

Figure 4.8: Benefit and change owners for FoodCo

other operational and administrative staff, as well as external parties, such as the growers, could be understood to prevent unexpected problems arising during implementation. This is discussed in Chapter 6.

Adding measures and evidence of achievement to the network

While adding owners of benefits and changes to the network, it is important to determine a measure for each of the benefits and define how the achievement of each change will be assessed. The initial measures identified by the owners of the benefits and changes are shown on the benefits dependency network in Figure 4.9. As can be seen, in some cases it is helpful to define two or more measures for benefits or changes in order to demonstrate that improvements in performance are due to the new investment and have not occurred for other reasons. The importance and implications of selecting appropriate measures are discussed in detail in Chapter 5.

The start of the benefits plan: completing benefit and change templates

Partially completed benefit and change templates for the FoodCo example are shown in Tables 4.4 and 4.5 respectively. Further information to complete the tables will be added during the development of the business case, as described in Chapter 5, and when stakeholder analysis, described in Chapter 6, is undertaken. Each table shows just two benefits or changes, but similar details were provided for all the identified benefits and changes.

The FoodCo example is developed further in the following two chapters.

Summary

This chapter has presented some of the key tools and frameworks used in the benefits management process. Additional tools will be presented in later chapters. As stated earlier, the use of these tools is to:

1. Understand the strategic rationale and agree the objectives for the investment.
2. Identify and explore the expected benefits from the particular investment.

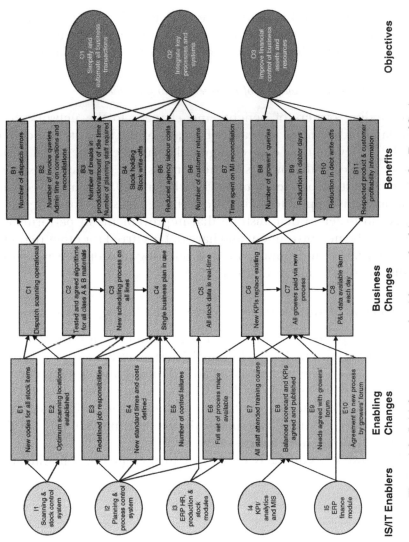

Figure 4.9: Initial measures and evidence of achievement for FoodCo investment

Table 4.4: Partially completed benefit template

Benefit no. and type, and related objectives	Benefit description	Benefit owner(s)	Dependent changes and responsibilities	Measures	Expected value (if applicable)	Due date
B2: Financial: O1	Eliminate invoice errors	Financial Controller	C1 – Production Manager	1. Customer invoice queries 2. Admin time on corrections and reconciliations		
B4: Financial: O2	Reduced costs of stock holding Including inventory reductions	Product Managers	C4 – Production Planners C5 – Purchasing Manager E3, E4 and E5 – Operations Director	1. Stock holding by product type for: (a) (RM) Raw Materials (b) Packaging 2. Number of stock write-offs		

Table 4.5: Partially completed change template

Change or enabler no. and dependent benefits	Description	Responsibility (and *involvement*)	Prerequisite or consequent changes	Evidence of completion	Due date	Resources required
E8 B7, B9 and B10	Develop new KPIs based on balanced scorecard	Executive Directors	P: None C: C6 Implement performance management process	Balanced scorecard and KPIs agreed by Board and published		
C2 B3, B4	Implement new raw material stock replenishment algorithms	Purchasing Manager and *Product Managers*	P: E1 Restructure Stock coding C: None	Tested and agreed algorithms for all A and B class materials		

3. Determine the feasibility of achieving them, by understanding the changes to organizational structures, processes and working practices that will be required to realize those benefits.
4. Identify potential owners for all benefits and changes.
5. Consider whether and how the achievement of each of the benefits and changes can be measured or assessed.

If the investment looks viable after a first pass at linking it to the drivers and having generated an initial benefits dependency network, then more work can be carried out to develop a more complete and accurate network. This should include a more detailed description of each of the benefits and necessary changes, including estimates of timescales required for the latter. If the investment is significant and involves a large number of changes to different areas of the business, then the development of a complete network may take some time and resources to complete. However, getting it 'as right as possible' at this early stage can avoid misunderstandings later in the project about what has to be done, by whom, to succeed with the investment. *It is therefore important to ensure that all the key stakeholders are involved in creating the network.*

This additional work is also essential to the development of a business case and benefits plan for the investment, which is described in Chapter 5. At the same time, for most projects, it is valuable to carry out a comprehensive analysis of how the investment and change programme is seen from the perspectives of the different stakeholders. This is discussed in Chapter 6. It normally will shed further light on how achievable each of the changes is, and may lead to further actions to overcome any particular stakeholder concerns or issues that could prevent the benefits from being realized.

The changes identified on the network will form the main work packages to be undertaken as part of the execution or implementation phase of the project. These work packages can be specified in more detail and then incorporated in a standard project management methodology, such as PRINCE2. The timing of each work package will be influenced by any dependencies identified on the network or any resource or other constraints identified in the project plan. Identified owners, particularly change owners, should be involved in the planning of the work packages relevant to their change activities.

Chapter 5

Building the business case

The main purpose in developing a business case for an IS/IT project is often to obtain funding for the financial investment. However, in the context of this book and the realization of business benefits, the term 'business case' has a wider meaning. In addition to providing information to decide whether or not to make the financial investment, it should also enable the organization to plan and manage the project to a successful conclusion.

The term 'business case' also implies that it is more than a financial justification for investment. The latter relies on identifying explicit, relatively short-term, performance improvements that will be achieved and excludes consideration of benefits that cannot be interpreted financially. While this may have been appropriate when the vast majority of benefits were accrued from efficiencies resulting from automation of clerical tasks, the integral and often critical role IS/IT plays in organizations today means that such a limited view will preclude the realization of many available benefits. These additional benefits are often associated with the term 'capability': the technology enables the organization to change and evolve over the longer term to achieve its strategic aims and create new opportunities. The business case, therefore, should include, where appropriate, arguments that define how it contributes to enhancing existing capabilities or creating new ones (Ross and Beath, 2002).

'In preparing business cases for investments in IT, organizations should take into account relatively intangible benefits including informational, transformational and strategic as well as the more easily quantified transactional benefits.'
Gregor et al. (2006)

As described in earlier chapters, it is the complementary investments an organization makes in changes to the way business is performed and resources are deployed that deliver the majority of benefits from IS/IT. It has been shown that the level of complementary investment required to fully exploit IS/IT assets is often five times the cost of the technology itself (Brynjolfsson and Hitt, 2000). Apart from IT infrastructure investments, which only create IT assets, the business case is therefore really concerned with justifying an IT-enabled business change project.

The business case is an essential 'document' in ensuring effective coordination and management of the complex set of activities and resources involved. Representing that complexity as a simple set of financial figures obscures the real nature of the investment, by losing the understanding of what has to change in order to achieve each of the business improvements. That is not to say that a financial appraisal of the case for investment should not be made in order to decide whether it should be funded. The business case must be developed in a way that enables a financial appraisal to be made. However, this should not be an independent decision, since at any time there will be a choice of possible investments and the decision will always be made in relation to the overall funds available and alternative ways of investing them. The investment has therefore to be understood from the viewpoints of both *what* benefits can be expected and *how* feasible it is to achieve them, in comparison with alternative uses of funds and resources. This implies that all IS/IT project business cases are developed and expressed in a consistent way so that management can compare 'apples with apples' when making decisions on funding priorities. It would be ideal if all business investments were expressed similarly and not just the IS/IT options and, for this reason, a number of organizations have adopted the approach described in this book for a wide range of investments involving business changes, such as office relocation and organizational restructuring.

The business case should also form the basis for assessment of technology and financial risks. An aspect that is often overlooked, especially for strategic investments, is the organization's capability to make the required changes and drive through all the benefits. These aspects of risk assessment are considered towards the end of this chapter.

Organizational risks can be assessed and understood at an overall level, but there are also more specific issues that can influence the success of the investment. These result from particular stakeholders' expectations, interests and priorities, which inevitably will affect their commitment of time and resources to making the required changes. How these stakeholder issues can be identified, understood and managed is discussed in detail in the next chapter. As will be discussed, it is sometimes appropriate to carry out a detailed stakeholder analysis prior to completion of the business case.

Arguing the value of the project

Developing any business case involves considering both the value and cost sides of the investment equation. While costs are often relatively easily calculated, or at least estimated, the major weakness in many proposals for investing in IS/IT is the inadequate expression or analysis of the benefits that the organization will gain. Box 5.1 presents the findings of a survey we carried out into the effectiveness of business cases.

As described in the discussion of the benefits management process in Chapter 3, developing the 'value' side of the case often requires two stages. An initial assessment based on the identification of the potential benefits, as per the dependency network, is needed to determine whether the project has any prospect of being funded and, if it has, to specify the further work needed to develop the full business case. This will involve activities to prove how the benefits can be measured and to determine which of the benefits can be quantified and expressed in financial terms.

The main differences between the benefits management approach to developing the value side of the equation, compared with more traditional approaches, are the continued emphasis on the relationship between change and benefit, the importance of benefit ownership and the need to be explicit about benefit measurement. From the benefit dependency network, it should be understood how each benefit relates to one or more of the investment objectives, who owns it and how it can be measured. This information and an understanding of the types of change required to achieve the benefit are the starting points for building and refining the business case. This chapter will discuss the additional requirement of applying appropriate rigour to the evidence needed for formal justification.

Box 5.1: Business cases in practice

In 2008, we undertook a survey of the practice and effectiveness of business cases (Ward and Daniel, 2008). Overall, the survey generated 84 responses from a broad spectrum of industries in many countries, including America (46%), Europe (24%) and India (11%). Large organizations (those with more than 500 employees) represented the majority of the sample (67%), with small and medium-sized organizations representing the remaining 33%.

With such a good response we were able to differentiate those organizations that are more successful from those that are less successful in delivering the benefits expressed in their business cases. More successful organizations are defined as those where more than 50% of their IT investments deliver the expected benefits (43% of the sample) and the less successful organizations as those where less than 50% of their projects deliver the expected benefits or those which do not know how many projects deliver the intended benefits (57% of the sample). The analysis that follows is based upon a comparison of the two groups – the more successful and the less successful organizations.

Our survey results showed that the majority of the organizations that responded always or often developed business cases for their IT investments, whether they involved new applications (69%), new infrastructure investments (61%), enhancements to both applications and infrastructure (73%) or business change programmes involving IT (66%). These results did not differ significantly between the more and less successful groups.

However, there are some significant differences in what the business cases contain and how effective they are between the two groups. Table 5.1 shows the more successful organizations were more likely to identify all the benefits available from the investment, gain commitment from business colleagues to realizing those benefits and achieve an acceptable return on investment (ROI) for the project. As a result of this, the majority of their business cases are funded, meaning they do not waste time developing cases that go nowhere.

The findings of the survey also show that the more successful organizations are more likely to establish appropriate measures

Table 5.1: Business case effectiveness

In addition to obtaining funding, preparation of a business case often or always . . .	More successful group	Less successful group	Total
Identifies all available benefits	50%	27%	37%
Gains commitment from the business to realizing the benefits	64%	44%	53%
Attains an ROI above a required hurdle rate	56%	33%	43%
Establishes appropriate measures for the benefits	36%	17%	25%
Adequately quantifies the benefits	47%	21%	32%
Overstates the benefits to get approval	25%	46%	37%
As a result, what % of business cases are approved?	78%	44%	58%

for benefits and, where possible, quantify the size of the expected benefit. Finally, we also found that nearly half the organizations in the less successful group often or always overstate the benefits in a business case to win funding. Whilst their honesty is laudable, this is obviously a dangerous practice. It inevitably leads to disappointment with the final result of the project, since the promised benefits were never achievable. And the next business case will probably need to be even more oversold if it is to win funding, establishing a vicious circle that damages credibility within the organization.

Maintaining dependency: benefits are the result of changes

The first statements in the business case should be clear about the business drivers that mean change is essential, and how the achievement of the objectives of the investment will address those drivers.

Then, the benefits expected to arise from achievement of each of the objectives should be classified in terms of the main type of change that will be needed to realize it, as shown in the columns in Figure 5.1. It may seem simplistic to relate each benefit to one of only three causes, but the vast majority of benefits arise because:

> 'To realize the benefits of change, departments need to ensure that business cases are not used solely as mechanisms to secure funding, but set out how the business changes will be achieved, what the benefits will be and what machinery will be put in place to drive the achievement of those benefits.' *NAO report (2006)*

1. The organization, its staff or trading partners can do new things, or do things in new ways, which, prior to this investment, were not possible.
2. The organization can improve the performance of things it must continue to do, i.e. do them better.
3. The organization can stop doing things that are no longer needed.

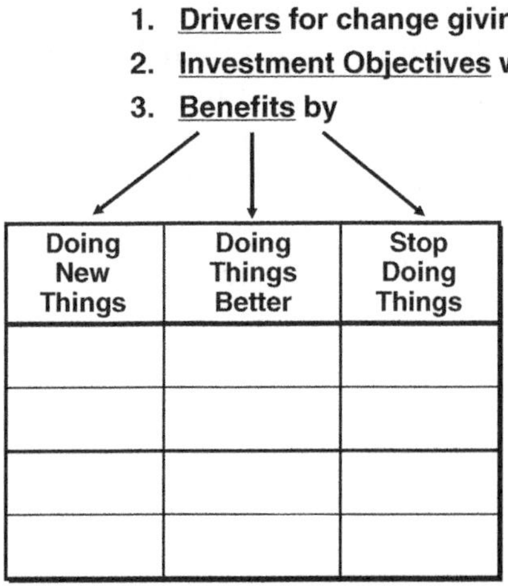

1. **Drivers** for change giving rise to
2. **Investment Objectives** which result in
3. **Benefits** by

Doing New Things	Doing Things Better	Stop Doing Things

Figure 5.1: The essence of the value argument: relating the benefits to change

It is reasonable to expect senior management to be more excited by the benefits, and therefore commit more time and effort to changes which allow new activities or innovations or those that stop wastage on unnecessary activities.

In some cases a benefit may be restated as two or more benefits, since, for example, by stopping one thing resources can be reused to do something new. This is only a first step in arguing the case for investment, but an important one, since it retains the understanding of the link between the drivers for change and benefit delivery and it also helps determine the nature of the measures that can legitimately be used to calculate the value of the benefit. Clearly, it should be quite feasible to quantify and value the reduction in resources required if an activity will cease, but it will be far more difficult to estimate the financial value that will accrue from a new activity. Equally, the change management associated with creating a new activity or way of working will have different challenges from eliminating an old working practice. That is not to suggest that one is easier than the other. Often, benefits fail to be delivered because old practices are still in place despite the implementation of new systems and technology.

A structure for analysing and describing the benefits

A business case is essentially a reasoned argument for investment. It should be based on the ability to measure each benefit and on specific evidence that enables the level or size of each expected improvement to be estimated. The matrix shown in Figure 5.2 defines four levels of 'explicitness' that are based on the ability to assign a value to the benefit and the degree of current knowledge about future improvement. Each benefit should be allocated initially to either the *observable* or *measurable* row, assuming that it at least meets the criteria, and then an assessment should be made of how much is already known or could be determined, such that it might be moved upwards in the table.

Observable benefits

Definition: Observable benefit

By use of agreed criteria, specific individuals/groups will decide, based on their experience or judgement, to what extent the benefit has been realized.

Degree of Explicitness	Do New Things	Do Things Better	Stop Doing Things
Financial	By applying a cost/price or other valid financial formula to a quantifiable benefit a financial value can be calculated.		
Quantifiable	Sufficient evidence exists to forecast how much improvement/benefit should result from the changes.		
Measurable	This aspect of performance is currently being measured or an appropriate measure could be. But it is not possible to estimate by how much performance will improve when the changes are completed.		
Observable	By use of agreed criteria, specific individuals/groups will decide, based upon their experience or judgement, to what extent the benefit has been realized.		

Figure 5.2: Classifying the benefits by the explicitness of the contribution

Observable benefits require a clear statement of the criteria to be used to assess their achievement and also who is qualified or appropriate to make the most objective judgement. This is often the only way of determining whether many of the 'softer' benefits, such as improved staff morale or customer satisfaction, have been realized. If these have been tracked for a period of time through surveys, it may be possible to actually measure, rather than merely observe, the benefit. While such benefits, even in total, are unlikely to be sufficient to argue the investment case, they should not be ignored or trivialized. They may accrue to large numbers of stakeholders, whose change in behaviour is essential for the realization of the more substantial organizational benefits. Such benefits should be retained in the business case and benefits plan, even if there are ample other financial and quantified benefits to obtain investment funding.

For example, in the introduction of new EPOS systems in a supermarket chain, although the main financial benefits were due to the speed at which transactions could be processed through the tills, the checkout staff would be less stressed at peak times, due to reduced queue lengths and fewer errors. This benefit made the thousands of staff involved positive about the introduction of the new systems, despite the disruption to work patterns that would occur during the changeover.

In a healthcare organization, a knowledge management initiative was failing to achieve its objectives of knowledge sharing among product development and marketing professionals. This was in spite of financial incentives to 'provide content'. When the authorship of the content was made explicit to users and the number of times the content was accessed was fed back to the author, contributions increased. Recognition of an individual's contribution by his or her peers was considered to be more significant than financial reward.

Measurable benefits

Definition: Measurable benefit

This aspect of performance is currently being measured or an appropriate measure could be implemented. But it is currently not possible to estimate by how much performance will improve when the changes are completed.

A measurable benefit is one where either measures exist or can be put in place that will enable the improvement in performance to be determined after the event. This obviously implies that the level of performance (or 'baseline') prior to the implementation can also be measured and that the improvement can be specifically attributed to the investment, rather than other changes. When looking at process improvements, measures may be of organizational inputs, activity levels, outputs or results. It may be necessary to have more than one measure to determine whether the benefit has been fully realized; for example, if the number of customer complaints has reduced, has that led to a reduction in the staff time spent dealing with complaints or even the number of staff involved? If the new process has meant that each complaint can be dealt with more quickly and requires less investigative effort, again has this resulted in less time spent by staff per complaint? These examples are intended to show that the measure should not only be relevant to the benefit itself but also to the changes that are needed to realize it, so that the improvement can be directly attributable.

Wherever possible, existing measures should be used and particularly when they are part of the organizational performance measurement system, such as a balanced scorecard or KPIs (key performance indicators), since this ensures that achieving the benefit is seen as important to the organization. It will also mean that the current baseline is already known. If, however, no relevant current measurement exists, which is often the case when the benefit results from doing something new, a decision has to be made as to not only what measure is appropriate, but also whether the effort required to establish the measure is worthwhile in relation to the significance of the benefit. If it is deemed too difficult or expensive to set up a measure, then the benefit should be 'relegated' to observable, and suitable criteria for evaluation identified.

Another important aspect to consider is whether the way the improvement is measured will encourage the types of organizational and personal behaviours required to deliver the benefit. For example, staff in a call centre were expected to spend, on average, less time per service call once a new system was installed. However, only average call times were used to measure staff productivity, and this did not reflect the range of types of call or the communication abilities of different customers. As a result, some staff cut off callers who were taking more than the average time, resulting either in another call or a dissatisfied customer.

A last consideration with both observable and measurable benefits is the time period required after implementation before a meaningful measurement can be made to determine whether and to what degree improvement has occurred. Few benefits are instantaneous and most require a few weeks or even months to accrue. An estimate should be made as to when sufficient effects of the changes should be visible as measurable improvements, but before the specific benefits may become obscured by the consequences of other changes or events.

Quantifying the benefits: the major challenge

Definition: Quantifiable benefit

Sufficient evidence exists to forecast how much improvement should result from the changes (i.e. the size or amount of the expected benefit).

As defined in Figure 5.2, the essential difference between measurable and quantifiable benefits is that for measurable benefits no pre-implementation estimate can be made of the size or degree of improvement to be expected. In order to quantify benefits, evidence is needed to 'calculate' the amount of improvement that the changes will produce. This is relatively easy in the 'stop' column on the matrix, but more difficult in the others. Having determined the most appropriate measures for a benefit, it is essential that the current baseline can be established, from which the estimate of performance improvement can be developed.

One of the weaknesses of many investment cases is the lack of evidence provided to substantiate the benefits. Without 'legitimate' quantification, it will be difficult, if not impossible, to agree a realistic financial value. Hence, the step between measurable and quantifiable is the most critical in converting a qualitative argument to a sound economic case for investment. Of course, as already considered, there is always the issue of 'materiality', i.e. is the effort involved worth it? This, in turn, depends on the likely increment in performance that could be achieved, but often the task is not undertaken because there are already 'sufficient benefits to justify the investment' or 'nobody will believe the figures anyway' or some similar rationale. This is understandable, but leads to misunderstandings of what the investment is actually intended to deliver and reduces the attention paid to ensuring that all the available benefits are achieved.

Ways of overcoming the quantification problem

As illustrated in Figure 5.3, there are a number of ways in which, assuming the potential benefit is material, the measurable-to-quantifiable 'barrier' can be overcome.

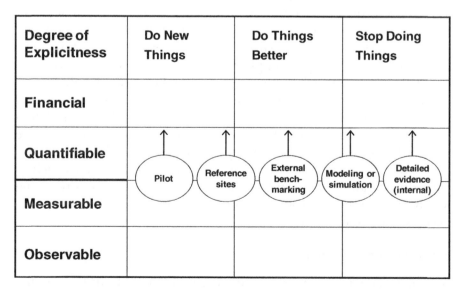

Figure 5.3: Converting measurable to quantifiable benefits

As stated earlier, quantification is more difficult in the new and better columns, relative to the stop column, and there is generally an increasing need to obtain external data or evidence to help develop the business case for these types of benefits. Organizations that have comprehensive activity and process performance measurement and variance analysis systems, especially those that include activity-based cost analysis, may well be able to calculate and quantify the majority of improvements from internal data. But even those organizations will find difficulty in estimating the degree of improvement that can be achieved by IT-based innovations.

The five approaches shown in the circles in Figure 5.3 are not exclusively aligned to the columns as shown. More sophisticated means, such as pilots and reference sites, could be used for the quantification of all types of benefit if the organization has no experience of implementing such changes. Using these approaches may also help to identify further benefits that could result from the planned changes. This is especially true when implementing large, enterprise-wide packages, where the integration benefits are difficult to understand and describe – especially from an existing situation of fragmented and incompatible systems.

Detailed evidence and modeling or simulation

Relevant detailed evidence to help quantify a benefit may take some 'digging out' from existing systems, which tend to record performance in relation to the organization structure rather than business activities or processes. It is also often important to establish evidence over a relevant time period, such as a year or through a peak in the trading cycle. It may only be necessary to sample the data to find sufficient representative evidence from which the overall value can be extrapolated.

Some software packages, mainly in transactional or operational areas, such as ERP, logistics and workflow systems, have simulation or modeling software that show the level of performance that can be achieved by adopting practices and processes embedded in the application suite. Many companies also use modeling tools in areas such as marketing planning, inventory management and sales forecasting which can be used to explore the potential implications of changes to processes and ways of working.

Benchmarking and reference sites

Benchmarking is commonly used in a number of industries as the starting point for improvement programmes. This can be a valuable approach to quantifying benefits, by evaluating the changes in relation to 'best practices' in the industry, or in comparable processes in other industries (Alshawi *et al.*, 2003; Johnson and Misic, 1999). For example, supermarkets study each other's EPOS systems performance in relation to store 'traffic', in terms of processing speed for transactions and queue lengths. The time and cost taken to process loan and mortgage applications or insurance claims are considered 'competitive' KPIs in the financial services industry, whereas in other industries, such as electronics and pharmaceuticals, time to market for new products is a critical benchmark.

Although benchmarking is helpful for identifying potential improvements to established processes and practices by comparing the performance of similar activities in other organizations, it is less useful when trying to quantify the benefits from innovations.

Unless the innovation is the first of its kind in the industry, there should be reference sites where similar changes have been made or examples where the technology is being used in other industries. The latter are usually available from the technology suppliers, which are keen to prove the benefits of their products to new customers via existing ones. Obviously, care is needed to select relevant implementations and to be able to compare not only how the technology has been deployed, but also to understand the changes that were made to deliver the performance improvement. It is also important to understand where the reference organization started from, in performance terms, to be able to assess how much of the improvement they have achieved is relevant and feasible. Where organizations believe they are achieving an advantage from an innovation, it is unlikely that they will be willing to share all the secrets of their success, so the information gained from reference sites has to be treated with a degree of caution.

Pilot implementations

Pilot implementations are becoming increasingly used not only to test the technology, but also to evaluate the benefits that can be achieved from new systems and ways of working. When there is no other feasible way of determining the degree of improvement that could result from the changes, a pilot implementation of the new process or practice is necessary if 'proof' of the benefits is needed. A pilot will normally test the new way of working on a small scale, so that the total benefit can be extrapolated. To provide the best evidence, it is essential to identify, if possible, a comparable control group still working in the old way, as the current baseline. For example, when Thomson holidays first introduced its online holiday booking system into travel agents, it was able to compare very accurately the sales of the selected pilot sites with a similarly representative sample of agents still making bookings over the phone. The pilot was undertaken in a sample of agencies selected to be representative of the range of different agencies that the company operated. The pilot was also run for several months, to ensure that improvements were genuine and not just due to the initial enthusiasm of agencies selected to take part in the pilot. The 30% average increase in business handled by the pilot site agencies was sufficient evidence to justify the major investment required for all agents.

Box 5.2 describes how modeling, benchmarking and a pilot implementation were used to develop the business case for a customer relationship management system in a major European paper manufacturer.

Box 5.2: Quantifying benefits in a European paper manufacturer

A major European manufacturer of fine and printing papers was considering the introduction of a customer relationship management system into its sales and marketing functions.

The company, which manufactures high quality papers and paper-based packaging materials, sold its products via distributors to printers, large corporations and packaging manufacturers. While these organizations were its main customers, the decision about which paper to purchase was often influenced by graphic designers working for these customers. These designers therefore

represented key influencers on sales and hence were also an important group for the manufacturer.

Sales were achieved by advertising and promoting (A&P) their products to both distributors and graphic designers. A key part of this A&P activity was a set of targeted marketing campaigns, in which marketing collateral about the products would be mailed out to the distributors and designers. This material was then followed up either by a visit from a member of sales staff or by a telephone call from the sales office. On average, the company carried out around 50 such A&P campaigns per year, costing a total of some 10 million euros. It employed 150 professional sales staff in 15 countries and had over 6000 end customers.

It was felt that the firm could achieve more sales from the significant amount it was spending by improving its knowledge of, and hence relationship with, its customers and support this via the use of IS/IT.

The specific drivers for the investment were identified as:

1. The need for improved customer retention and increased market share in the high value market segments.
2. Maintenance of brand leadership despite increased marketing activity of competitors.
3. A desire to achieve more sales from the significant amount being spent on A&P.

The two main objectives of the new system and associated business changes were agreed to be:

1. Improving the effectiveness of A&P expenditure (defined as the ratio of sales revenue generated/advertising and promotion (A&P) cost).
2. Increasing sales volume and value from new customers.

Benefits associated with these objectives included:

(a) reduced costs by avoiding wasted mailings and product samples to 'irrelevant' customers;
(b) increased response rates from A&P campaigns;
(c) increased rate of following up leads generated by campaigns – earlier and more customers;
(d) increased conversion rate of leads to sales.

(Continued)

Developing a benefits dependency network identified a number of significant business changes that were essential to delivering the benefits, including a complete restructuring of the customer database into new market segments to reflect customer lifetime value and purchasing patterns, rather than just industry sector; a new key account management process and sales commission system; a telesales centre for customers placing small orders and a new process for campaign planning, response tracking and sales targeting, based on the new customer and prospect database.

The main benefits of this investment were measurable, but the company insisted that every IS/IT project should deliver a financial return, which was difficult to prove unless a number of the benefits could first be quantified and then converted to financial values. The only two benefits that it was considered would lead to financial figures were (a) and (d) in the list, but the value of benefit (d) was dependent on quantifying benefits (b) and (c)!

Detailed analysis of historical data

To calculate the direct A&P cost savings, a representative sample of campaigns from the previous year was analysed. This analysis sought to understand the types of leads generated and to identify patterns in responses including those customers who never responded to campaigns. As a result, it was estimated that some 30% of the costs could be saved, without reducing the response rate.

Modeling and benchmarking

To quantify the expected improvement in responses from better campaign targeting, comparisons of the results from database marketing to industrial customers were obtained from a specialist consultancy. A modeling exercise on the new database within the paper manufacturer was then carried out, to show how targeting based on the timing in buying patterns would produce higher levels of response. This pattern was compared with the customer sales information held by a number of key distributors to confirm the likely improvements. This led to additional cost savings of some 10%.

To estimate the number of additional customers that could be visited by the sales force or contacted by the telesales staff, depending on which was appropriate, all the sales staff logged their time and customer visits for two months. The mix of activity across different customer value profiles, leads generated from campaigns, regular customer meetings and time spent with different types of customer were analysed in relation to the sales that resulted over the next two months. Based on best practice benchmarks and information from similar organizations that had implemented the same key account management process, it was clear that by using the telesales approach to follow up many of the lower value enquiries, the sales staff could increase the time spent with potentially high value customers by some 20%.

A pilot implementation

The remaining issue was whether the more productive use of sales staff would actually deliver more sales. No comparable information to help quantify the value of additional sales was available and although a few companies that had introduced similar changes were visited, none had the same combination of sales and distribution channels. The only remaining option was to pilot the new system and processes of managing the campaigns and sales follow-up. This was done by using a PC-based prototype of the system and paper-based 'workflow' control of activity on one typical campaign in one market. In order to provide a control for comparison purposes, existing processes were followed for the same campaign in another, similar-sized market. The pilot study lasted two months and sales from the two markets were monitored for a further two months, the normal 'depreciation' period for a campaign.

At the end of the pilot, comparing the sales patterns in the two markets as accurately as possible, sales in the pilot market resulting from the new approach were some 50% higher than in the control market. If these figures were extrapolated across all campaigns and all markets, the increased contribution from these sales would cover the investment costs in a few months. However the figure had to be moderated by the fact that the sales team involved in the pilot had, due to being under the spotlight, undoubtedly worked far harder to prove they could succeed than could be sustained over time by the whole sales force. It was agreed by the sales director that a 20% increase was achievable and sustainable across the whole business, and hence this more realistic figure was included in the business case (Figure 5.4).

(Continued)

Degree of Explicitness	Do New Things	Do Things Better	Stop Doing Things
Financial	d) Increased conversion rate to sales (p.a.) Additional Conversions Contribut'n Enquiries (+20%) £400K Mailings (+15%) £250K Samples (+20%) £350K Specif'ns (+40%) £200K Total £1200K (p.a.)		a) Reduced cost by avoiding waste on irrelevant customers 30% + 10% cost saving = £950K p.a.
Quantifiable	c) Increased rate of follow up of leads by category (p.a.) New (Old) Enquiries 2000 (800) Mailings 15000 (<5000) Samples 5000 (2000) Specif'ns 600 (400)		
Measurable		b) Increased response rate from defined target group and earlier response from defined group Target group response rate increased from 5% to 10% 55% of responses received within 2 weeks of campaign (previously 45%)	
Observable			

Figure 5.4: The business case for the European paper manufacturer

Financial benefits

Definition: Financial benefit

By applying a cost or a price or other valid financial formula to a quantifiable benefit, a financial value can be calculated.

The aim of any business case should be to express as many of the benefits as possible in financial terms, so that the expected return on investment can be ascertained. Many organizations use primarily financial criteria to decide on IS/IT projects, although, as discussed in Chapter 1, this can lead to a number of issues, for example:

- a lack of innovative uses of IS/IT since the financial benefits are uncertain;
- a focus purely on efficiency gains from IS/IT, which improve individual processes, but often at the expense of overall organizational effectiveness;
- 'creative' calculations of financial benefits based on inadequate evidence;
- making assumptions that enable sufficient financial benefits to be claimed to provide the necessary return in relation to the costs;
- only declaring enough of the available financial benefits to offset the expected cost;
- minimizing the costs of the system either by removing functionality, especially that which is not deemed immediately essential (e.g. integration of processes or information resources) or understating the organizational costs of implementation, such as training.

Overall, undue emphasis on purely financial returns will limit the range of investments largely to support or key operational applications, since it is only for these that sufficient knowledge normally exists to quantify the improvements and hence calculate a financial value.

The use of financial and economic appraisal techniques is discussed in overview later, with references to more detailed sources of information about the techniques. The emphasis in this section is on converting quantifiable benefits to financial ones, as in the benefits analysis structure shown in Figure 5.2.

Due to the essential attributes of IT, its application to business processes frequently results in three types of benefit that can be quantified in advance. These benefits are related to increases in *efficiency* – using less resource to complete activities – improved *accuracy* – greater precision and consistency or higher quality outputs from activities – and increases in *speed* – completing activities more quickly. Often these are combined under the heading of *greater productivity*, but productivity is not in itself a financial benefit, unless it results in the ability either to reduce real costs by using fewer resources or reusing the resource, or time savings to gain new revenue. How productivity gains are 'taken' as benefits varies considerably across organizations, especially those which save staff time. Box 5.3 describes two different ways in which a financial value was, or was not, derived from benefits which saved the time of staff within the organization.

In essence, financial benefits are only realizable from reductions in cost and from increases in revenue or avoidable revenue losses.

Box 5.3: The productivity conundrum

Frito-Lay, the snack food manufacturer, decided to equip its sales/delivery force with handheld computers (Applegate, 1993). The pilot implementation showed that this saved three to four hours' administrative effort each week. The sales managers were asked to decide what that time saving could deliver as a benefit. It was agreed that each sales/delivery person should be able to increase their sales by between 3 and 10% per week, given the increased selling time available and allowing for their different customer mixes. This was measured shortly after implementation and an average of 6% over and above market growth was achieved.

An enterprise portal was implemented by a major healthcare company. Although they, too, calculated the daily time saving (in the order of 10–20 minutes), this productivity gain was not converted into a financial benefit, since it would be possible neither to measure the saving after the event nor to attribute it to the portal. The main objectives of the investment were to ensure all staff members were better informed and to reduce staff frustration in finding information and carrying out administrative tasks, as well as saving IT costs associated with supporting the proliferation of intranet sites built in non-standard ways.

Obviously, cost reductions are easier to identify, quantify and 'prove' than additional revenues, but in both cases the final calculations are relatively easy provided the quantification, as described and exemplified in Box 5.2, has been based on legitimate assumptions and relevant evidence.

Not targets

'Goodhart's law states that "when a measure becomes a target, it ceases to be a good measure."' *Strathern (1997)*

When producing a justification for an IS/IT project, it is often tempting to include target figures in the business case. Management may have stipulated a cost saving figure or an increase in revenues or some other quantified performance improvement they wish to realize from the investment. Hence, it appears necessary to include such figures if funding is to be obtained. However, we would caution against this. Rather, we would suggest that the approaches described in earlier sections are followed, with the value of benefits being justified from evidence that is as objective and verifiable as possible. This approach will test how reasonable, and hence achievable, the targets that have been set are. Even if the target appears feasible, providing detailed evidence of how it will be achieved is not always straightforward, since it may depend on the cumulative effects of several smaller individual improvements. While management may be willing to fund achievement of an overall target, gaining involvement of other stakeholders often requires them to understand how they can achieve the target that has been set.

Cost reductions

To determine and verify cost reductions, it is necessary to consider how the combination of efficiency, accuracy and speed that creates the benefit can be converted to cost savings. This is a relatively simple calculation, based on the change in volume of activity and reduction in resources, people and other activity costs.

One issue with all types of cost reduction benefits is to determine whether the saving is in direct or variable costs only or if certain fixed costs will also be reduced. It is usually possible to calculate the variable element, such as direct labour, travel or materials, and it is also possible to estimate the notional savings in fixed costs that could occur – for example, savings in employment costs and accommodation. However, it is partly a matter of determining whether or not these savings will actually be realized and partly an issue of the organization's accounting policies as to whether and how they are included in the business case. Some organizations include a time element that allows for the direct cost saving immediately after implementation but postpones the inclusion of indirect savings for a period within which they can be realized.

For example, an engineering design company introduced a document management system, which would reduce the storage space required for documents and drawings in its London offices by several hundred square metres. By reorganizing and rationalizing the use of space, most of the 'floor space' saved could actually be released and sublet until the current lease expired, when the company could reduce its accommodation in the building. Given the cost of office space in London at the time, this produced a saving of over £100 000 p.a., which was included in the business case for year two onwards, to allow for the time taken after implementation to rationalize the space used.

Alternatively, some organizations take a longer-term view and allow the savings to be included by transferring costs, normally from operational to overheads, in the understanding that other actions will be taken later to address those areas of cost. For example, the implementation of a new stock management and online purchasing system in a builders' merchant operating over 100 branches, would reduce the yard area needed for 'heavy-side materials' by up to 40% in many of the larger branches. One performance measure for each branch site was 'profit per square metre', which would now provide misleading comparative performance information if it were not based on the area actually in use. The policy decision was to reduce the area to that actually in use in the branch profit and loss accounts, and include the area not in use in a head office business development account. Later, decisions would be made as to whether the space would be used to increase the branch product range and generate more revenue for the branch or, alternatively, sell the land and realize the value of the asset.

Whatever the policy or reason for a specific decision to include elements of fixed costs, it is important that the arguments and calculations are consistently applied across all investments, not just IS/IT projects.

Revenue increases

The effects of specific changes on existing costs can usually be estimated with some certainty, but the same is not true of many changes in revenue. Also, the period over which any estimated revenue increases from the investment will be sustained is uncertain and, in most cases, probably shorter than for cost reductions, many of which are permanent. Therefore, not only are revenue increases less easy to predict in terms of their likely value but the way in which they are included in the overall calculation of the financial return will also differ.

Some revenue increases can be estimated reliably, especially those that involve improved financial systems to ensure revenue earned is actually received, for example by more accurate invoicing and contracts or better bad debt control. If there are known causes of lost revenue, such as unavailability of product, unacceptable delivery or service response times or uncompetitive prices, it is possible to make an informed estimate of the sales that can be recovered by changes to correct the causes of poor performance. Of course, other factors will simultaneously influence sales; for example, supply problems of a competitor, a successful promotion campaign or, more negatively, a quality problem with a product or the launch of a better service by a competitor. This makes it difficult to prove, following implementation, that the increase in sales was due to the changes made. And of course there may simply have been a change in customer demand between making the case and completing the project.

Most examples of increased revenue result from improving current performance or eliminating causes of problems. Such benefits would be shown in the *better* or *stop* columns of the matrix shown in Figure 5.2. It is clearly more difficult to quantify, and therefore put a reliable financial value on, benefits resulting from doing new things – for example, opening up an online sales channel – or doing things in entirely new ways – such as applying workflow tools to new product development processes in order to bring new products to market faster.

Market research is needed when the revenue is expected from a new product, sales channel, type of customer or geographic market. It is important that any claim of revenue increases is supported by evidence about the causes of the increase.

It may only be possible to provide a series of potential benefit levels, each based on a different interpretation or extrapolation of the evidence available – '*if the following interpretation of the evidence is made, then the increase will be between 5 and 10%, but if this other interpretation is made, then it could enable a 15% improvement*', etc. Different figures would then be input into the return on investment calculation to determine how sensitive or dependent the investment case is on the accuracy of the revenue estimates. 'What if' calculations can also be carried out to assess the effects of the sustainability of the increase over different time periods. If the business case is dependent on a particular revenue increase, then further work would be worthwhile, for instance, by testing the assumptions with customers to narrow the range of probable outcomes. However, it will always be a judgement rather than a clear-cut yes/no decision, implying that if any assumptions prove incorrect later in the project, the business case should be reassessed.

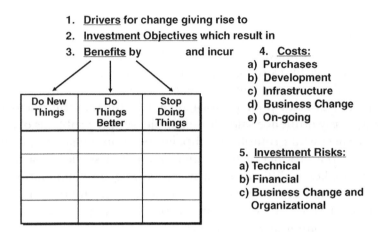

Figure 5.5: The full content of the business case

The preceding sections have described the ways in which the value side of the business case can be developed into a comprehensive, substantive and robust argument. The full business case must obviously include these, as shown in Figure 5.5, but it is important that they are considered and evaluated in the context of the complete range of costs that will be incurred and the risks involved in undertaking the project. Project costs and risks are discussed in the following sections.

Project cost assessment

As has been discussed earlier in this chapter, estimating the benefits, both quantitative and financial, is complex and difficult. Equally, predicting the costs associated with an investment is not simple. Any financial assessment of the return or payback is sensitive to the potential inaccuracies in both. The types of cost that should be included in the financial justification are shown in Box 5.4.

Investment appraisal techniques

Once a total financial value of the relevant benefits has been determined and the expected costs have been identified, a financial assessment can be made. It is not the purpose of this book to include a detailed description or critique of different financial appraisal

Box 5.4: Cost types in financial justification

Purchase costs of hardware and software, plus any external consultancy or specialist technical resources required.

Internal systems development costs, i.e. the costs of specialist internal resources for business analysis, designing the system, processes and procedures, developing or procuring the software, commissioning and implementing the technology and the system. How these are calculated varies across organizations depending on the accounting policies. In some cases they are considered a fixed cost and not allocated to individual projects, in others the direct salary costs are allocated and in many organizations the full costs of internal resources are recovered across the range of developments through an hourly or daily charge-out rate. The last of these provides the most realistic view of the full costs involved, which is necessary when comparing different options for resourcing the project, but implies the costs are discretionary and will not be incurred if the project is not funded.

Charge-out or cost allocation policies have a significant influence on investment decision making, as discussed by a number of authors (see, for example, Earl, 1989; Ward and Griffiths, 1996), and understanding the implications for different types of IS/IT project decisions is essential in managing a comprehensive project portfolio.

Infrastructure costs that are incurred exclusively for the new system should be included, but again it will depend on accounting policies, including the policy for depreciating IT assets, as to whether the costs of shared infrastructure are allocated indirectly, for example, based on the number of workstations or recovered as a per unit cost based on the level of usage of the system. The options and issues associated with different ways of dealing with infrastructure costs are covered in the references mentioned above.

Costs of carrying out the business changes should also be included to provide a complete financial view of the investment, although apart from obvious costs associated with training, staff relocation or redundancy and refitting buildings (e.g. recabling or new office equipment), these are rarely included, being considered 'business as usual'. This is realistic if there is no way of identifying the costs actually incurred by the project.

(Continued)

Ongoing costs associated not only with the operation of the new system, but also additional permanent costs involved in the new ways of working. For instance, many organizations are enabling staff to work remotely, which saves on travelling but increases telephone costs. These costs can either be included explicitly as additional costs or 'netted off' against the benefits from the changes to working practices.

techniques. The techniques applied to IS/IT projects are all derived from investment appraisal approaches for other forms of capital or revenue investment (Ballantine and Stray, 1998). Common approaches include return on investment (ROI) or net present value (NPV), which can be compared with alternative uses of funds, and the required return on assets (ROA) or return on capital employed (ROCE) for the organization's shareholders, or as needed to remain competitive in the industry.

While surveys such as that by Ballantine and Stray show that 90% of organizations perform some form of financial assessment on all IS/IT projects, that does not imply that the decision to invest is based exclusively on the estimated economic return. The limitations of financial appraisal techniques are well known and, given the many uncertainties of IS/IT projects, even those organizations that apply them rigorously appreciate that basing decisions solely on estimated financial values will limit the types of business investment they make (Kohli and Devaraj, 2004). A comprehensive analysis of the types of accounting technique and their applicability to IS/IT projects is included in books by Hares and Royle (1994) and Renkema (2000).

Variations in benefits and changes across the investment portfolio

The investment portfolio was introduced in Chapter 2 as a strategic management tool to enable the contribution of different types of IS/IT project to be understood. It has already been mentioned in this chapter that certain types of benefit and their required changes are associated with the different application types identified by the portfolio.

High potential investments are essentially research and development (R&D) activities to identify the benefits that could be achieved by innovative use of IS/IT. Benefits are therefore likely to be associated with changes that are new to the organization or associated with radically new ways of working. By definition, in such cases it is likely that little will be known about the benefits at the time of considering the investment. Hence, the possible benefits associated with such investments can only be described in outline terms, based on external 'evidence' or from experience and judgement, and can at best be considered observable or measurable, as the potential improvement is not yet known. At this stage, the nature of the changes required will not be known, except in the general sense of the potential differences from the current ways of working.

The purpose of most high potential evaluations is to provide sufficient evidence of the potential benefits and the costs and feasibility of the business changes required to achieve them, to justify initiating a major investment. The initial investment will not result in a working system at this stage, merely a 'proof of concept'. In many cases the work will demonstrate that further investment is not worthwhile.

Strategic investments are intended to achieve future advantages by creating new business and organizational capabilities which are superior to those of competitors. This usually implies significant change and innovation in the ways of conducting business or using resources; benefits will be associated mainly with doing new things, although some will result from performance improvements in existing activities. It is also possible that the new processes completely replace existing ones and elimination of those activities will save costs. Apart from the removal of old processes, the financial outcome cannot be predicted with much certainty. Benefits are therefore likely to be predominantly measurable, although some may be quantifiable or even financial if the new processes have been successfully piloted to provide evidence to quantify them. If the investment is significant, then it is often worthwhile undertaking a pilot or proof of concept first, so that more can be understood about the benefits, and the associated changes that will be required, before significant resources are deployed.

Key operational investments are intended to ensure that the organization is not disadvantaged by the inadequacies of its essential processes and systems. Since these applications are aimed at improving existing activities, the majority of benefits will result from 'doing things better'. The focus on existing activities also implies that there is sufficient knowledge of the fact that the level of improvement required can be quantified and also of how those targeted improvements could be achieved. It should be possible to estimate the financial value of many of the benefits. In the process of removing the causes of potential or actual disadvantages, some new activities can be undertaken with the resources released. These benefits are less likely to be provable in terms of quantifiable or financial values.

Changes associated with key operational applications can be extensive and complex, given the degree of integration and interdependence of such systems, but due to the role they play in making the core business processes operate, the changes would not normally be radical.

Support investments are intended to improve organizational efficiency and eliminate unnecessary costs. They are therefore often related to *stopping doing things*, automating activities and reducing the costs of the resources required to perform the processes. While cost savings are the primary aim, improvements in performing necessary processes and activities should also be achieved. It should be possible to predict the financial value of the majority of benefits in advance, since they are activities that the organization has been undertaking.

It might appear that because the changes largely involve automation, simplification and elimination, they are easier to define and implement. However, they normally result in labour savings of some kind and this frequently creates resistance from those whose jobs are threatened or whose roles will be changed significantly. Critical to achieving benefits from support investments is the removal or decommissioning of old systems, many of which may be 'informal' systems that were developed by individuals or small groups to address local problems. Figure 5.6 summarizes these differences across the portfolio.

The importance of recognizing the variation in benefits

It should be stressed that while different application types within the portfolio will give rise to the majority of benefits in different 'columns' in the business case, many investments do not fit neatly into one segment of the portfolio and will give rise to a large number of benefits spread across the matrix.

A broad spread of benefits across the entire matrix, or clusters of benefits in different rows or columns, may be indicative of an investment that has a number of the different application characteristics within it. For example, the investment being considered may have elements of improving existing operations (key operational) and also new value-adding capabilities (strategic). In such cases, it is worth

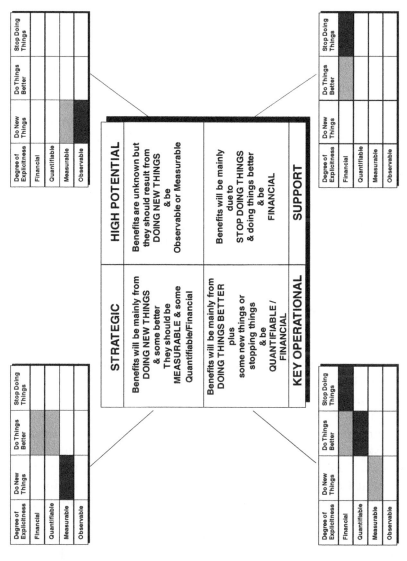

Figure 5.6: Variations of benefits across the investment portfolio

recognizing that these are intrinsically different types of change and it may well be appropriate to phase the project to address them separately. Often, the key operational part of the investment needs to be implemented first to remove constraints and problems in the current ways of working, before the innovations become achievable and the more strategic benefits can be realized (Peppard and Ward, 2005). Also, when the operational part of the project has been implemented successfully, it is likely that more will be known about the benefits that can actually be achieved from the strategic part of the investment.

Another implication of the variation in types of benefit that arise from different applications, and perhaps the most serious one, is that organizations should not expect all investments to produce similar business cases. In particular, high potential and strategic investments are unlikely to be able to yield a fully financially justified business case.

Risk assessment

There are many well established approaches to risk analysis. Apart from the consistently obvious factors that increase risk, such as project scale, duration and technical or business complexity, there are often organizational contextual issues that can create specific risks for certain projects at particular times. Comprehensive and practical sources of understanding the causes of risks, frameworks for assessing IS/IT project risks and approaches to managing them can be found in Jordan and Silcock (2005) and, for business projects in general, the Office of Government Commerce (2002) publication *Management of Risk: Guidance for Practitioners*. Despite the obvious need to assess and minimize the risks of the investment, there is a tendency to interpret risk management as the maintainence of a 'risk register', rather than understanding and dealing with the uncertainties involved in the project (Gibson, 2003). As a result, the emphasis is moving towards organizational rather than procedural approaches to risk management (see Pullan and Murray-Webster, 2011).

For most IS/IT projects, three aspects of risk need to be assessed as early in the project as possible to enable a realistic appraisal of the probability of achieving the objectives and benefits. These risk types are described in Box 5.5.

Although the technical and financial risks of IS/IT projects can be significant and must be assessed and addressed, there is an increasing

Box 5.5: Risk types associated with IS/IT projects

Technical risks are those associated with the chosen technologies and suppliers and their ability to deliver the functionality, security and performance required. Whether the organization has the internal knowledge, skills and required infrastructure, and is using the most appropriate process to implement the technologies, must also be considered. Approaches to assessing and then managing technical risks, and risks associated with processes of development and implementation, are built in to most systems development and project management methodologies via risk registers.

Financial risks concern the predictability of the costs and confidence in the financial benefits. Such risks can be estimated by conducting sensitivity checks on the financial case assuming higher costs and reduced or delayed benefits. Other techniques, including scenario planning and real options analysis, can be used to compare the relative financial risks of alternative investments.

Business change and organizational risks include the capability of the organization, and in some cases external stakeholders, to carry out the enabling and business changes that are essential to realize each of the benefits. A detailed analysis of stakeholder perspectives and concerns is the most effective way of taking action to reduce organizational risks, mitigate their effects or adjust the scope of the project to avoid them. This is described in detail in the next chapter.

consensus that risks due to organizational issues are the most critical to the success of many projects, especially when the implementation affects large parts of an enterprise.

A checklist of risk factors that need to be considered under each of these headings

'The problem (IT project failure) stems from senior and project management failing to assess the risks of the changes up front: the most serious are the business changes, not changes to the technology.' *Gibson (2003)*

is shown in Table 5.2. The factors have been included in the category where they are likely to have the most impact, but clearly many will have secondary effects in the other categories. For example, the longer

Table 5.2: Checklist of the most common risk factors

Technical risk factors	Financial risk factors	Business change and organizational risk factors
Complexity of the system functionality	Size of the investment	Senior management commitment to the project
Technical novelty – to the organization and supplier	Project duration	User commitment of resources and knowledge
Number of system interfaces and systems being replaced	Degree of confidence in all the elements of project cost	Stability of organization and key staff
Certainty and stability of the business requirements	Confidence in the evidence for investment benefits	Extent of changes to business processes and practices
Technical skills of project team	Appropriateness of project cost control mechanisms	Number of departments, functions and business staff involved and affected
Business knowledge of the project team	Reliability of external suppliers' estimates and enforceability of contract conditions	Degree to which organizational and role changes are needed to realize the benefits
Degree to which formal methodologies and standards are adopted	Rate of change of the external environment	Other change initiatives that will affect the same areas of business
Extent of the changes needed to IT infrastructure	Business criticality of the areas affected by the system	Existing change management capability and experience
Degree to which the system can be prototyped or piloted	Dependence of the benefits on other projects	Existing user IT and information skills and knowledge of 'how the business works'

the duration of the project, the more likely it is that key personnel will change, new requirements will emerge and resources will be required for other projects.

Risk variation across the investment portfolio

Earlier in this chapter we discussed how the benefits expected and the nature of the associated changes will vary across application types. As shown in Figure 5.7, the type of risks that may be expected will also vary across the portfolio.

High potential investments are, by definition, high risk and the risks are mitigated by controlling the time and costs allowed for the evaluation. This usually implies a limit on the scale or scope of the evaluation. It has to be accepted that, in many cases, the right outcome of the evaluation is not to proceed further, due to technical, financial or organizational risks being too great.

Strategic investments normally involve significant innovative change and the implementation of new ways of conducting business or using resources. Neither the costs nor the financial benefits can be predicted

STRATEGIC	HIGH POTENTIAL
Risks are likely to be of all kinds TECHNICAL, FINANCIAL & ORGANIZATIONAL	Risks are likely to be high and of all kinds TECHNICAL, FINANCIAL & ORGANIZATIONAL Minimized by limited scale/scope
Major risks are likely to be ORGANIZATIONAL Financial and technical risks are addressed by strict application of methodologies	Major risks are likely to be ORGANIZATIONAL due to vested interests Low financial risks and technical risks minimized by use of proven technologies
KEY OPERATIONAL	SUPPORT

Figure 5.7: Variation of risks across the investment portfolio

with certainty at the outset. The IS/IT requirements and business changes will evolve as it becomes clearer how the benefits can best be achieved and perhaps some potential benefits will prove impossible to deliver. If deploying new technology is integral to the project success, this, in turn, will introduce additional risks. Therefore, the number of risk factors across all three categories is likely to be high and the approach to managing the project must allow for this.

Key operational investments are normally undertaken to improve existing essential processes and systems. Technical risks should be reduced by using established, proven technology as far as possible. However, many key operational applications are complex and have multiple interfaces to other systems. The strict application of systems development, quality assurance and project management methodologies, including risk registers, is needed to ensure that the system design and operational performance meet the business needs. Any financial risks should be relatively low, since the expected benefits should be financial or quantifiable and the costs associated with known technology should also be relatively easy to determine. However, such investments often require significant simplification of processes, resulting in widespread changes to organizational roles and responsibilities and the development of new skills or performance measures. Since these systems are at the core of the business, changes have to be carefully controlled to avoid deterioration in performance during the implementation.

Support investments are intended to improve organizational efficiency and eliminate unnecessary costs. Given that the benefits should be achievable using proven technologies, the investments should be relatively low risk. However, the achievement of many of the benefits will rely on changing and standardizing organizational practices to make effective use of the technology available. Many of the efficiency savings rely on individuals or groups changing their ways of working and may also result in reducing the number of staff required. Consequently, the main risk factors are organizational, due to the unwillingness of some users to change their previous ways of working and concerns about the loss of jobs.

A financial services company applied this understanding of the different degrees of investment risk across the portfolio to include standard financial contingencies in the approval process. For example, overruns of up to 5% of costs were allowed for support investments, 10% for key operational and 20% for strategic, before further funding had to be authorized through a revised business case.

Completing the business case

Organizations vary in the way they require proposed investments to be described, the criteria used to make funding decisions and the process by which those decisions are made. This chapter has described tools and techniques for converting the knowledge created by the development of a benefits dependency network into an argument for investment. Considerations of the costs and risks of the investment have been addressed, but only in summary. The emphasis has been on creating a more realistic, comprehensive and substantive case for the benefits that should accrue and how those benefits can be realized. The business case should be supported by a detailed benefits plan, which can be based on the templates described in Chapter 4 and the benefits dependency network itself, to show the interrelationships of enabling and business changes and how, in combination, these can lead to the realization of each of the benefits. Details of responsibilities and how achievements will be measured should be clearly stated, to demonstrate the commitment of all the main stakeholders to carrying out their agreed tasks.

An example of a completed benefit template from the FoodCo case study is shown in Table 5.3, building on the earlier version shown in Chapter 4 (see Table 4.4). The corresponding change table is completed after undertaking a stakeholder analysis and is shown in Chapter 6 in Table 6.1.

For each of the benefits, a more detailed description of both the benefit and the actions required to track its delivery will be included in the project documentation, so that progress can be monitored during implementation.

The business case itself should, if possible, be structured in a similar way to the process through which it was derived, to reflect the way in which the argument for investment was developed:

1. The business drivers that are causing the need to change.
2. The objectives of the investment and the contribution that their achievement will make to the relevant drivers.
3. The benefits that will be realized in meeting those objectives and whether they will occur due to new innovations or by improving the performance of essential processes or stopping unnecessary activities.
4. The quantified improvement expected and the financial value of those improvements where possible.
5. Further measurable and observable benefits that will be delivered.

Table 5.3: Example of a completed benefit template from FoodCo

Benefit no. and type, and related objectives	Benefit description	Benefit owner(s)	Dependent changes and responsibilities	Measures	Expected value (if applicable)	Due date
B2: Financial: O1	Eliminate invoice errors	Financial Controller	C1 – Production Manager	1. Number of customer invoice queries	Reduce by 90%	Oct 2004
				2. Admin time on corrections and reconciliations	Reduce by 15–20 hours per week (0.5 FTE)	Sept 2004
B4: Financial: O2	Reduced costs of stock holding including inventory reductions	Product Managers	C4 – Production Planners C5 – Purchasing Manager E3, E4 and E5 – Operations Director	1. Stock holding by product type for: (a) (RM) raw materials (b) Packaging	Reduction of holding RM by 10% and Packaging by 15%: One-off saving of £125 000	Oct 2004
				2. Number of stock write-offs	Annual saving of: RM (50%) £180 000 Packaging (80%) £40 000	Nov 2004

6. Expected costs involved and a calculation of the overall financial implications such as return on investment. This should include sensitivity calculations due to uncertainties in some estimates.
7. An analysis of the potential risks involved and actions that can be put in place to address them.

The following sections present part of the business case for the FoodCo example developed in Chapter 4. Some of the benefits (for example, B2 and B3) have been split into components, depending on the parts of the benefit that could be quantified in advance. Some benefits could be quantified in the future if more work was undertaken, such as undertaking a pilot. However, they are left as measurable in the table until such further work has been undertaken, or because the work involved might not be justified, given the expected value of the benefit.

Although most of the benefits arise from carrying out processes and activities more effectively (better), some have been entered into the 'stop' column, when problems will be eliminated (or almost eliminated) by the systems and process changes. Equally, some have been entered in the 'new' column because they occur due to the implementation of new processes and systems. This spreading out of benefits across all three columns, particularly having benefits in the stop and new columns, makes a more compelling case, demonstrating how the planned investment is going to stop wasteful activities and enable new ones.

The company was growing rapidly and needed to retain good staff to achieve the growth. Therefore, although efficiency gains through automation would release several operational staff, they would not leave the company, so no financial savings were claimed. Equally, the small savings in financial staff costs were 'notional', in that the staff would be offered alternative jobs in other areas, where vacancies existed.

The benefits dependency network shown in Figure 4.7 was appended to the business case, as were the full set of completed benefit and change templates.

Summary business case for the FoodCo project

Business drivers

Forces acting on the organization that require the company to invest in new systems and change its processes in order to achieve its intended strategy of continuing profitable growth through product innovation and high levels of customer service are:

- **External** – price pressures due to the power of large customers, the need for traceability and for continuous product innovation.
- **Internal** – the need to improve grower relations, reduce the unacceptable levels of material wastage and reduce the cost and improve the effectiveness of internal processes.

Investment objectives

These primarily address the internal drivers but will also produce changes that will enable the company to improve its performance with respect to the external drivers. The investment objectives are:

1. To simplify and automate all business transactions.
2. To integrate key processes and systems.
3. To improve financial control of business assets and resources.

Benefits

The benefits that will be realized by achieving these objectives are shown in Table 5.4.

Project costs

Purchase of new hardware and software	£250 000
Cost of scanning equipment	£85 000
Cost of implementation: technical consultants	£120 000
Internal systems development costs (for configuration)	£150 000
Infrastructure upgrade costs	£75 000
Business change costs	£170 000
Training costs	£80 000
Total	**£930 000**
Net increase in ongoing systems support and licence costs	£40 000 p.a.

Table 5.4: Benefits table for FoodCo

	Do New Things	Do Things Better	Stop Doing Things
Financial		**B3a:** Improved production planning and control: release 4 FTE planning staff, cost saving £150 000 p.a. **B4:** Reduction in stock holding costs: one-off saving from reduction of stock holding of £200 000 and savings of £250 000 p.a. from reduced stock write-offs **B10:** Reduction in bad debts: reduced payment write-offs: £35 000 p.a.	**B2b:** Eliminating invoice errors: release 0.5 FTE staff in reconciliations, cost savings £30 000 p.a. **B5:** Stop unnecessary use of agency staff: £110 000 p.a. **B9:** Improve cash flow: reduce debtor days by 15: £25 000 p.a. reduction in interest charges
Quantifiable	**B8b:** Improved speed and accuracy of grower returns: 90% reduction in queries		**B2a:** Eliminating invoice errors: reduce customer queries by 90%
Measurable	**B1:** Reduce number of dispatch errors due to scanning: number of dispatch errors	**B3b:** Improve business/production planning and control: number of breaks in production schedules/ reduction in idle time **B6:** Reduced costs of customer service failures: number of returns	
Observable	**B8a:** Improved accuracy and speed of grower returns: improved grower relations	**B7:** Access to accurate and timely KPIs and management information: less time spent reconciling MI, more time spent on decision making and performance analysis **B11:** Better knowledge of customer and product profitability: credible and respected product and customer profitability information	

Financial project return

A financial return for the project can be calculated by looking at the financial benefits shown in the top row of Table 5.4 and comparing these to the project costs.

One-off savings (B4) = £200 000, resulting in a one-off net investment of (£930 000 – £200 000) = £730 000

Recurring savings (B2b + B3a + B4 + B5 + B9 + B10) = £600 000, resulting in a recurring net saving of (£600 000 – £40 000) = £540 000

Payback period = (£730 000/£540 000) = 1.4 years (an NPV or IRR can also be calculated if required)

Risk analysis

The following risks are identified that could prevent the realization of all or some of the benefits and need to be addressed in the approach to managing the project. Initial actions to address and mitigate the risks have been identified and a risk review agenda item established for each project management meeting.

- **Technical risks:** complexity of the systems functionality; number of system interfaces and systems being replaced.
- **Financial risks:** confidence in some elements of the project cost; confidence in the evidence for some of the benefits; business critical-ity of areas affected by the system.
- **Organizational risks:** extent of changes to business processes and practices; number of departments/functions/staff involved; signifi-cant organizational changes needed to realize the benefits; limited existing change management capability.

Summary

The structure and logic for a business case, presented in this chapter, are intended to ensure that the rationale for investment is clearly understood by those who have to decide whether to proceed, and also by those who will be involved in managing the project. In many organi-zations the story is told largely in reverse – the costs are presented first and then the benefits are described – hence the origin of the term 'cost–benefit analysis'. This approach proposes a 'benefit–cost analysis', which enables management to clearly understand the benefits that they can expect from an investment and hence decide how much they are willing to invest. Using the pro forma we have suggested in this chapter, the benefits that can be expected are clearly linked to the nature of business change required and hence management can also consider whether they are willing to make the complementary investments in change needed to realize the benefits.

The techniques have been described in terms of their ability to improve the quality of the business case. Later chapters explain how they can be adapted to ensure that the benefits management process can be used in different contexts. The next chapter describes the finalization of the benefits plan, including a detailed assessment of stakeholder issues. It also considers the approaches needed to manage the business changes that are essential to achieving the expected benefits.

Chapter 6

Stakeholder and change management

Many studies have shown that IT, of itself, delivers few benefits. It is the complementary business and organizational changes that produce the majority of benefits (see, for example, Gregor *et al.*, 2006). Other studies have shown that it is organizational issues that either pre-date or arise during the project, which cause many benefits not to be realized (Markus *et al.*, 2000; Doherty and King, 2001). It is necessary to understand the reasons why changes may be difficult to carry out and then to adopt an approach to managing each change that deals effectively with the causes of any problems as well as the effects. It is not the 'organization' that makes the changes, but individuals and groups of people – stakeholders – who have to change what they do or how they do it. Stakeholders include the beneficiaries of the investment, those who have to make changes to bring about the benefits and, in some cases, others who are indirectly affected by the project, for example if they will have a reduced level of service during the change period.

Some studies have suggested that IT-enabled change (or 'techno-change' as described by Markus, 2004) creates particular sets of issues due to both the reality and perceptions about the overall effects of IT. Not understanding these different views, and the reasons for the consequent behaviours, can create major problems in managing the changes required and for the project team's relationships with different stakeholder groups.

It is important to understand how the benefits are distributed across organizational

> 'Problems are often the result of either a lack of common understanding of the purposes of changes or different perspectives on how to achieve them successfully.' *Swanson and Ramiller (1997)*

stakeholder groups and whether the balance of 'pain' from change and 'gain' from the benefits is acceptable from each stakeholder's perspective and for the organization as a whole. Without an understanding of, and ways to address, this balance, the activities and actions of some stakeholders may be inappropriate or even destructive.

It is not necessarily the explicit changes that cause the resistance, but often the real or perceived secondary effects of the changes. For example, in many enterprise resource planning (ERP) implementations, line managers are concerned about changes that cause closer integration across processes and functions and the interdependencies this creates, such as:

- increased accountability with less discretion and autonomy of decision making;
- the performance of their area of responsibility is more visible to others;
- they have to rely on others to achieve their performance targets;
- recognition and reward structures reflect collective rather than individual performance;
- the significant learning curve required for them to manage in new ways and place greater reliance on the ERP system.

Another common concern of line managers is that, during implementation, conflicts and issues will inevitably arise due to the difficulty in resolving priorities between delivering the change programme and sustaining 'business as usual'. The success of the project may depend on managers releasing time for their most able and experienced staff – the same people they rely on to ensure existing operations run effectively.

This chapter first considers how stakeholder analysis can help understand how to deal with real and perceived issues. Then, approaches to change management are discussed in relation to the different types of issues. Finally, completion of the benefits plan is described.

Assessing the feasibility of achieving the benefit

Once a business case for investment has been developed and an overall risk analysis completed, a more detailed analysis is needed to determine how the organization can achieve each of the changes required to deliver the benefits. This can be considered an aspect of risk analysis, based on an assessment of how able or willing the main stakeholders involved in the project are to take the necessary actions and commit the time and resources required. In projects involving either significant changes or a wide range of diverse stakeholders, it is advisable to do an initial analysis of stakeholder perceptions prior to preparing the business case, to decide if any of the benefits are unlikely to be delivered.

During implementation, many issues within or outside the project could arise that affect stakeholder perceptions, interests and priorities, which, in turn, may change their commitment to the project. Therefore, the stakeholder analysis will probably need to be revisited during implementation.

In many cases a detailed stakeholder analysis will result in the identification of additional changes; these are most often additional enabling changes required to address stakeholder issues, either before implementation starts or at particular stages during implementation. Based on the issues that arise from the stakeholder analysis, different options for managing the changes can be identified, responsibilities finalized and the benefits plan completed.

There are many different techniques for stakeholder analysis. In this chapter we present two of the most commonly used techniques. The first of these considers the power of stakeholders and their interest in the project (Figure 6.1). The second approach, which fits well with the benefits management frameworks presented in earlier chapters, considers the balance between the benefits gained by stakeholders and the nature of the changes they are involved in (Figure 6.2). We then present a third approach that combines both of these approaches. This combination allows a full analysis of stakeholder attitudes and, most importantly, allows actions to be identified to address those attitudes. Whilst it is appropriate at the early stages of the assessment to refer to stakeholder analysis, we prefer the term 'stakeholder management', since this clearly indicates that the analysis should lead to actions to address stakeholder issues.

The purposes of stakeholder management are to:

- identify all the stakeholders whose knowledge, commitment or action is needed to realize each benefit;
- determine the view held by each stakeholder (or stakeholder group) in terms of '*what's in it for me?*' and any disbenefits they perceive;
- understand how the change activities affect each stakeholder group and their motivation to achieve or resist the changes;

- identify the actions needed to gain the required involvement and commitment of all the stakeholders and develop action plans to enable or encourage the necessary involvement.

It also has to be recognized that there will be existing relationships or 'coalitions of interest' among stakeholders which will also influence their perceptions. These interrelationships can either be a concern, if they cause empathy with groups that are against the project, or an asset if those who support the project can persuade others that, overall, the organizational benefits justify the amount of change.

Increasingly, many IS/IT projects are enterprise-wide and the number of stakeholder groups affected can be considerable and it may well cause working relationships among groups to change. It is also unlikely that all the stakeholders' issues can be addressed, and neither is there always time in the project to reach agreement with everyone concerned on every issue. Therefore, it is important as a first step to assess which stakeholders' commitment of time and resources are most critical to delivering the main benefits, either as benefit owners or change agents.

Many new systems are aimed at improving or creating new ways of working with external stakeholders, such as customers, suppliers and other trading partners. An understanding of their perceptions of the benefits they will receive and willingness to make changes is necessary, but any actions to address external stakeholder issues will normally have to be undertaken by managers within the organization who have responsibility for those external stakeholders. If customers or suppliers will benefit without having to make significant changes, they may be very supportive, and this can be a strong argument to persuade some reluctant internal stakeholders of the real need to change – external pressure can often create internal unity of purpose.

Identification of stakeholders will be based on the benefits dependency network in terms of benefit owners and those involved in making the business and enabling changes. These will include named individuals, people in defined managerial roles, specialists such as in human resources or regulatory functions and often large groups of operational staff or external parties, such as customers or even the public. Large groups are unlikely to be homogeneous in terms of their perceptions of the benefits or changes and it may be necessary to break them down into subgroups to reflect those different views and consequent issues.

Subdividing the group may be needed to allow for different levels of experience, time in the job, the age ranges of people or the location in which they work. For example, when introducing workflow systems in a call centre in an insurance company, the operators split into two groups based on their attitudes to working overtime and shifts – the younger staff relied on overtime and shift payments to 'pay the mortgage', whereas those with families preferred to work fixed, normal working hours. The project was expected to result in significant reductions in overtime required. Having identified the two views, the work groups were reorganized to include people with both preferences and they were then allowed to agree the shift and overtime patterns among themselves.

Stakeholder analysis and management techniques

Power and influence

The role that the power and influence of particular stakeholders play in IS implementations has long been known to have a significant effect on the outcome, depending on how individuals choose to exercise that power and influence. The power of stakeholders in projects may arise from their role in the organization, for example, the CEO, but other sources of power may be from the control of scarce resources or of the processes involved or access to specialist knowledge. Hence, understanding the viewpoints

> '. . . the realization of (the benefits of) an IS implementation largely occurs because of a collective consent where various stakeholders align their power and intentions.'
> *Dhillon et al. (2011)*

of different stakeholders with varying abilities to influence events and anticipating or dealing with the consequences is a critical success factor in many IS projects and other change programmes (OGC, 2007). The implementation of some new systems also reconfigures organizational power and influence, due to the changes that it brings about or the roles that individuals have to play in the implementation process (Dhillon *et al.*, 2011). Therefore, it is important for the project team to appreciate the potential implications of any changes in the balance of stakeholder power or influence as the project evolves.

A technique which is frequently used by experienced project managers, implicitly if not explicitly, is shown in Figure 6.1. It considers the relationship between the power or influence of certain stakeholders and their interest in the project.

A key purpose of this analysis is to provide guidance about the approaches to be adopted by the project team in engaging and

		Low ──── Power or ability to influence project success ──── High	
Attitude towards project	Supporting	Keep informed, in order to retain their support.	Keep well-informed, particularly if there is a problem with the project, to retain their confidence.
	Indifferent	Get them on board if only limited effort is required to persuade them. Pay more attention to them if their support will encourage other supporters and/or help to manage opposing groups.	Engage in dialogue to develop more favourable attitude towards the project and to limit the influence that groups opposing the project might have on them.
	Opposing	Usually require more effort to change their attitudes than is worthwhile. However, may be necessary to counter their negative influence on important groups.	Require substantial time and effort to develop a positive attitude to the project and to manage their demands. Effort may also be needed to counter their impact on other groups.

Low   High

Power or ability to influence project success

Figure 6.1: Power and interest of stakeholder groups (adapted from OGC, *Managing Successful Programmes*, 2003)

communicating with the different types of interest group. Clearly, the main efforts of the project team should focus on gaining and retaining the commitment of those who have the greatest power. The communications and engagement approaches will be different for those who have high power and have a high interest in the project, compared to those who have high power and have a low interest, are unaware of the project or who may actually oppose it. In the latter case, much of the communication will involve negotiating with the stakeholder group to reduce any potential negative effects they may have on the project. At the same time, the project team needs to identify other stakeholder groups whose influence may be less critical at first but who could become more important as the project evolves.

This technique can often be used as a 'first-cut' analysis and is particularly useful in large projects that involve many functions or business units which are starting from different levels of satisfaction with the current situation and therefore have more or less interest in the project. This situation is also quite common in international organizations, where units have different relationships with the centre and different cultures, creating further divergence of interests and attitudes among apparently similar stakeholder groups.

Benefits and change

The second technique is based on the work of Benjamin and Levinson (1993) and fits well with the benefits management frameworks described in previous chapters. It considers each stakeholder's perspective on the project from the balance of change and benefit affecting them.

The first step is to identify, from the benefits dependency network – normally by asking the stakeholders themselves – how significant the benefits that they will receive or recognize as benefits for the organization are, and also the scale or complexity of the changes in which they are involved. An initial analysis can be made on a matrix, as shown in Figure 6.2, which plots the relative positions of stakeholders on two axes, those of benefits received and changes required.

While the relative positions on each of the axes are important to show the gradations of views held, this analysis identifies four basic groups of stakeholders, by what they expect to get from the project:

1. **Net benefits** – those who should champion the project because they will receive benefits with little change. These stakeholders should be able to influence others, provided they are sensitive to the need for

	High	NET BENEFITS	BENEFITS BUT ...
		Should champion the project - but must be aware of implications for others and use their influence	Will be positive about benefits but concerned over changes needed - ensure sufficient enabling changes are identified to offset any resistance
Benefits Received		*'Collaborators'*	*'Compromisers'*
		FEW BENEFITS BUT ...	NET DISBENEFIT
		Must be kept supportive by removing any inertia/apathy which may influence others	Likely to resist the changes - must ensure all aspects of resistance dealt with by enabling projects
	Low	*'Accommodators'*	*'Resistors'*
		Low	Changes Required High

Figure 6.2: Summary of stakeholders' balance of benefits and changes

others to make or undergo changes for their benefit. They should behave as *collaborators*, willing to work closely with the project team and should be kept actively involved in the project planning. Their opinions should be sought when any issues or uncertainties arise.

2. **Benefits but . . .** – those who will obtain worthwhile benefits, but have to make considerable changes to obtain them. Inevitably, the changes come first and if the benefits are not certain or the project begins to have problems, their commitment may waver as the benefits seem either a long way off or look unlikely ever to be achieved. If the project can deliver some early visible benefits or 'quick wins', it will increase confidence that the more difficult changes are worthwhile. It is likely that throughout the project this group will change their views and some renegotiation of the change programme or further actions to address emergent issues will be needed, hence they will have to make some *compromises* at times. This will be particularly the case if they are balancing the changes with existing workloads involved in business as usual. If their interests are not continually and explicitly addressed, they may gradually become less committed and even resist some of the change aspects of the project.

3. **Net disbenefits** – those stakeholders who have to make changes largely for the benefit of others, while they have little or nothing to gain. In the worst case they may feel that the project will only result in disbenefits or have a negative impact for them. These groups are likely to *resist* the changes and it will normally require specific actions to be taken early in the project to address their concerns. This may even require making changes to the benefits plan, especially if they are influential stakeholders. It is important to make it clear that their concerns are being considered seriously and addressed as far as is possible. These groups are always likely to give priority to maintaining performance levels in existing business as usual activities rather than devoting time and resources to the change programme.

4. **Few benefits but . . .** – those who are only marginally involved in or affected by the investment: they will see few benefits and have little, if any, change to make. Provided that they are kept informed of how the project is proceeding, and specifically when and how their time or involvement is needed, they will normally *accommodate* the project within business as usual. This may change if they begin to empathize with other stakeholders who are negatively affected by, or are struggling to cope with, the changes.

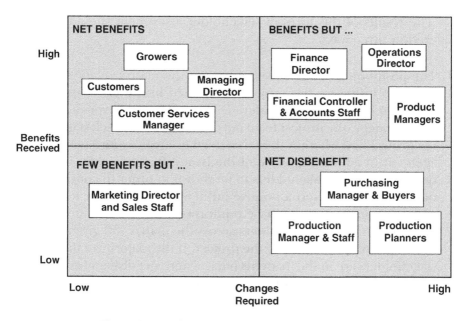

Figure 6.3: Stakeholder assessment from FoodCo

An initial assessment of the stakeholder positioning in the FoodCo example discussed in previous chapters is shown in Figure 6.3. The pattern is a positive one: there are clearly a number of stakeholders, including the managing director, who will gain significant benefits with little effort. However, the growers and customers are external stakeholders and need to be informed about the benefits that they can expect. It is unlikely that this view will directly influence the other stakeholder groups, but in the case of the customers, the customer services manager and marketing director should represent their interests in discussions with other stakeholders.

There are also three groups of internal stakeholders who have to make significant changes for little, if any, 'personal' benefit: the purchasing manager and buyers, the production manager and his staff and the production planners. These groups could form a powerful alliance to reduce the scope of the changes, given the critical parts of the operations they control. Four other groups or individuals are in the 'benefits but...' category and will need to be convinced that the changes required justify the expected benefits, if they are to use their influence to persuade others to make changes. This example will be considered in more detail later in the chapter.

The results of this form of stakeholder assessment should be considered in three ways:

1. The positioning of the stakeholders on the matrix relative to their ability to influence the project, as defined in the previous analysis (Figure 6.1) should be considered. This suggests the type of 'engagement strategy' the project team needs to adopt with each stakeholder (or group) and whether there is a need to involve more senior management in addressing some of the issues. It also enables interrelationships among stakeholders to be shown in order to consider how one group could exert a positive influence on others, or to identify where negative views might be reinforced.
2. The pattern of the stakeholders across the matrix will give an initial indication of the viability of the project. If the majority of influential stakeholders are in the 'benefits but...' and 'net disbenefits' groups, it will probably prove difficult to obtain the commitment needed to achieve the business changes. The project scope may have to be revised, either to find more benefits or reduce the extent of the changes required. Alternatively, the project could be broken into stages that deliver some early benefits from limited changes.
3. The assessment helps to identify those whose position must be considered in depth using the more detailed analysis described in the next section. This more detailed analysis, which combines elements of both of the previous techniques, identifies specific actions required and who is responsible for taking the actions identified. This more detailed analysis should always be carried out for all stakeholders in the 'benefits but . . .' and 'net disbenefits' categories, but may also be undertaken for influential stakeholders in the other segments to ensure their perceptions, and hence involvement, will be sustained over the duration of the project.

From analysis to action

Having identified stakeholder groups with views that could lead to failure to achieve some or all of the benefits, actions need to be defined to address those views. The table in Figure 6.4 is a means of eliciting and exploring those issues in a way that can lead to relevant and practical action plans.

The first step is to list the stakeholders or stakeholder groups. It is important to ensure that this list includes all of those that may have

Stakeholder Group	Benefits Perceived (Disbenefits)	Changes Needed	Concerns or Potential Resistance	Commitment: Current & Required				
				Resist	No view	Allow it to happen	Help it happen	Make it happen
List of stakeholders and stakeholder groups (especially 'resistors' and 'compromisers')	Individual and organizational benefits for each stakeholder and group	Changes to be made by or which affect each stakeholder or group	Resistance of each stakeholder or group, if applicable, and reason for it	Are against the project & will attempt to stop it or hinder progress	Are either unaware the project is going on or do not think it affects them	Will comply, when requested to do tasks required by the project, e.g. attend training	Will provide knowledge, time & resource to ensure the project meets objectives & timescales	Will instigate, oversee or carry out changes and ensure that all relevant changes are completed successfully

C ⟶ R

C ⟶ R
Action1?

Action?

Action 2?

C ⟶ R1/C1 ⟶ R

Figure 6.4: A comprehensive stakeholder analysis including actions required

difficulty with the project due to significant changes they are involved in (the resistors and compromisers in Figure 6.2). For each stakeholder, the benefits they receive directly and their view of the other organizational benefits should then be summarized in the second column. It may be that a benefit to the organization overall is a disbenefit to a particular stakeholder group, such as the need to relocate or a threat to their long-term job security, and this should be expressly shown in the analysis. The changes that they either have to make or which will affect them should be summarized in the third column of the table.

Then, preferably in discussion with the stakeholders themselves or their representatives and based on the balance of the benefits and changes, any potential concerns or reasons for resistance should be explicitly identified in the fourth column. Reasons for resistance may be due to the particular changes affecting them or more general issues, such as: 'change fatigue', the need to learn new skills or apparent deskilling of their role, new systems being too prescriptive or the introduction of detailed measurements of individual performance, leaving little or no discretion in the job. Often, concerns are about introducing the changes and simultaneously maintaining current levels of performance, without any additional resources during the transition. Alternatively, they may just be due to scepticism that the new system will actually work, based on experience of other investments in the past. In the worst cases, there may be cynicism that there is a hidden agenda and that these changes are only the start of more extensive reductions in staffing or deskilling of jobs through technology. There may be other reasons due to the current context of the business and other changes taking place.

The current view or position of each stakeholder is then indicated (C) in one of the five columns using the definitions:

1. **resist** – will overtly try to prevent the changes due to the overall negative effects on them;
2. **no view** – no commitment to what is needed to be done or perhaps unaware of the need for change or that the changes affect them;
3. **allow it to happen** – will do the minimum needed: compliant rather than cooperative;
4. **help it happen** – will cooperate and actively support actions as requested;
5. **make it happen** – will instigate the necessary actions and ensure that they are completed successfully.

Based on the role the particular stakeholders need to play in achieving the changes, the required level of commitment is then agreed and indicated (R). It is the extent of the gap between the current and required levels that will determine the nature of the action and who is best able to take it.

If the current and required positions are identical, clearly no action is needed. If they are in adjacent columns, no additional action is required, since good project management practices plus attentive and consistent communication should be sufficient to address the concerns.

When the gap is over two columns, for example from *no view* to *help it happen*, then some specific action is required, which becomes another enabling change on the benefits network, linked to the relevant changes affecting that stakeholder. As with other changes, responsibility and evidence of achievement need to be identified explicitly. For many of these further enabling changes, responsibility will lie with line managers, or specialists in other business areas, rather than within the project team itself.

Where the gap extends over more than two columns, especially in the case of *resist* to *make it happen*, either the feasibility of achieving the dependent benefits has to be reconsidered or a series of actions is needed, first to reduce the antipathy towards the project and later to achieve the level of positive commitment required. Again, the need for action and the nature of that action will also depend on the degree of influence of the stakeholder.

An interesting variant that can appear in this analysis is the need to reduce the enthusiasm of some stakeholders, often including the project champion, to personally *make* everything happen as quickly as possible, without being willing to allow others time to understand and buy into the changes.

Figure 6.5 shows a detailed analysis of some of the stakeholder groups in FoodCo – those who were in the high change segments of Figure 6.3. In five cases, further actions were needed to address the genuine concerns that might prevent the stakeholders giving the project the necessary level of commitment. In the case of the production planners, action would be needed in two stages: first, to overcome existing resistance, due to the fear that jobs would be lost, and then to obtain the cooperation required to implement the new system successfully.

Many stakeholder views can be changed by appropriate actions to address their concerns, but their perceptions are also likely to change over time as the project evolves, especially if problems arise, and also

Stakeholder Group	Perceived Benefits (Disbenefits)	Changes Needed	Concerns or Potential Resistance	Commitment (Current & Required)				
				Resist	No view	Allow it to happen	Help it happen	Make it happen
Finance Director	Improved cash control & info	New KPIs and controls	None				C ——→ R	
Fin. Controller & Accounts staff	Fewer errors, better control	New systems & procedures	*Extensive retraining*			C	Action ——→ R	
Operations Dir.	Reduced stock costs	New planning processes	None				C ——→ R	
Production Manager & Staff	Fewer production problems	New systems and technology	*Fear of new technology & lack of skills*			C—	Action ——→ R	
Purchasing Manager & Buyers	None	Inventory-driven procurement system	*Reduced discretion & tougher KPIs*		C	Action ——→ R		
Product Managers	Better cost info & accurate grower payments	New grower system and inventory KPIs	*Risk that grower needs will not be met*			C Action ——→R		
Production Planners	None – (*but fewer planners needed*)	More automated scheduling	*Fear of job losses*	C Actions ——→R				

Figure 6.5: Stakeholder analysis from FoodCo

due to factors outside the project. In projects that last more than a few months, the stakeholders themselves are also likely to change and reorganizations may change the roles of stakeholders in the project as well as the individuals involved. Therefore, it is important to revisit the stakeholder analysis whenever any influential stakeholders change or events have changed the views of stakeholders.

Completing the benefits plan

Having carried out a comprehensive stakeholder analysis, the final details can be completed on the benefits plan – the set of 'tables' that define the activities, interdependencies, timing and responsibilities involved in managing the changes and benefits. The stakeholder analysis may have added further enabling changes to the benefits dependency network, clarified or redefined some of the business changes and may even have amended some of the benefits, based on the practicalities of achieving them.

In Chapter 4, templates for describing the benefits and changes (see Tables 4.4 and 4.5) were introduced. At that stage, initial information derived from the benefits dependency network could be entered into the tables. In Chapter 5, as the business case was developed, the benefits information could be completed, as described and exemplified in Table 5.3.

The final stage in completing the change elements of the plan involves ensuring that all the stakeholders who have to contribute to effecting the changes understand the roles they are expected to play and the resource commitment needed. The timing of when each change activity needs to be started needs to be identified. By estimating the resource commitment from each stakeholder for the change activity, standard PERT networking techniques can be used to schedule the work within the overall project plan. This will almost certainly result in some compromises from the ideal sequence of activities due to resource constraints. If this impacts the critical path, the overall timescale of the project will need to be revised.

The information from this planning process can then be used to complete the details required for the benefits plan, as per the example in Table 6.1, for the FoodCo project. As for the benefits, the change activities will be described in more detail in the project manual and will be updated as implementation proceeds. For complex or extensive changes, it is probably necessary to develop a more detailed

Table 6.1: Completed change template – example from FoodCo

Change or enabler no. and dependent benefits	Description	Responsibility (and *involvement*)	Prerequisite or consequent changes	Evidence of completion	Due date	Resources required
E8 B7, B9 and B10	Develop new KPIs based on balanced scorecard	Executive Directors	P: None C: C6 Implement performance management process	Balanced scorecard and KPIs agreed by Board and published	April 2004	2/3 Executive Meetings + 1 day per Dept Manager
C2 B3, B4	Implement new raw material stock replenishment algorithms	Purchasing Manager and *Product Managers*	P: E1 Restructure Stock coding C: None	Tested and agreed algorithms for all A and B class materials	June 2004	20 days of inventory controllers, 10 days of Product/ Purchasing Managers + 4 days of Accounts staff

'sub-project' plan and to manage and track the progress of all the activities required to complete the change.

Approaches to managing change

There are a number of ways to address stakeholder attitudes to change management issues in the project environment. Ury *et al.* (1993) suggest three different types of management approach, which can be used to bring about change successfully, although each can also cause both helpful and adverse stakeholder behaviours:

- **Top down** – imposition of the changes by senior management. This can be quick and effective but, although it usually obtains compliance in the short term, it can breed feelings of resentment and reduce future cooperation, especially when there are genuine causes for the concerns that appear to have been ignored.
- **Coalition** – working together to understand and resolve the concerns and, if possible, the causes of those concerns, at least for the duration of the project. Concessions will probably have to be made in terms of the change plan or by finding additional benefits to encourage the required commitment.
- **Negotiation** – making specific trade-offs between the organization's need for the benefits and the means by which the stakeholder group will help those benefits occur. This may involve agreeing to terms and conditions to protect the jobs of staff or new incentive or reward schemes to 'buy in' the new ways of working. The danger here is that special treatment for those taking a negative stance may reduce the commitment of others who initially were in favour of the project.

Which of the approaches should be adopted is also dependent on the nature of the organization, the culture and existing management style. In an organization with a strong command and control structure, such as the police, change can be implemented from the top down. In an organization with devolved professional responsibilities, such as a law firm or a hospital, a negotiated approach is more likely to be successful.

An alternative approach described by Markus and Benjamin (1997) is to recognize that 'change is a contact sport' and establish specific change management and change agent roles and allocate responsibilities for change 'advocacy' and 'facilitation'. These roles should, preferably, be filled by experienced line managers and organizational development specialists, who are not part of the project team and therefore wedded to the particular IT solution, and who will be open to different options for achieving the changes.

Matching the management approach and stakeholder behaviours

Kumar *et al.* (1998) identified three commonly held perceptions of IT-enabled change projects that can provoke quite different responses by stakeholders. The terms they use – system rationalism, trust-based rationalism and segmented institutionalism – are easier to understand (and remember!) as follows:

- **Rational** – the behaviours of those stakeholders who subscribe to the economic goal of maximizing the organization's efficiency and effectiveness through technology.
- **Trust** – those stakeholders who trust that others will only make changes that are mutually beneficial and are willing to collaborate with certain other stakeholder groups.
- **Self-interest** – those stakeholders who focus on satisfying their private interests and agendas, at the expense of others if necessary. This behaviour can, in the worst case, undermine the investment.

As noted in the previous section, the approach adopted for managing the project can be essentially one of three types: *top down, coalition* or *negotiation*.

These are inevitably simplifications of all the possible alternatives available, but they are helpful, when combined, to understand how the interplay between the approaches adopted by management and the project team and the different stakeholder behaviours can influence the outcome of the investment.

In a study of international enterprise systems implementations, Ward *et al.* (2005) used these classifications to analyse the stakeholder and project team interactions over the course of the projects to understand how effectively the management approaches addressed different stakeholder behaviours, in terms of the effects on time, cost and benefits delivered. The study revealed that the different management approaches provoked responsive behaviours from certain stakeholder groups that influenced the outcome. Table 6.2 summarizes the main

Table 6.2: Interplay of stakeholder behaviours and management approaches

Stakeholder behaviours	Management approach		
	Top down	Coalition	Negotiation
Rational	1 Clear vision of potential benefits – business case and overall plan	2 Mutual benefits from changes and shared learning – but tends to reduce scope to changes that can be agreed by all	3 Agreement on timescales, resources and local benefits, but tends to reduce scope and lose some major benefits
Trust	4 Shared vision of potential benefits and acceptance of the need to change to overcome problems	5 Cooperative change management to achieve mutual benefits	6 Trade-offs in resources, benefits and changes can be agreed across interest groups
Self-interest	7 Localized view of benefits only – resistance to change if no local benefit, leading to software customization	8 Trade-offs between coalitions to minimize negative effects of changes (and probably reduce benefits)	9 Detailed 'contracts' on all aspects of implementation – benefits, resources, changes, etc. with each interest group

effects of the different combinations of management approach and stakeholder behaviour on the projects.

A more detailed discussion is given in Box 6.1.

The nature of IT-enabled change management: is it different?

Like Ward and Elvin (1999), Markus (2004) considers that the interdependency of technology implementation, business changes and the benefits to be realized, has to be recognized in the way IT-enabled

Box 6.1: Implications of interactions of management approaches and stakeholder behaviours

1. Top down/rational

At the start of a project it is essential to ensure that the project is consistent with the stated vision or strategy of the senior management through a rational discussion of the drivers for change, the investment objectives and business benefits expected and to present these in a business case. Senior executives are more likely to agree to and support a well-argued business case which links the investment benefits to the business strategy and it is often their confidence in the business case that enables them, individually and collectively, to persuade others of the need or change. The business case also provides a 'mandate' for the project manager and team.

However, senior management may be unaware of some serious issues that may prevent delivery of all the benefits and they will want the benefits delivered by minimum resources and change effort.

2. Coalitions/rational

From the project mandate, the project team, supported by senior management, needs to establish the appropriate relationships with 'coalitions' of key stakeholders to develop the change plan that will deliver the benefits. If the project requires significant innovation, then new knowledge will be required to create and achieve the changes. This can take some time to develop or acquire and can require more effort than expected to achieve agreement among the affected stakeholders.

The rational view will tend to balance the change effort with the importance of the benefits, which may result in a reduction in scope in order to deliver what the coalitions perceive as the major benefits, within an acceptable timescale and manageable change plan. Given that these coalitions need to see the mutual benefit from their agreements, their existence may not be sustained if the situation changes.

3. Negotiation/rational

The project team's relationship with the business managers will tend to focus on rational negotiation about the facts: costs,

(*Continued*)

schedules, resources and the most obvious benefits. The more complex issues, such as change implementation and new working relationships, require more subtle types of negotiation to resolve. The project team can use the business case to argue the need for other changes to deliver the benefits, but the line managers will argue it is 'their job to deliver the benefits' and the project team's job to deliver the necessary technology at the right time and cost. This often leads to a focus on the project costs and the technology rather than the business changes. As a result, the relatively easy benefits will be obtained but many of the more difficult benefits are likely to be lost.

4. Top down/trust

When senior managers attempt to impose 'their' plan without allowing time and effort for understanding how the changes will be made, existing relationships among stakeholders based on 'who trusts whom' will often be reinforced. They may well agree with the benefits, but the attitude to change will be acceptance rather than commitment to make it happen. The project team will be faced with stakeholder groups who represent the current organization structure, and senior management's inability to delegate to or empower the groups can inhibit achievement of consensus about the change plan.

5. Coalitions/trust

This is the best combination for moving from 'intent' through planning and into implementation when major business and organizational changes are needed. It requires the same actions by senior management and the project team as in 'coalitions/ rational', but recognizes the existence of current relationships and the need for a facilitated process to enable those stakeholders to determine the changes in working relationships required. Line managers are allowed discretion to define new working arrangements, or perhaps conclude that not all the changes are worthwhile in relation to the benefits. This should mean that the investment objectives can be converted into a viable plan, so that the majority of benefits can be achieved because the changes will actually be made.

6. Negotiation/trust

This enables the more complex organizational issues to be addressed, since the existing trust among stakeholders will enable a degree of trade-off between both benefits obtained and changes needed, as well as the resources and timescales required to achieve implementation. Again, the effect may be to reduce the overall benefits delivered to those where balanced, 'fair' trade-offs can be agreed. However, the trading process is likely to delay the project, since the trade-off arrangements may well produce a non-ideal implementation schedule in terms of the use of the project team's resources.

7. Top down/self-interest

When senior managers attempt to impose a 'solution' without reference to existing stakeholder issues and constraints or trust their line managers to achieve the plan using their knowledge and resources, the riskiest combination can occur. It is often compounded when the project team has only focused on its relationship with senior management and paid little or no attention to line managers' change and resource issues.

Many of the line managers will only accept the need for change relating to the specific benefits they will obtain and will not cooperate in changes that result in benefits to others or the organization overall. This often happens in multi-unit, multinational implementations where a corporate solution is imposed without consultation and involvement in the initial planning. When the project team consists primarily of 'head office' staff, the problems are often compounded.

8. Coalitions/self-interest

This combination can be a problem when the coalitions required to work together and the project team have little confidence and trust in each other's motives. Behaviour close to self-protection can occur, especially if those outside the coalitions have more to lose than gain. Trade-offs with the project team and among the groups are likely to result in reducing the benefits to those

(Continued)

achievable by minimal change. It is this combination that often turns the implementation into a 'software project' to avoid contention between stakeholder groups and the project team.

9. Negotiation/self-interest

At the point of implementation and changeover to the new system and associated ways of working, each individual line manager needs to be clear about the 'contract' they, and their staff, have to achieve the new performance levels implied by the benefits. The project team also needs clear criteria as to priority areas of business concern and to have contingency plans for any deterioration of business performance following implementation. It is more likely that the conditions for constructive negotiations will exist close to implementation if the self-interest behaviours that are now acceptable have not prevailed earlier in the project.

In large projects with multiple stakeholders, all three management approaches are likely to be required during the project, and even used simultaneously to deal with varying stakeholder behaviours. It should be remembered that the project team can choose its management approach but the stakeholder behaviours are not under its control. Therefore, the project team has to be sensitive to the stakeholders' views in selecting its approach, but also aware of the possible adverse or disruptive behaviours a particular approach may cause.

Alternative routes through the matrix

Figure 6.6 suggests three main routes through the matrix, leading to varying degrees of probable success. The routes discussed are not intended to be prescriptive, but do reflect experience of analysing different types of project using the framework. All avoid the top-down/self-interest box, a combination that can cause major setbacks and delays, increase risk and may even derail the whole project. Each route is workable and will produce success to a degree, but the top and bottom routes (dots and dashes, respectively) are likely to deliver fewer benefits.

The 'best' route is shown by the full line, since the management approach adapts to match the organizational behaviours as they often evolve during the project. The top-down/rational combination in the planning phase is effective in establishing the

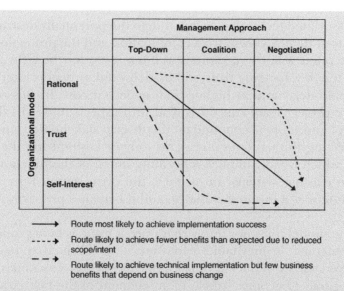

Figure 6.6: Routes through the matrix

investment intent, expected benefits, business case and project structure. But then a change to coalitions/trust is best for developing and agreeing an achievable change plan which will deliver the majority of the benefits. This needs to continue through the early stages of implementation, but move to negotiation/self-interest close to final implementation in order to provide the effective control needed to operate the new system and processes.

If, following the project set-up, the purely rational view prevails, it is likely to move the project to the coalitions/rational box (*dotted route*). In which case, the project may be redefined to some extent to reduce the scope to enable changes to be managed with fewer problems. If agreement among the stakeholders who gain most from the investment is not reached quickly, the project may well proceed to more detailed negotiations about 'facts', such as the system specification, project timescales and resources (negotiation/ rational), rather than resolve the more subjective or sensitive organizational aspects. Again, these changes to the scope will probably cause a reduction in the benefits.

The third (*dashed*) route is likely to produce a successful IT project in terms of moving the organization onto new software

(*Continued*)

and associated technologies but, due to the potentially destructive aspects of the top-down/trust combination and the protectionism which often follows (coalitions/self-interest), few benefits apart from the 'low-hanging fruit' will be delivered, probably after considerable delay and at higher than expected cost. In this route, all the project team can do is deal with aspects under its direct control and try to accommodate the diverse stakeholder interests by meeting the basic requirements only or customizing the software, which usually implies replicating much of the functionality in the existing systems. In essence, the organization rejects the investment as a business initiative and it becomes primarily an IT project.

The model does not imply that once a route is being followed the outcome is inevitable. However, it is likely that benefits achieved will be reduced, timescales extended or costs increased if the project becomes 'stuck' in an element of the matrix where the management approach and mode of behaviour are conflicting, rather than reinforcing.

change projects are managed. This is in part due to the uncertainty of the outcome of the combination of changes, but also due to the limitations of traditional IS/IT project management and organizational change management approaches – the former focus on delivering a working solution and the latter on the ability of people to adapt to new organizational processes, roles and structures. Markus lists a wide range of types of change, which are very similar to those described as typical business and enabling changes in Chapter 4. The critical difference between the 'technochange' perspective and more traditional approaches is that the benefits realized depend on the design of new technology-enabled ways of working and the synchronized implementation of technology and organizational change.

While many IS/IT implementations can be planned in detail based on prior experience and by adopting best practice methodologies in design and

'Using IT in ways that can trigger major organizational changes creates high-risk, potentially high-reward, situations and is what I call technochange (for technology-driven organizational change).' Markus (2004)

project management, many more require significant new knowledge to be created during the project. This implies an iterative, or 'agile', development approach, often involving prototyping or piloting key IS/IT solution components *and* the new ways of working, to understand both the potential benefits and whether they can actually be realized. This, according to Markus, is important not only when new technology is involved, but also when the organization is resistant to change and prototyping is used to create the ability to change ways of working incrementally, rather than risk major business and IT changes at the same time.

Interestingly, the UK National Health Service's 'Connecting for Health' programme, which had many aspects with the characteristics of 'technochange', was initially set up to be managed with separately defined roles, responsibilities and even structures addressing technology delivery, change management and benefits realization. The need to integrate and synchronize these streams of activity soon became apparent to the clinical and managerial staff involved.

Alternative change management strategies

The discussion so far implies that different change management strategies are required for different types of IS/IT investment, to deal with the inherently different interactions between the IS/IT and organizational changes needed to deliver the variety of benefits available.

Research by Simon (1995) proposed four types of change control or management to be used in different circumstances, depending on whether senior management wished to encourage *contribution, performance, innovation* or *initiative.* Achieving these different intentions requires senior management and the project team to apply varying degrees of control over the change activities and the extent to which decision making can safely be delegated.

This will, of course, vary across organizations and depends on the nature of the application, the business and the organizational culture – for example, in retail organizations with many branches or stores. In contrast, in the R&D functions in pharmaceutical companies, different communities of scientists will be given much local discretion in how they make best use of knowledge-sharing applications.

These different forms of management control are closely related to the different benefits, changes and risks to be managed across the four segments of the investment portfolio (see Chapter 2). They also recognize the need to address many of the change management issues, described earlier, that are characteristic of 'technochange'.

Boundary control

This is appropriate when the intended *contribution* – the benefits – can be stated clearly, but senior managers are indifferent as to how they are achieved within some stated parameters, such as the cost they are willing to incur or the timescale that can be allowed. Within these constraints, people are empowered to achieve the stated benefits in the way they think most appropriate, given the resources available.

Boundary control is most effective when the benefits can be expressed in financial or quantifiable terms and the changes needed to achieve them explicitly defined in terms of cause and effect. It also requires a clear statement of the extent to which software will be customized or whether a 'vanilla' IS/IT solution will be accompanied by changes to procedures and practices. This normally implies that the stakeholder implications can be identified early in the project and action taken to mitigate any adverse issues. Discretion is then allowed for the project team and the line managers involved to negotiate the detail of when and how the required changes can be made.

All these attributes imply that this approach is most feasible when the changes are mainly to make efficiency improvements and therefore it is most suitable for *support* (see the investment portfolio in Chapter 2) investments which do not have any significant interdependencies with other projects.

Diagnostic control

If the required benefits can be specified in detail, but their delivery is dependent on a complex or interrelated set of changes, then the change management components of the implementation need to be carefully monitored to ensure that all the benefits remain realizable. This can be especially difficult if decisions have to be made during implementation regarding whether to make changes to the IS/IT or to business practices. There may be a clearly stated rationale for the changes in terms of how performance improvements can be achieved, but influential stakeholders may have different views about the best way of achieving them.

It is also likely that new stakeholder issues will arise as the project progresses, due to problems of detail in the changes or alternative options for achieving the benefits. As shown in Box 6.1, these emergent issues often result in trade-offs being required between stakeholders and also between benefits and the costs or risks of some changes. These trade-offs are most easily understood and negotiated when the target benefits are explicitly quantifiable or financial.

This form of control is used when achieving *performance* improvements is the main objective, but it relies heavily on the stakeholders' ability to describe in detail at each stage what has to be delivered and how it will be done. It is most appropriate for *key operational* or large, organization-wide *support* investments, which involve many, often inter-related but not radical, changes to business processes or structures.

Interactive control

The previous two approaches are appropriate when the benefits can be stated explicitly, even if the change plan may have to be modified during implementation. In other investments, senior management is unable to state in detail what it expects, beyond an outline vision with perhaps some explicit objectives. Iterations are then required to iden-tify the benefits that can be delivered from different change options.

These uncertainties mean that it is difficult to identify or address all the stakeholder issues at the start of the project. In this case, senior managers need to share their knowledge by facilitating and supporting an organizational learning process to identify more precisely what the benefits could be and the risks the organization is willing to take to achieve them. In these circumstances, senior managers need to monitor the evolution of the project and the business case and be able to intervene to make critical decisions, as and when appropriate, while encouraging *innovation* and creative thinking. This is a delicate balancing act, which relies on effective, trusting working relationships between stakeholders as well as adhering to good project management practices. It requires senior management to be informed of any stake-holder conflicts or issues that require changes to organizational roles and responsibilities.

Clearly, these situations are more likely to arise in large, complex projects where significant, even radical, business changes are involved, with a range of possible trade-offs between technology investment and business changes. *Innovation* through 'technochange' or radical busi-ness change based on proven technologies is most frequent in *strategic* investments or for *key operational* investments intended to carry out existing processes in significantly different ways.

Belief system

If senior management wishes to encourage *initiative* and empower people to create something radically different, then it must establish a belief system, or set of values, that enables people to explore options that align with the strategic intentions of the organization. The belief system also gives guidance regarding the types of change the organization is willing to undertake and the rationale or justification needed to initiate different types of change programme. In many organizations, the argument for 'technochange' programmes has to be particularly compelling, given senior management scepticism about the business benefits. In this case, the only means of control is through actively facilitating behaviours in line with the organizational values they have established.

This form of management control is most commonly used in conjunction with a variant of boundary control, such as a limit on authorized expenditure for each project stage, to reduce the potential business and financial risks associated with the degrees of freedom being allowed.

STRATEGIC	HIGH POTENTIAL
Benefits: from innovation Characteristics: organizational learning Stakeholder issues: uncertain, evolving & complex Risks: technical, financial & organizational Change Control: INTERACTIVE	Benefits: to be determined Characteristics: create knowledge Stakeholder issues: unknown Risks: all types but minimized by limited scale/scope Change Control: BELIEF SYSTEM + BOUNDARY CONTROL
Benefits: by performance improvements Characteristics: knowledge application Stakeholder issues: predictable but complex & interrelated Risks: organizational mainly - financial and technical reduced by application of methodologies Change Control: DIAGNOSTIC	Benefits: from financial savings Characteristics: automation with empowerment to deliver savings Stakeholder issues: predictable but often negative due to cost savings Risks: mainly organizational, due to vested interests. Change Control: BOUNDARY
KEY OPERATIONAL	SUPPORT

Figure 6.7: Change management approaches and the investment portfolio

High potential evaluations exploring new business opportunities or the potential benefits of new technologies, including prototypes or pilots to test the concepts, would fall into this category. If the evaluation is successful, then the form of control should change to one more appropriate to the nature and purpose of the resulting major investment.

Figure 6.7 summarizes the relationship between these four change management approaches and the nature of the benefits, changes, risks and stakeholder issues that are commonly associated with each segment of the investment portfolio.

Summary

While stakeholder analysis and management can be considered a component of risk assessment, its real value is in anticipating and determining the actions needed to address stakeholder issues as early as possible in the project. This enables the planning and management of the organizational and business changes to accommodate and deal with the genuine, legitimate concerns of individuals or groups of stakeholders.

Many organizations now understand that benefits realization is both an organizational competence and a major component of IS/IT implementation (see, for example, the OGC (2007) guidelines, *Managing Successful Programmes*). However, it is often considered an activity separate from change management and, all too frequently, responsibilities for change management and benefits realization are assigned to different people. This tends to reinforce the belief that the benefits largely result from the implementation of technology. This can lead to resistance to change, since the reasons for the changes seem, to many people, to be merely due to the implementation of the technology. Coupled with scepticism resulting from many IS/IT disappointments or inflated promises, this can cause many stakeholders to avoid becoming actively involved in the change programme, resulting in the perception that 'IT is being done to them'.

Adopting a change management strategy appropriate both to the stakeholders' interests and what the organization is trying to achieve increases the ability to realize the investment benefits. Change management and benefits realization should be closely integrated and the approaches to stakeholder and change management discussed in this chapter explicitly recognize this interdependence. There is considerable literature on how to manage organizational change, but very little of it makes specific reference to the issues arising from technology-enabled change. Hence, this chapter has concentrated on the particular aspects of IT-enabled change projects.

The next chapter considers how the benefits management process can be aligned and integrated with other established best practices and methods of IS/IT implementation management and governance. Chapter 8 then describes how it can be adapted to different organizational contexts and for different types of investment.

Chapter 7

Implementing a benefits management approach

Business managers in most organizations realize that benefits from IS/IT projects do not just happen, but there is less appreciation of the fact that to achieve greater success, an organization must change the way it thinks about and manages those investments. As stated in Chapter 3, merely improving existing processes and methodologies is insufficient, because that does not address the central issues involved in managing the benefits. However, having new processes, tools and techniques is only the first step. These are just the *means*, and it is how they are used that will determine whether the *ends* of improving the value from investments are realized. Therefore, the 'mode of engagement' – that is, the *ways* that IT specialists, business managers, users and executives are involved and contribute to the project, the roles each play and how decisions are taken – also has to change if these new tools are to be used effectively.

The previous three chapters described a suite of tools and techniques that enable organizations to change the way they identify business benefits, build business cases and manage the changes needed. Through consistent application of these techniques, an organization can develop the competences needed to manage the variety of investments it undertakes more successfully. This chapter describes how these new ways of managing IS/IT projects can be introduced and made effective in the day-to-day conduct of project activities.

First, the reasons why organizations introduce a benefits management approach, and the implications of those different rationales for how the process and tools are implemented, are considered. Then we return to the process outlined in Chapter 3, to describe how the approach and process can be operationalized in practice. This includes how benefits management can be integrated with existing methodologies for planning and managing IS/IT projects. Throughout the chapter, the discussion reflects the experiences of a wide range of organizations that have adopted this new way of managing their IS/IT projects.

Rationales for introducing benefits management

Having been involved in the introduction and observed the adoption of the benefits management techniques described in this book in many organizations over the last ten years, there are a number of reasons that commonly lead to the recognition that a new approach is needed. Different reasons often influence the extent of the implementation, ranging from the introduction of new organizational processes and governance mechanisms to simply the addition of new tools and techniques to existing methods.

Perhaps the four most common causes of adoption are:

1. **A crisis:** a major investment is out of control, costs are escalating and it appears that few, if any, of the benefits will be delivered. The benefits management toolkit is then used to reappraise the project's business case and develop a benefits plan to redefine the overall scope or revise the implementation plan. This would include, in some cases, cancelling the project. Use of the tools and techniques is then usually extended to other projects to prevent them from suffering the same fate.
2. **An intervention:** business managers are reluctant to engage in the development of business cases for IS/IT projects or to play an active role in delivering the changes and benefits. Instead, they prefer to leave it to the 'project team'. This often occurs when the project team insists on following rigorous systems development and project management methods that are not 'user-friendly' ways of working. This can result in managers feeling that, rather than being involved in the process, it is being 'done to them'. The introduction of the tools and techniques plus the new process can enable business managers to apply their knowledge in a simple and effective way. If, however, the focus remains exclusively on short-term financial payback, there is a danger that the tools are used merely to provide better-argued financial figures, rather than follow through the change management and benefits realization.

3. **A new initiative:** either as a result of an IS/IT strategic planning process or due to the initiation of a number of significant IS/IT projects, the organization realizes that its current methods are insufficient. The complexity of such projects indicates the need to take into account a wider range of stakeholder interests and how the balance of benefits and changes will affect their commitment to the programme or project. The introduction of a benefits management process in this context is seen as a means of improving collaboration between project teams and line managers over an extended period. As such, it tends to lead to the adoption of the approach as a central component of the ways in which all major IS/IT projects, as well as many other change programmes, are conceived, assessed and managed.

4. **Improved governance:** as organizations become aware that the range of IS/IT projects they make has a significant effect on current and future performance, the need for more effective and adept governance processes becomes paramount. The intention is not only to manage the IS/IT projects and change initiatives more effectively, but also to improve the decision making that instigates those investments. This view also requires the 'loop to be closed', by using formal post-implementation reviews to understand how well investments that have been made have achieved their objectives. This 'top-down' governance usually recognizes that there is a gap in current methods which is preventing the organization from exploiting the IS/IT capabilities it has or can acquire.

The first two causes are perhaps characteristic of organizations that do not have comprehensive IS strategies aligned with their business strategy, but tend to be problem driven and opportunistic in terms of IS/IT projects. This 'point solution' approach tends to foster a similar attitude to the disciplines required to carry out the projects consistently well. This results in new tools and techniques being implemented reactively to overcome problems, rather than improve organizational competences in managing IS/IT. These new ways of working are normally introduced to the organization by the IS/IT function, which can be interpreted by business managers as the IS/IT function alone needing to improve its competences. Having said that, in some instances, these modes of introduction have led, over time, to the approach becoming used for all IS/IT projects as well as other types of organizational projects.

Figure 7.1: Different rationales for implementation of a benefits management approach

These four different starting points are depicted in Figure 7.1. When a benefits management approach is implemented due to reasons 3 and 4, it is able to make a significant improvement, not only in benefits realized from individual projects, but also in the ability of the organization to identify the most advantageous projects to undertake.

Box 7.1 describes in more detail how a major UK retailer introduced the approach, not only as an initiative to improve the value delivered from each of its major IS/IT projects, but also to improve the governance of the whole IT-enabled transformation programme.

As shown by the example in Box 7.1, the benefits management approach provides additional value when applied to the multiple projects within a programme, as discussed in detail in Chapter 9. Use of the benefits management process allowed the organization to combine the individual project benefit plans into a coherent programme plan that recognized dependencies between the individual projects and, importantly, recognized when multiple projects were claiming the same benefits. Basing the programme benefits plan on the detailed individual project plans ensured a more realistic assessment of the benefits expected from the programme, allowing expectations

Box 7.1: Adoption of benefits management within a major retailer

A major supermarket in the UK had embarked on a multi-million pound programme to replace many of its core information systems and redesign its operational processes. In order to ensure that the programme did not simply become a technology replacement initiative, but would deliver benefits that addressed the strategic drivers on the organization, it decided to adopt the benefits management approach throughout. However, introducing the process was also seen to require significant changes in how the organization initiated, managed and evaluated the success of its IS/IT and change projects. Therefore, a benefits management approach was used to plan the new process introduction. This demonstrated the improvements expected and ensured that the key stakeholders, the business managers, would become more appropriately involved in the projects. The benefits dependency network that was developed to identify the benefits from adopting this approach across the programme and the changes to working practices is shown in Figure 7.2.

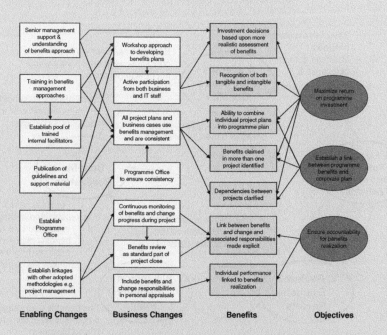

Figure 7.2: Benefits dependency network for benefits management adoption

to be set particularly among the shareholders of the organization who were watching the significant investment with extreme interest.

Initiating and managing a benefits-driven project

As shown in Figure 7.3, the benefits management approach involves a different way of carrying out the activities associated with initiating a project and developing the business case for the investment. It also involves a specific focus during implementation on tracking the achievement of each of the benefits. The ability to achieve the maximum benefits from the project will depend on the degree of certainty of the benefits plan and, during its execution, identifying if and when it needs to be amended and adjusting it appropriately. Therefore, it is important that all the necessary knowledge is included during the planning stage and that everyone understands the implications of the plan and their role in its execution.

As described in earlier chapters, success in the first two stages of the benefits management process depends on the effective sharing of

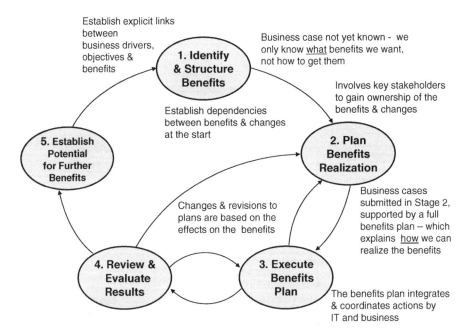

Figure 7.3: Key differences of the benefits management approach in the project initiation and implementation stages

knowledge between business managers and IS/IT specialists, an exchange which is facilitated by conducting workshops rather than holding meetings or one-to-one discussions. Overall, the workshops should ensure that all the necessary links with the business drivers are made and can be sustained, and that the relationship between benefits and changes is made explicit. The ability of all stakeholders to commit the time and resources required by the project should also be ensured. The outputs from the workshops will form the basis of the business case and benefits plan and should become integral components of the overall project plan. The number of workshops needed to develop the benefits plan will vary depending on the scale and complexity of the project, but normally at least two will be necessary. Each workshop should involve the key stakeholders in order to agree the investment objectives, elicit the benefits, define the scope of the change programme and understand the potential risks.

Between the workshops, a considerable amount of work will have to be done by both the project team members and other key stakeholders. This will include documenting and reviewing outputs from the first workshop, obtaining the further information that was identified as being needed. While it is impossible to prescribe a guaranteed way of achieving the best benefits plan and business case, there are a number of areas where good practices can improve the process – both in the content and management of the workshops. Figure 7.4 suggests

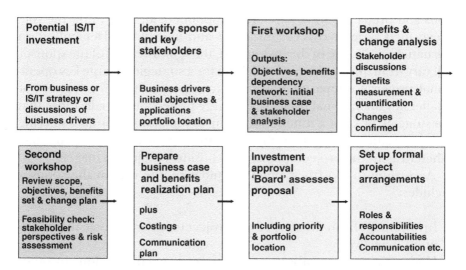

Figure 7.4: Initial activities in a benefits-driven project

the main activities that are involved in the establishment of a benefits-driven approach.

A potential investment need or opportunity may have arisen through a formal strategic assessment, from the operational issues or as a new business idea or due to the availability of new technology. In the last case it may be more appropriate to consider it a high potential opportunity to be evaluated, rather than require the development of a rigorous business case and benefits plan. How the benefits management approach and techniques can be adapted for high potential evaluations are considered later in this chapter.

Before considering the details of the project set-up activities, it is helpful to define and describe two roles that are critical to making the benefits-driven approach effective: the project sponsor and business project manager.

The project sponsor

At the start of the project a business project sponsor or champion should be appointed – a senior business manager who will take overall responsibility for ensuring that the investment produces the maximum value for the organization. The need for this senior business management leadership and involvement has been identified in many surveys as a factor that can significantly affect the outcome of IT investments, as well as other types of business change initiative. This is recognized in most organizations and project sponsors are often appointed, although how the role is executed varies across organizations and individuals. Depending on the nature and scope of the investment, the seniority level of the sponsor will vary from, probably, executive level for a strategic or large key operational project to departmental or functional manager for support or smaller key operational projects. For large projects, especially those that are strategic or span a number of business functions, a project steering group of senior managers from all the functions involved is often established to assist the project sponsor and business project manager.

According to most best practice guidance, the role of the sponsor includes:

1. Involvement from the start of the project to set or endorse the investment objectives.
2. Having the power, authority or influence to get things done by other managers, especially ensuring resources are made available and that organizational issues that may affect the project are addressed.

3. Understanding and articulating the vision of the project in terms of how the new ways of working and other business changes will result in the benefits.
4. Being the managerial link between the project and the wider organizational and other business initiatives.
5. Chairing the project steering group or review meetings, when decisions regarding any changes to the investment plan are made.

These imply that the sponsor should give the project strong, public support, actively monitor the progress from the business improvement perspective and be available, at any time, to the project manager and team to help resolve issues that arise. The sponsor should see the success of the investment as a significant personal objective and demonstrate some personal contribution to the project.

The attendance of the sponsor at the benefit workshops is essential, and the sponsor should preferably convene them to ensure that other senior managers attend. At the first workshop he or she will articulate and confirm the business drivers and ensure that clear investment objectives are defined and agreed, thereby setting the aims, scope and high-level success measures for the project. The scope is particularly important, since the temptation for extra functionality to be added needs to be challenged, as does over-engineering and unnecessary integration.

The business project manager

A business project manager should also be appointed, preferably before the project starts, although in some cases it may not be clear who the best person would be until after the first workshop when the scope is better understood. Many organizations now appoint business managers to project manage IS projects. However, the role is not always clearly defined and can often be summed up as 'to ensure the project proceeds in the best interests of the business'. This is too vague and can lead to misunderstandings and uncertainties of how the role relates to the IT project manager or leader who has responsibility for the 'technical' aspects of the project.

As has often been repeated in this book and elsewhere, it is the organizational issues associated with IS/IT projects that most frequently lead to failure to deliver the benefits. The appointment of a business project manager is intended to deal with these aspects of the investment. The term *business* project manager is used to distinguish the role from that of the IT project manager or leader and to ensure that the management of the investment is seen as an investment in business change, enabled by IT. He or she must ensure that the non-IT activities and responsibilities are defined, understood and executed. This includes many of the enabling changes and all of the business change management and benefits realization tasks. But it is not the responsibility of the business project manager to personally carry out the tasks. Benefit and change owners have to fulfil their responsibilities and be held accountable for activities assigned to them in the benefits plan. The role of the business project manager is to coordinate all the non-IT activities, ensuring that they are planned and controlled as integral components of the project.

The primary roles the business project manager fulfils are:

1. Coordination and monitoring of the change and benefits management activities on the benefits dependency network.
2. Development of the benefits plan and preparation of the business case and ensuring that the benefits measurement and tracking mechanisms are in place at the appropriate points in the project.
3. Custodianship of the benefits plan on behalf of the senior management.
4. Project management of the non-technical elements of the plan.
5. Responsibility for the communication strategy that keeps all stakeholders and other business managers informed about the investment and progress towards the objectives.
6. Maintaining a continuous dialogue with the key stakeholders to maintain their commitment and participation and to help them address issues as they arise.
7. Ensuring that the education and training programmes are developed and delivered at the required times so that everyone is able to fulfil their responsibilities.

These are extensive responsibilities and require expertise and knowledge of project management techniques. In many cases we have observed, people who are appointed to such positions have little experience of managing projects. Even if they are excellent operational managers, they find that the skills required to manage large projects are quite different. Therefore, it is important to select a business project manager who has both a good knowledge of the business area being addressed and practical experience of project management.

For small projects, the business project manager is likely to be a part-time role, but for large or strategic investments, a full-time role will be necessary. In very large investments, the business project manager may need specialist support to assist in coordinating, and perhaps facilitation of, the change management activities and also to develop and monitor the measurement processes that ensure the benefits are delivered.

The role of project management offices (PMOs)

A number of studies have shown that the majority of large organizations now have a form of Project Management Office, or PMO. Although they have existed in some organizations for nearly 20 years, these studies suggest the rate of PMO adoption has increased significantly since 2003 (do Valle *et al.*, 2008).

The reasons given for establishing a PMO are to improve project performance in a number of ways:

• to make more efficient use of project resources by using a shared service;
• to make more effective use of scarce skills and resources across projects and programmes;
• to reduce the risk of projects failing to deliver to time, cost and quality (TCQ) targets;
• to increase the success of projects and programmes in delivering the business value expected.

How PMOs contribute to benefits management activities is discussed in box 7.2.

Box 7.2: PMO involvement in benefits management

Surveys we have undertaken (Ward *et al.*, 2007) have included questions about the role and impact of the PMO on the realization of benefits. The results confirmed previous findings (Dai and Wells, 2004), which show that having a PMO does not affect the proportion of the projects that are successful in delivering benefits. This is not surprising when the aspects of IS/IT project management process and life-cycle that most PMOs are involved in are considered (see Table 7.1).

(*Continued*)

Table 7.1: Involvement of PMOs in the IS/IT project management process

IS/IT investment activity	% of organizations with a PMO where the PMO is often or always involved in the activity
Identifying and quantifying benefits	26%
Identifying costs	85%
Business case development	52%
Technology planning	70%
Change and benefit planning	23%
TCQ reviews	26%
Change and benefit reviews	12%

In the majority of organizations, the PMO is normally involved in two activities – identifying costs (85%) and technology planning (70%). This is to be expected, as the majority of PMOs are formed in order to increase the use of methodologies across the organization and bring in controls, and reporting and identifying costs and technology planning are areas where methodologies are most mature.

A minority of PMOs are also involved in activities aimed at increasing the value delivered from the projects as well as ensuring practices are consistently and effectively deployed. In about 25% of the organizations in our study, PMOs are involved in some or all of: identifying and quantifying benefits and planning change and benefit realization, which are core activities in the benefits management process model. The analysis showed that PMO involvement in these activities was correlated with higher levels of success. Interestingly, PMO involvement in these practices was also associated with greater satisfaction with the quality of business cases and the value achieved from TCQ reviews.

Another finding was that in organizations that were more successful in the realization of benefits, the PMO was involved in the review of benefits realized at the end of projects, as well as the identification of benefits at the start of projects. It appeared that there were a number of explanations for this. Firstly, if it was known that benefits would be reviewed at the end of a project, the original benefits plan tended to be more realistic and colleagues maintained a focus on the delivery of benefits. Also, the involvement of the PMO in review of projects offered the opportunity for the PMO to play a key role in transferring learning to subsequent projects.

PMOs which support large programmes are considered further in Chapter 9.

The first workshop

The purpose of the first workshop is to establish whether the investment looks viable in terms of the potential benefits and whether those benefits are relevant to the organization's strategy. This assessment requires input from the key stakeholders who are likely to be involved in the project. Their involvement ensures that their knowledge is included and also gets their commitment to the investment objectives and the work needed to produce an achievable business case and benefits plan. The project sponsor should identify who those key stakeholders are, personally invite them to the workshop and brief them on what is expected from the workshop.

The main tasks at the workshop are to:

1. Review the business drivers to ensure there is clarity about why changes are needed. The organizational context within which the project has to be undertaken should also be assessed to identify any factors that will influence the feasibility of the project, such as other strategic change initiatives or impending reorganization. The location of the investment on the investment portfolio should be clarified in order to enable the appropriate management processes to be established.
2. Discuss and agree the objectives and overall scope of the investment and develop an initial benefits dependency network that identifies the benefits expected and the main business and enabling changes needed to achieve them.
3. Carry out a preliminary structuring and assessment of the benefits, including whether or how they can be measured.
4. Agree ownership of all the benefits and changes to ensure that both the necessary work to refine the details will be carried out and also that there is longer-term commitment to the benefits plan.
5. Conduct an initial stakeholder analysis to identify any additional stakeholders who will be affected by the project. Stakeholders who

will suffer 'disbenefits' should also be listed and possible solutions identified. An assessment of any potential organizational issues that will affect the success of the project should also be made.

The outputs from the workshop are agreed investment objectives, an initial benefits dependency network with identified owners and measures, an outline business case and an understanding of the organizational and stakeholder issues that will need to be accommodated or addressed. An action plan to refine each of these in time for the second workshop should be established.

Activities between workshops

The activities that need to be undertaken before holding the second workshop involve ensuring that all stakeholder implications of the project, their perceptions about how it will affect them and their consequent ability and willingness to fulfil their expected responsibilities have been understood. This includes their view of any 'disbenefits' that may result from the investment, so that any concerns and potential resistance have been identified and can be considered at the next workshop.

Additionally, each of the proposed benefits needs to be examined in more detail to define measurements and, if possible, quantify the benefit if it is material to the business case. For those benefits which will need considerable effort to quantify, for example a pilot study, the work required should be specified and the implications for the timing of the business case submission considered. Between workshops, those involved may also need to investigate and understand in more detail the implications of the changes and their interrelationships, so that the benefits plan will reflect the timing and resources required to carry out the changes.

The technical feasibility of the project should also be evaluated during this period and an initial estimate of the likely IT costs made.

The second workshop

The main purpose of the second workshop is to decide whether it is worth proceeding with the investment. This will be based on the best estimate of the expected benefits and the feasibility of providing the required IS/IT components and carrying out the business changes. Although the objective is to find the best way to proceed, it is also the time to stop investments that do not appear to have a viable business case. Alternatively, only parts of the project may provide significant benefits, some of the changes may be deemed too risky or elements of the technology solution may be too expensive or not sufficiently proven, such that the project scope has to be revised.

Clearly, it may not be possible to have all the required information available for this second workshop, unless there is a lengthy gap between workshops. Even if this is the case, a second workshop should be held when the 'value side' of the business case is reasonably clear and then either a third workshop planned to produce the final business case, or actions put in place for the project team and stakeholders to complete the plan. In any project it is important to maintain the momentum and keep the main stakeholders involved and interested in the investment planning. Therefore, it is better to hold more workshops at reasonable intervals (probably one to two months apart) than to wait until the business case is perfected and then 'present' it back to those whose commitment is critical to the project.

The main tasks to be completed at the second workshop are:

1. To review and refine the investment objectives and scope in terms of which changes can be achieved successfully and deliver the most benefits, without undue risks. This will inevitably be iterative and depend on the other tasks described here. At this stage, a risk analysis, as described in Chapter 5, should also be formally undertaken.
2. Each of the benefits and changes on the benefits dependency network should be revisited, such that the connections shown in the network are fully understood by all the stakeholders. In particular, the enabling changes need to be reviewed to ensure that the organization will be able both to adopt the new system and to make the essential business changes.
3. For each of the benefits, either the current performance level or the timing of when such baseline measures will be taken should be confirmed.
4. The need for all the proposed IS/IT functionality should also be reconsidered. This is in order to determine whether all of it is essential to the realization of the benefits or if some of the benefits could be obtained by changing working practices, processes or roles and responsibilities, without introducing new technology. Equally, if the IS/IT comes as a 'package', the possibility of achieving further benefits from the deployment of functionality that will effectively be obtained 'free' should be explored. However, as discussed in earlier

chapters, if such functionality offers little or no benefit or will require significant additional business changes, the temptation to implement it, simply because it was free, should be resisted.

5. All stakeholder responsibilities should be confirmed, or amended if necessary, and actions put in place to address the organizational issues that have been identified from the stakeholder analysis, as described in Chapter 6.

6. The overall structure of the dependency network should be reviewed to identify potential benefit 'streams': sets of changes and benefits that are capable of being delivered more or less independently of the rest of the network. In that case, it may be better to phase the implementation to deliver each benefit stream separately, enabling some benefits to be achieved early and reducing the overall project risks. Although from a technology perspective it may appear more economic to install all the technology as one implementation, from a stakeholder perspective it may be preferable to realize some of the 'easier' benefits earlier, especially those that require less extensive or sensitive changes. This is a matter of judgement, but it is based on the general experience that large projects have the most risks and hence breaking a project down into more manageable phases can reduce risk. Also, the realization of some early benefits can increase the commitment of some stakeholders to the rest of the project, as discussed in Chapter 6.

The main outputs from this second workshop are the business case and benefits plan with completed benefits and change 'templates' for all the activities. This documentation should be completed as soon as possible after the workshop, although, as stated earlier, it may, for large or risky investments, be necessary to convene a further workshop or meeting to confirm some elements of the business case.

Although workshops are commonly used in organizations to bring people with different knowledge sets together to agree what needs to be done, experience of conducting many benefits management workshops has identified some useful 'tips' or guidance on how to make them work successfully. These are listed in Box 7.3.

As has been stated earlier, documentation arising from the benefits management process should be kept up to date as the project proceeds, so that, at any time, it reflects what has been agreed and achieved so far. Any changes will need to be recorded, so that after implementation the review of the success or otherwise of the investment can take due account of anything that influenced the eventual realization of each benefit.

Box 7.3: Guidance for conducting benefits management workshops

It is important to ensure that the right stakeholders can attend the workshops; that is, those who have the knowledge required, are of appropriate seniority and also have the ability to commit time and resources to the project. It is always preferable to delay the workshop to enable those key people to attend rather than go ahead without them, even if there is pressure to 'get on with it'.

Remember that it is a workshop and not a meeting; this encourages everyone to participate fully without concern for the organizational hierarchy or roles. It is often the more junior staff who have the detailed knowledge required to identify potential benefits, be specific about the changes and understand how others affected by the investment might respond.

The quality of the facilities is also important. Workshops require more space than meetings so that people can stand up, move about and have small group discussions as well as plenary sessions. This emphasizes the relative informality of the working relationships and also increases the energy people put into the work. The 'mental energy' that will be applied is higher when people spend time standing rather than sitting. It is tempting to suggest

(Continued)

removing chairs altogether, but people need a rest from time to time! However, the 'furniture' should be pushed to the side to avoid people sitting round a table, as in a meeting.

The room should have large areas of whiteboards or wall space, on which can be 'pinned' large sheets of paper to record and structure the work produced. These working sheets will become the output from the workshop, so it is best to record them on paper or an electronic whiteboard to avoid transcribing time and potential errors. It is important that everyone can see the wall-charts and work on them, which again requires a good working space.

Use Post-its to construct the network and other outputs. During the process, many Post-its are created, changed, discarded or moved about to develop the agreed output.

Following the initial workshop, the outputs should be con-verted to an electronic form, using a suitable drawing package, and, at subsequent workshops, this can be displayed on a white-board or wall and changes made either via more Post-its or directly. An interactive whiteboard is ideal for this.

Do not channel all the comments through one person who 'has the pen'. It is preferable that each individual writes down his or her own knowledge and then, once it is displayed, he or she can explain their reasoning and others can question, comment or add to it and then the group can reconcile different views where required and agree the final version. It may be appropriate to subdivide a large group into smaller teams, partly because of the practical problems of large group discussions being dominated by some individuals. These subgroups should consist of people who do not normally work together to facilitate the knowledge sharing.

People should be encouraged to be as explicit as possible when writing on the Post-its, to avoid uncertainty later about what was meant. For instance, 'reduce costs' will frequently be a benefit, but the specific costs in question should be stated. 'Change the culture' is often identified as a necessary business change. However, a change in organizational culture results from changes in the behaviours and working practices of groups and individual staff. So, the necessary changes, together with the individual(s) who should be making them, need to be specified.

The process requires a facilitator to ensure that all that could be done by those present, in the time available, is achieved. The facilitator should be someone not directly involved in the project – so definitely not the project manager – but who is familiar with the business areas being discussed. He or she needs to have expert knowledge of the tools and techniques of the benefits management approach plus skills and experience in facilitation. The facilitator should identify when conflicting views need to be reconciled.

At this stage it is also valuable to define a communication strategy for the project, to ensure that everyone in the organization (and perhaps external parties such as customers, suppliers and regulatory bodies) is informed at the earliest possible time of the intentions and implications of the project. This is normally the responsibility of the project sponsor and business project manager. When there are significant organizational change implications, it is important that everyone is told what is actually planned, as openly and honestly as possible, rather than allowing rumour and speculation to create a different, and almost inevitably less favourable, impression of what is going to happen. It is also important to tailor the communication content to particular stakeholder groups, based on the implications for them and their role in the business. Poor communication at this stage can introduce unnecessary additional risks. For example, in the 'Connecting for Health' programme in the UK NHS, failure to communicate with general practitioners and other clinicians in a language that encouraged their involvement in the programme caused delays and created resistance to some of its key components.

Inclusion of the benefits plan in the management of the project

From this stage onwards the activities identified in the benefits plan should become integral components of the project plan and be monitored accordingly at all progress review meetings. Often, such meetings focus mainly on the IT delivery plan and issues resulting from any problems with functionality, cost or timeliness. These are, of course, important, but the same discussions should also include updates on progress towards implementing the business changes and delivering the benefits and the resolution of any issues affecting these aspects of the project. Chapter 3 discussed the use of project 'health checks,' which are undertaken during implementation to ensure that the expected benefits are still likely to be realized. The overall success of the investment relies on the accurate alignment and synchronization of the IT and business activities, and that is less likely to happen if they are reviewed separately or at different times.

It is important that the project sponsor is involved in the review processes, to ensure that the project team and other stakeholders are aware of any changes in the organization or business context that could affect the project. Changes in the business drivers or strategy could require a reappraisal of the whole investment to decide whether it is worth continuing as planned or whether it should be changed significantly. Equally, other events or external changes that have made some of the benefits more or less important may require the business case to be revisited or revised. Should the expected costs or timescale for the project increase significantly, then achieving the investment objectives or realizing net benefits may have become problematic. If the investment is dependent on deliverables from other projects or business changes in those projects, the sponsor and business project manager should consider the implications of delays or changes in these to the viability of the project.

In most cases, changes affecting the project identified at review meetings will result in revisions to the implementation plans, but in some cases they may cause the project to be abandoned. This is clearly a difficult decision, especially when implementation is well under way or close to completion. However, many failed projects could and should have been stopped before all the expenditure was incurred, because they were no longer going to deliver any benefits to the organization. There are always other investments competing for the funds and resources available and it is better to free up those that are being wasted than to continue to deploy them when failure is seen to be inevitable. Equally, people working on a project that is clearly of little or no organizational value will become demoralized and this is likely to decrease the chances of 'salvaging anything of value from the wreckage' even further. In spite of this, in too many cases, a 'we've started, so we'll finish' rationale causes projects to carry on, as if they had developed a life of their own.

Evaluating the results and establishing the potential for further benefits

Following the full implementation of the new IS/IT and business changes, the achievement of the business case and benefits plan should

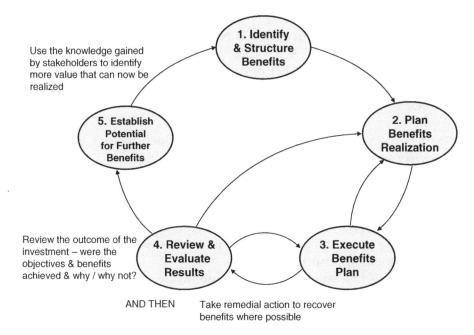

Use the knowledge gained by stakeholders to identify more value that can now be realized

Review the outcome of the investment – were the objectives & benefits achieved & why / why not?

AND THEN   Take remedial action to recover benefits where possible

Figure 7.5: The key activities in the review process

be formally reviewed, as indicated in stage 4 of Figure 7.5. The purposes of the review include a detailed assessment of whether each of the expected benefits has been achieved or not. If they have not been achieved, the reasons for this should be established and any remedial action that could allow them to be realized should be identified. It is also important to ascertain any unexpected positive or negative consequences of the new technology or business changes.

At the same time as reviewing the delivery of the intended benefits, the meeting should also consider the opportunity for further benefits, as shown in stage 5 of Figure 7.5. Using the knowledge that has been gained from the project, new benefits that are now available from further business changes or IS/IT developments should be considered.

While these are the purposes of any particular benefit review, the reason for carrying them out systematically for all major projects is to learn how

'Although some project managers are learning from experience, the failure rate does not seem to be decreasing. This may be due to . . . the reluctance of many organizations to perform retrospectives (reviews).' *Nelson (2007)*

> **Box 7.4: What a benefit review is NOT**
>
> Because there are a number of reviews or audits that can occur at the end of a project, it is probably worth stating what a benefit review is *not*.
>
> - It is *not* a project management review, which focuses on variances in time and cost from the project plan.
> - It is *not* a system quality or performance review, which assesses the conformance of systems functionality and performance with the requirements specification.
> - It is *not* a financial audit, although in public sector organizations an audit is an official requirement to ensure that funds have been spent appropriately.
> - Neither is it a 'witchhunt' to allocate blame!

to improve the overall value that the organization derives from all its IS/IT projects, by learning from success and failure. Those lessons should be communicated to the managers of other projects.

In order to gain the most from a benefit review, and avoid the potential downsides, the process has to be managed effectively. It is also important to be as consistent as possible in how the reviews are conducted across projects, to ensure that the outputs provide valid comparisons and enable lessons to be transferred to future projects. Visible consistency and objectivity will also encourage people to engage in the process openly and honestly, rather than attempting to ensure that any blame belongs elsewhere. Figure 7.6 shows the main inputs and expected outputs of the review meeting.

The review should be planned in advance in order to gain maximum value from the process. Ideally it should be clearly identified as a key date or milestone in the project plan, probably about two to three months after implementation is complete and when it should be possible to determine whether the benefits have occurred or are beginning to be realized. It should follow any project or systems quality reviews, since they may provide some relevant explanations concerning the lack of achievement of some of the benefits.

The review meeting should be convened by the project sponsor and the business project manager; the IT project leader and all the main

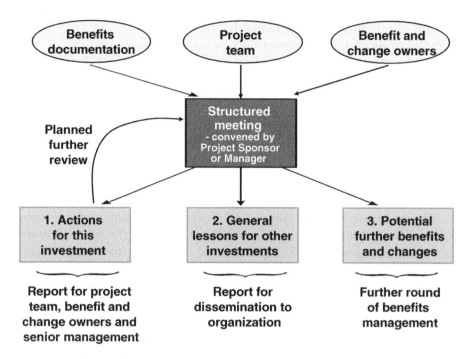

Figure 7.6: Main elements of the benefits review meeting

stakeholders should be invited to attend. In respect of the benefits, each of the benefit owners should prepare a statement, with the appropriate evidence, as to what extent the benefit has been realized and, if it has not been achieved, any reasons that might explain this. Documentation that will probably be essential to the discussions includes: the business case and benefits plan (both the original and the latest versions); any project or system quality review reports and a summary of key decisions that were taken to alter the scope or other aspects of the project during implementation.

The review meeting itself should be run as a structured discussion based on what has happened as a result of the investment, with emphasis on the final outcome rather than what happened during the project. In order to gain the most from the meeting time, the order of discussion should match the objectives of the review; that is:

- it should commence with the intended benefits that have been achieved and any unexpected consequences, both positive and negative;

- it should then consider benefits that have not, as yet, been achieved, the reasons and any actions that can be taken to retrieve them;
- any benefits that have to be 'written off' should be identified, including the reasons for this;
- actions and responsibilities should be agreed for any benefit that could still be retrieved and to deal with the effects of unexpected 'disbenefits';
- finally, the meeting should identify any further benefits that can now be realized and instigate actions to investigate the feasibility of actually realizing them.

The meeting should conclude by identifying the main lessons learned from the project, in terms of how the use of the benefits management process within the organization could be improved and advice for other projects that could improve the way they are managed, or implemented, in order to increase the value delivered. For example, it is worth revisiting the initial risk analysis and identifying which risks actually materialized, how they were dealt with and the overall effect on the project outcome. As shown in Figure 7.6, the outputs from the review meeting should be three 'reports':

1. A full review of the investment in terms of benefits realized and any actions still outstanding to achieve the business case. This should be confidential to the meeting attendees and the appropriate senior managers, such as the investment board that sanctioned the funding. They should agree the extent to which the review report can be made public. If there are significant actions still to be taken, this report will probably be the basis of a further review meeting to be held when the actions have been carried out.
2. A summary of the lessons learned that may benefit future investments. This should be communicated as soon as possible to all other current project sponsors and managers, and made available through updates to 'best practice guidelines' for future projects.
3. A report describing the further potential benefits now available and actions that have been put in place to examine them. For instance, an engineering organization installed imaging technology as a more efficient way of archiving diagrams and documents. Once the new technology was working well, it became clear that improving the whole document management process was now possible, leading to an ability to provide more effective exchanges with clients during design and to shorten the time taken to respond to invitations to

tender for new contracts. If, as in this case, the further opportunities require significant resources, they will become new projects to be evaluated against alternative future investments, but often they can be achieved through low-cost, small projects that are part of the organization's continuous improvement. For example, if a new stock control system improves the accuracy of stock figures, it might lead to revisions of replenishment policies in planning systems through sharing information with suppliers. Alternatively, some may be innovative or speculative ideas that should progress as high potential projects.

It should be stressed that these reports do not need to be long documents. Indeed, it is better, particularly in the case of the general lessons to be shared with other projects, that such reports are brief and to the point. In the case of the general lessons learned, it may well be worth sending this summary directly to the business project managers of other current projects to ensure that it is seen. Many organizations have found that posting such documents on intranets or in electronic knowledge bases ensures that they never see the light of day again!

The overall contribution that benefits reviews make to an organization's ability to increase the benefits derived from its IS/IT cannot be overstated. However, ensuring that the review process makes such a contribution relies on three critical factors: that the review is rigorous in understanding cause and effect relationships regarding changes and benefits; that the meeting concentrates on what can be done now and in the future, rather than dwelling on the past (or even trying to re-manage it!); and that no blame is allocated or seen to be, however difficult this may be. If the last of these cannot be achieved, it is likely that many people will be suspicious of the process.

Monitoring the benefits after implementation

The benefits review should normally be held as soon after implementation as it is possible to assess, with sufficient evidence, whether the intended benefits have been achieved. This would normally be some two to three months after the system and associated business changes have been made, although some benefits may materialize immediately. However, it may be necessary to wait longer to evaluate some benefits adequately, especially those that were dependent on using new capabilities created by the investment. In many cases it is wise to implement new systems when business activity or volumes are at their lowest, to reduce the risk of the changes causing performance to deteriorate. The benefits may involve the ability to deal with 'peak loads' and it will only be when volumes are high that the benefits can accurately be measured. Benefits associated with more accurate and timely information leading to more effective decision making are notoriously difficult to prove after the event, because there is likely to be a time lag between the information being available and its use in decisions.

Another concern is that, although benefits do occur soon after implementation, they can 'decay' once the changes have become the normal practices and people's enthusiasm for the improvements has waned. It therefore may be worth having a second review some months after the first to determine whether certain, vulnerable benefits have been sustained. Some organizations also want to be able to prove that their IT investments have delivered the expected value over an extended period, even several years. This cannot really be done project by project, since, after a year or more has elapsed, other changes have been made that will obscure the benefits realized from any particular investment. Any such assessment, therefore, is probably best done through an annual review of investments completed during the previous year and the cumulative benefits delivered, verified by the reviews of the individual projects. As discussed later, this can be considered an aspect of governance and relates to managing the overall investment portfolio.

> 'Management of IT payoffs begins prior to the investment and continues through post implementation.' *Kohli and Devaraj (2004)*

Fit with other methodologies

As was described in Chapter 3, the benefits management process complements other methodologies. Appropriate systems development methodologies should be used to develop the IS/IT enablers identified for the project in order to ensure conformance to requirements. While it is not possible to be prescriptive, the highly structured methodologies (such as SSADM) are usually more appropriate for key operational and support application investment, whereas the more iterative or 'agile' methodologies (such as DSDM) are needed for strategic and high potential applications.

A range of change management methods can be employed to achieve the changes identified in the benefits dependency network. The nature, scale or impact of a change may require or suggest the use of a particular approach to effecting the specific change, and other changes that depend on it. If it involves redeploying, or even no longer employing, significant numbers of staff, the organization's employment policies and practices will influence or determine the approach to be taken. Equally, corporate communications policies will influence the way in which the implications of the project are communicated to internal or external stakeholders and may require different groups to be informed at different times in different ways.

The benefits management process also complements the most commonly used project management (PM) methodologies. These tend to focus on conformance to cost, time and quality issues, rather than explicitly identifying the benefits the organization is seeking to achieve. Even when such methodologies refer to benefits, they rarely describe how to identify and manage them. The benefits management process should be used in conjunction with PM methodologies in order to ensure that the organization is explicit about the benefits it is seeking and that it remains focused on these throughout the project. Most PM methodologies also require that the project is broken into a number of discrete steps or work packages, to define the deliverables and time and resources required and then focus on identifying the optimum order in which to carry these out, often by using a Gantt chart or some form of critical path analysis. Use of the benefits management approach can help identify the project work packages, their dependencies and suggest a schedule for them. How the benefits management process can be used in conjunction with the well-known PM methodology PRINCE2 is described in Box 7.5.

Organizational benefits management maturity

From our surveys of benefits management practices mentioned earlier, we have been able to develop a maturity model which helps organizations to consider what they can do to improve the value delivered from their IS/IT projects. The model was developed from a sample of 138, mainly large, European organizations in both the public and private sectors. The survey identified:

- the levels of success in delivering benefits from IT and management satisfaction with the business value derived from IT;
- the comprehensiveness and effectiveness of organizational practices related to the benefits management process model over the whole

Box 7.5: Benefits management and PRINCE2

PRINCE2 (Projects IN Controlled Environments 2) is an example of a structured project management approach that is used widely in both the private and public sectors. It was developed by the Office of Government Commerce (OGC) and is the recommended approach for UK government projects (see *Managing Successful Projects with PRINCE2*, OGC, 2009).

The OGC was involved in the early stages of the research that led to the development of the benefits management process described in this book. There is, therefore, a high degree of consistency between the two approaches, allowing them to be used together in a way that draws on the specific strengths of each approach.

PRINCE2 defines eight processes for the effective management and governance of a project. Each process is described briefly here, followed by a discussion on how benefits management and PRINCE2 can be combined to complement each other.

1. **Directing a project** – this is a process for senior management responsible for the project to direct its activities and resources. The process lasts for the full duration of the project and has five major strands within it: authorizing the development of a business case and project plan; approval of the business case; review of the project at stage boundaries and ensuring the project comes to a controlled close and that lessons are shared with other projects.
2. **Starting up a project** – this tends to be a short process in which the project management team is appointed and the aims of the project are communicated.
3. **Initiating a project** – this process seeks to develop a business case for the project, which is contained in a project initiation document (PID). It is suggested that a PID contains:
   objectives;
   critical success factors and key performance indicators;
   impacts and assumptions;
   constraints and option evaluations;
   benefits analysis;
   project costs;

cost/benefit analysis;

risks;

delivery plan – including stages or milestones.

4. **Controlling a stage** – a key principle in PRINCE2 is to break projects into manageable stages. This process describes the monitoring and control activities required to keep a stage on track.

5. **Managing product delivery** – specifies the contract between the project and suppliers. PRINCE2 calls the work agreed in this process a 'work package' and seeks to ensure agreement on issues such as timing, quality and cost.

6. **Managing stage boundaries** – this process includes reporting on the performance of the previous stage, approval from senior management to move to the next stage, updating the project plan and detailed planning of the next stage.

7. **Planning** – the planning process continues throughout the project. A key recommendation of PRINCE2 is that detailed planning is only carried out for the next stage of the project to be undertaken.

8. **Closing a project** – this process seeks to understand the extent to which the objectives of the project have been met, ensure follow-up actions are undertaken and to share lessons learned with other projects.

While PRINCE2 is very comprehensive, provides very detailed guidance to improve project management practices and is widely used, its treatment of benefits tends to be cursory. In particular, while it is suggested that the PID in the project initiation stage includes a full benefits analysis, including linking benefits to the changes required to deliver them, appointing benefit owners and setting measures for each benefit, little detailed guidance is given on how to do this. The benefits are the most important outcome from a project, since that is presumably why the project is being undertaken. This limited treatment of benefits is therefore a noticeable area of weakness. We would suggest that the tools and techniques relating to the first two stages of our five-stage process are used to develop a full benefits plan, as has been described in earlier chapters. If the organization has mandated the use of

(Continued)

PRINCE2, then this benefits plan can be incorporated into the PID in an appropriate form.

The simplicity of the benefits management approach is also important in this early stage of a project. The strength of PRINCE2 lies in its comprehensiveness, formality, attention to detail and its robustness. However, it is inevitably complex and most business managers do not want, or have the time, to learn the methodology, or even be subjected to it. The simple frameworks of the benefits management approach, coupled with the participative workshops, ensure that individuals, both from the business and specialist areas, can input and combine their knowledge in a way that they find intuitive – and occasionally even fun! This willingness to participate early ensures that agreement for the project is gained from those who will be impacted and, importantly, knowledge within the business is captured in the benefits plan.

We would therefore suggest that the PRINCE2 processes of controlling stages, managing stage boundaries and managing product delivery are used to undertake the third stage of our benefits management process: the execution of the benefits plan. A key part of the PRINCE2 approach is the breaking down of projects into phases. The benefits plan, particularly the benefits dependency network, can prove a means of identifying and comparing possible phases. The identified dependencies between changes and benefits allow an understanding of which benefits can be expected from undertaking a certain set of changes. An identification of such linkages can enable the delivery of benefits early in a project, which may be important if the project is a long one or if there is particular stakeholder resistance.

Finally, while the closing of a project process in PRINCE2 suggests a review of the success of the project and a sharing of best practice, these are not focused explicitly on benefits. Also, it does not expressly include the important stage in the benefits management process of identifying the potential for further benefits. Given the centrality of benefits delivery to the success of the project, we would suggest that the benefits management process is adopted for these activities. For organizations that have mandated the use of PRINCE2, the evaluation of benefits realized from the project and the identification of further benefits should be included in the project closing process.

Figure 7.7 illustrates how the benefits management process and PRINCE2 are related and which approach we suggest should lead at each stage.

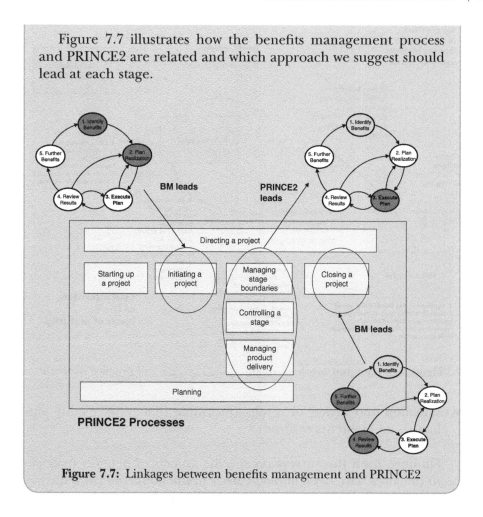

Figure 7.7: Linkages between benefits management and PRINCE2

investment life-cycle – this includes the extent to which decisions and accountability lie jointly with business and IS/IT management.

The management practices included were:

- project appraisal and selection: portfolio management;
- identifying and quantifying benefits;
- identifying costs;
- business case development (including risk assessment);
- delivery planning (including technology, process, organizational change and benefit planning);

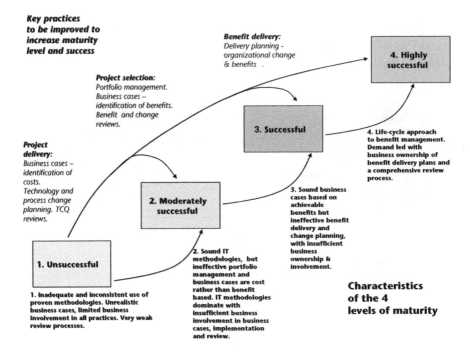

Figure 7.8: The four levels of organizational success and practice maturity

- evaluation and review of results (including time, cost, quality plus changes and benefits realized).

Findings from the surveys on specific aspects of benefits management practices have been quoted earlier in the book, but from further analysis it was possible to identify the relationship between the practices listed above and project success.

The resulting model has four levels of practice 'maturity' and related success, which are summarized in Figure 7.8 and described in more detail below.

Level 1 – Unsuccessful

Organizations were classified as unsuccessful when the majority of projects failed to achieve time, cost and quality (TCQ) and benefit targets. As a result, there is little management confidence that IS/IT projects will improve business performance.

To become more successful at this low level of maturity, it is necessary to prioritize the management of the IS/IT supply-side activities more consistently and professionally, by adopting and using proven project methodologies so that the IS/IT function can cope better with the business needs. Introducing the rigour of the benefits management process and tools at this level of maturity is likely to be unsuccessful, since business managers will be reluctant to get involved in projects that will probably fail. To improve performance at this level, organizations should:

- ensure that they can deliver most projects to time, cost and quality targets – this might include not undertaking projects that are risky or difficult to estimate;
- mandate and police the use of project management and other methodologies;
- review how successfully they achieve the TCQ estimates;
- improve the approach to costing to include more of the actual costs that will be incurred, not just direct expenses.

This can be summed up by saying that before organizations can expect greater success, they must improve *project delivery*. The introduction of a Project Management Office (PMO) can help to ensure that proven methods are not only in place, but also used appropriately.

Level 2 – Moderately successful

At this level of maturity, the majority of IS/IT projects fail to deliver the expected benefits even though they are normally delivered to time, cost and quality targets. As a consequence, managers are comfortable that IS/IT projects are well managed, but will not risk making the business changes needed to deliver the benefits available.

Once the organization has achieved a high level of supply competence and is delivering projects successfully in terms of TCQ, the focus has to change to become more responsive to the business demands by selecting and prioritizing projects based on business benefits. The benefits management tools will help improve the early stages of managing the investments and in enabling IT and business managers to work together more effectively. To improve performance, these organizations should:

- introduce a comprehensive portfolio management approach that takes into account both demand- and supply-side factors when selecting which investments to authorize;

- develop more rigorous business cases, which are more realistic in terms of deliverable benefits;
- change how IT and the business work together, involving the business managers more in prioritization and identifying the benefits and costs in the business cases;
- extend the review process to include the benefits and changes – if business cases are not realistic, reviews serve little purpose.

This can be summarized as improving *project selection* in order to deliver more business value from the capability in place. The existence of a PMO can help in this through enabling consistency of approach in investment decision making, which is a key aspect of this stage of development.

Level 3 – Successful (but inconsistent)

In these organizations, many projects deliver the expected benefits but there are inconsistent levels of success across the investment portfolio. This is mainly due to inadequate approaches to implementation management in some projects, leading to failure to achieve the benefits in the business case. Ownership of the benefits by the business managers becomes possible when the business cases are realistic in terms of both the benefits expected and the required changes.

Having improved project selection, prioritization and investment decision making, the emphasis should move to improving the implementation processes that realize the benefits. This means further increasing the involvement of the business managers throughout the investment life-cycle, rather than in the pre-implementation decisions. The temptation is to assume that the improved business cases will actually be delivered by following proven methodologies, but this is not the case unless business managers take responsibility for those parts of the process that affect benefits delivery. To further improve performance, organizations should:

- develop process and organizational change plans that are integrated with the technology delivery plan;
- extend the range of benefit types that are included in the business cases to increase the business commitment to achieving investment success;
- develop benefit delivery plans with accountability for each benefit assigned to individual business managers;

- increase the scope of the review process to consider not only benefits realized, but also the changes that were required to achieve them;
- have an effective process that ensures lessons from all completed projects are passed on to future projects.

This can be summarized as the need to improve the management of benefit delivery to achieve the potential value created through better investment selection.

Level 4 – Highly successful

At the highest level of maturity, the majority of projects deliver the expected benefits. Achieving ongoing success in terms of both benefits realized and management satisfaction implies not only delivering to the business cases of the selected projects, but also responding objectively to all types of management demands for new investments. Being willing to undertake more risky projects on the understanding by senior management that some might fail is a sign of a mature organization. This relies as much on the degree of confidence the business managers have in their specialist colleagues as the presence of comprehensive practices. It also implies that the organization is willing to stop projects that are heading for failure, before it occurs.

To sustain this level of performance, comprehensive practices, strong working relationships, collective, consistent decision making and the ability to learn from previous investments are essential to ensuring *business value* drives the investment programme.

In most organizations, the level of success is easy to identify and, through a set of diagnostic questions, the maturity of each of the main practices can be determined. This normally shows that, for an organization at a particular success level, most practices will be at the expected level of maturity, but a few will probably still be underdeveloped and preventing progress.

Carrying out this assessment should identify both the priority areas for improvement of the practices and what should happen as a result. As with most maturity models, it is almost impossible for organizations to jump from low to high levels without developing the knowledge and competences involved in the intermediate stages. However, from experience of working with many organizations, improvements from one level to another can often be achieved within six months to a year. But a word of warning: our experiences with other organizations suggest that it is also possible for careless, inconsistent or inept management behaviour to reduce the level of maturity quite quickly, causing an inevitable reduction in the level of success achieved.

Summary

This chapter has described how the benefits management process can be introduced and implemented in organizations and has provided practical guidance on how the tools and techniques can be used effectively. Much of the emphasis of this chapter has been on the first two stages of the benefits management process. This was quite deliberate. As has been said earlier, developing a business case and benefits plan is more than a means of obtaining funds. How it is done will not only affect the integrity of the investment case, but also the viability of achieving each of the benefits, through the willingness and ability of all the stakeholders to fulfil their commitments. The level of commitment is often dependent on the benefits they perceive and the extent to which they understand, and are involved in defining, the scope and nature of the business changes required.

Without stakeholder commitment at the outset of a project, the issues that inevitably arise during implementation can prove difficult to resolve, leading to increases in cost and time as well as failure to realize some or all of the benefits. With a comprehensive and detailed benefits plan, it is easier to assess the implications of events that occur during implementation and then adjust the appropriate elements of the plan. The evidence from both project failures and successes strongly supports the argument that careful planning at the start, combined with identifying and resolving contentious issues early in the project, leads to higher levels of success. The more complex and extensive the programme of change, the more important it is to plan and re-plan for the benefits as the project proceeds. The outputs from the benefits framework are relatively easy to update and the techniques can, and should, be reapplied throughout the project when either uncertainties arise or more becomes known.

This chapter has discussed the general aspects of introducing and adopting the benefits management approach. Chapter 8 considers factors that influence its use in different situations and organizational contexts.

Chapter 8

The importance of context

In previous chapters, we have emphasized the linkage between the realization of benefits from IS/IT projects and the need to make organizational changes. The particular changes that an organization needs to make will depend on its current situation as well as the investment objectives. Even if implementing similar applications, some organizations may be starting from 'further behind' than others and hence will need to make more changes in order to achieve the same benefits. Alternatively, an organization may not be able or willing to make certain changes, due to resource or capability constraints or the risks involved, and hence may only realize a limited set of the available benefits. For example, smaller businesses, on average, have fewer financial and human resources at their disposal (Pollard and Hayne, 1998) and less internal IS/IT knowledge and capability to manage change projects (Cragg *et al.*, 2011). They are often unable to accomplish large change programmes and might, therefore, expect a more modest set of benefits. However, those benefits may improve their performance in a greater proportion than larger organizations.

Context is also important when considering benefits themselves: what is considered a benefit will depend on the current performance level of the organization relative to its competitors or business targets. For organizations that are investing to overcome business disadvantages, the benefits expected will be of different types from those intending to create advantage from innovative uses of IT. What is viewed as a benefit will also depend on the strategy of the organization and its external and internal drivers, as discussed in Chapter 2. Although some drivers may be common to many organizations, such as improvements to customer or client service, others, particularly internal drivers, are likely to vary across organizations, giving rise to differences in what are perceived to be benefits.

Factors to take into account

Generic benefits

The importance of organizational context on the realization of benefits means that it is not possible to develop a generic set of benefits and associated changes for given application types, for types of organization or for IS/IT supply arrangements such as outsourcing. The fallacy of the 'silver bullet' approach to IS/IT projects (Markus and Benjamin, 1997), when vendors describe product features or functionality as a list of standard benefits, has already been discussed in earlier chapters. Then, it was noted that the lack of consideration of organizational change was a significant problem in this view of technology. However, it is also flawed in that it disregards the context of individual organizations and suggests the improvements listed can be achieved by all organizations and are beneficial to all of them.

This leads to a health warning: although we have shown a number of completed frameworks in this book, these are simply to illustrate their use and they should not be applied wholesale to other projects, however similar these may appear.

Even in projects where the implementation of the same system is being replicated across different units within an organization, or in public programmes where the same system is to be deployed in multiple settings, the temptation to generate a standard version of the frameworks, such as the benefits dependency network, should be resisted. It makes an assumption that the benefits are the same or similar for each unit and can be achieved through a prescribed set of changes. Not only is this rarely the case, but it can significantly reduce the commitment of the unit's management and staff to the project implementation.

Different types of organization

Organizations can be classified in many different ways. The factors that are most likely to have a bearing on the benefits realization process described in this book and are most frequently encountered are:

- Whether the organization is in the private sector, when a significant driver is always to maximize returns to shareholders, members or partners, or whether it is in the public sector, where the drivers are more likely to be related to service provision and providing value for money.

- The size of the organization – that is, if it is large or if it is what is termed a 'small or medium-sized enterprise' (SME), which is usually taken to mean an organization with 250 employees or fewer.

- If the organization is a single business unit or consists of multiple distinct units, for example, for different lines of business or geographic territories.

We have already presented a number of examples that relate to investments by large organizations in the private sector in single business units, and so, in this chapter, we consider investments by other types of organization; that is: the public sector, small businesses and multi-unit businesses.

The public sector

Some examples of public sector investments in IS/IT have been mentioned in previous chapters. These examples show that the benefits management process can be applied successfully in such contexts, although a number of issues are frequently encountered in public sector organizations.

Imposed drivers

The drivers acting on public sector organizations are often the result of government policies. While private sector firms will have significant external pressures, they can choose how and when to respond to these. In the case of the public sector, the drivers are often in the form of a requirement to meet a specific target and by a given deadline, whether or not this is feasible or appropriate for that organization.

Such imposed drivers can often make it appear that benefits identification and management is unnecessary, since there is a feeling of 'we have to do it anyway'. We would argue that the benefits management frameworks and ways of working are highly beneficial because:

- Agreement of the objectives of the investment will begin to ensure that all those involved have a common and shared view of what the organization is seeking to achieve.

- Most investments yield a range of benefits and by identifying them, a focus can be placed on those that are most important to the organization.
- It will demonstrate to stakeholders what they might expect to gain from the investment.
- While not undertaking the project may not be an option, identification of the business changes needed may well show ways of making changes that are more acceptable or effective than others, and also determine those that are critical to realizing the benefits that are of most value to the organization. Indeed, identification and successful achievement of the business and enabling changes can ensure that an imposed investment does actually yield benefits to the organization, rather than just becoming a bureaucratic requirement that absorbs resources, or worse, an expensive and time-consuming failure.

An example of the benefits approach used to ensure benefits from a mandated project is described in Box 8.1.

Many stakeholders

Another common feature of public sector projects is that they often have a wide range of different stakeholder groups, some of which are very large in terms of the number of people involved. Many public sector organizations also have strong social and consultative cultures, due to the nature of services they provide and the mix of professionals employed. The staff members expect to be able to express their views on how the investment will affect their work and roles, and, importantly, to have these views taken into account in the development and implementation of the project.

Many projects also often include stakeholders outside the organization itself, including the general public. The realization of benefits may rely on changes to ways in which external stakeholders access or make use of the services or how they contribute to them. In addition, there is a need for most public sector projects to be inclusive. Unlike private companies, public sector organizations can rarely decide to serve only some of their clients or users. Instead, they must ensure that all parts of their community are served properly.

For example, the NHS 'Choose and Book' system, introduced in Chapter 4, enables patients to book hospital appointments at a time convenient to themselves. This may sound simple, but for it to work effectively and deliver benefits to both patients and healthcare

Box 8.1: Choice-based lettings of public housing

In the UK, the government is pursuing a far-reaching programme of change in the public sector. In many cases a central element of these programmes is the modernization of services through process redevelopment and the adoption of new information technologies and systems. A major element of the vision for the future is that all, or almost all, public services should be accessible online.

The housing department within a local authority was considering how it might meet this government requirement. A key area of responsibility for the department is the provision of council, or social, housing to families and individuals. The housing team wished to take the opportunity to improve the services they offered to residents and families needing housing. Traditionally, those seeking social housing were held on a waiting list and sent details of properties thought to be appropriate. Considerable time was wasted as the properties were often not suitable and, while details were sent back and forth, the properties stood empty. The department therefore decided to explore the development of an online service to show available properties and allow prospective tennants to indicate their interest in specific properties.

Using the benefits management process, the team was able to identify the benefits that could be expected from the new online service. A simplified version of the benefits dependency network they developed is shown in Figure 8.1. Benefits included increased rental income. However, when exploring the necessary changes, it became apparent that, in order to ensure there were sufficient properties to provide choice, the maintenance team had to refurbish previously let properties more quickly and adhere to agreed service levels. It was recognized that this would not be easy, as the maintenance team was part of a separate department and heavily unionized. Achievement of the changes by the maintenance team would therefore require an influential change owner. A well-respected senior manager in the maintenance department was asked to join the project team. He broke the necessary changes down into a set of smaller changes that could be implemented sequentially. He also linked each of these changes to the performance targets for his own teams and ensured that they

(Continued)

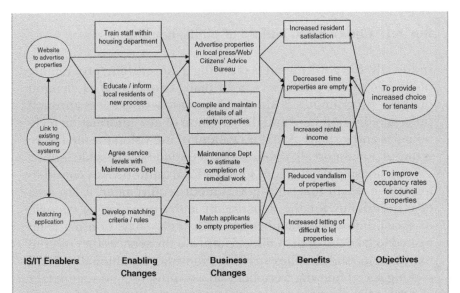

Figure 8.1: Benefits dependency network for a social housing department

understood the rationale for the changes they were being asked to make.

Although there was some initial resistance from the maintenance staff, their understanding of the reason for the changes and the stepwise approach meant that they were achieved successfully. Concern about the possible transfer of this activity to the private sector also helped to ensure the changes were made. Not only did the authority meet the imposed deadline from central government, it has realized significant benefits in terms of both increased client satisfaction and occupancy rates, leading to increased revenues.

organizations and professionals, many different groups need to change how they work, and work with each other. Figure 8.2 shows the stakeholder groups associated with arranging appointments for X-rays (see Figure 4.4 for the dependency network for the project). It can be seen that while there are a significant number of stakeholders within the hospital trust, the project must be viewed as a partnership with the primary care sector, since there are also important stakeholders in this sector, such as the GPs who must encourage their patients and their practice managers to adopt this new way of booking appointments.

Stakeholders within the Hospital Trust (Acute Sector)	Stakeholders at Regional/National Level within Healthcare Service
• Head of Radiology Department • Radiologists and radiographers • Departmental administrators • Central booking staff • Clinical Director • Radiological protection staff • Trust Board • ICT department • Ambulance and transport	• Regional Health Authority • Department of Health • National Institute for Clinical Excellence • National Radiological Protection Board • NHS Direct
Stakeholders Primary Care Sector	**External Stakeholders**
• GPs • GP practice managers / administrators • Primary Care Trust (PCT) Board • PCT commercial managers • Allied professionals e.g. district nurses, dentists, optometrists	• Patients and carers • Social services • IT suppliers • Private healthcare providers

Figure 8.2: Stakeholder groups for the 'Choose and Book' project

While all the stakeholders would agree on the need to improve patient treatment, they would have different views on the best way to achieve this and also how best to use scarce resources and funds, all of which are affected by the new approach.

Figure 8.2 also highlights that public sector projects often have a number of regional or national bodies as stakeholders, since they have set the initial intention or targets that are driving deployment and will wish to monitor progress, or they issue overall guidelines and monitor activity in the sector. Finally, such projects are likely to have a number of groups of external stakeholders, in this case the patients who will benefit from the improved service.

Small and medium-sized businesses (SMEs)

As well as having more limited human and financial resources than large organizations, SMEs are less likely to possess, or will have less access to, technical resources and capabilities when compared to their larger counterparts (Cragg *et al.*, 2011). However, smaller firms do have the advantage of flexibility to try new approaches because their processes, structures and systems are normally simpler than in larger firms (Chang and Powell, 1998). This implies that while smaller firms can often easily adapt to new ways of working, their limited resources mean that they must select these new ways very carefully. Hence, rather than being less relevant to smaller organizations, it could be argued that the process and tools presented in this book are more pertinent. They can help to ensure that benefits are realized from those projects that are undertaken and, equally importantly, they can be used to avoid projects that are likely to waste the limited funds and resources available.

The benefits management approach can be applied in a small business in a similar manner to that for larger organizations, but there are a few particular issues that arise in its use in SMEs. In very small businesses, it is likely that most of the staff will be involved in both benefit planning and realization activities. Some of them may not benefit from the investment directly, but they will probably be involved in, or affected by, the changes needed. Another important consideration is whether the organization has the capacity or capabilities to carry out the changes that have been identified. As is shown in the example described in Box 8.2, thought should be given to both the organization's ability to undertake the necessary changes and who should be responsible for ensuring that they occur.

Multi-unit businesses: replicated deployments

Most large businesses are composed of a number of different business units. These units may produce the same goods or services as each other, but operate in different geographic territories, or they may be organized according to product and service lines. In order to implement organization-wide strategies, realize operating synergies, provide a consolidated picture of performance across the different units and also achieve IT economies of scale, many organizations attempt to deploy the same IS/IT applications across all their units. Some public sector initiatives also require the same or similar systems to be deployed in a large number of locations and separate organizations, such as local authorities, state schools or publicly funded hospitals.

As discussed earlier, while it may be tempting to assume that the benefits and necessary changes for such similar implementations will be the same and hence save the time and cost of developing individual benefits plans, this temptation should be avoided. Each unit, even when

Box 8.2: B2B e-commerce in a gift manufacturer

A small, UK-based gift manufacturer was considering the implications of extending its Web catalogue facility by implementing an online distribution channel for use by retailers who stocked and sold its gifts. These retailers ranged from small, single-site newsagents and gift shops to large, national chains. The sale of gifts by supermarkets in the UK was also growing and the manufacturer hoped that this online offering might help it win business from these important and powerful players.

The planned online offering would allow retailers to enter their orders for gifts online at any time of day. The manufacturer would then receive orders immediately, cutting out the errors and delays that were being experienced with the telephone ordering system. It was also expected that the online ordering facility could provide a point of differentiation from other gift manufacturers.

A simplified version of the benefits dependency network developed by the management team is shown in Figure 8.3. A number of significant benefits were identified, including speeding up and improving the accuracy of order fulfilment to retailers, increasing

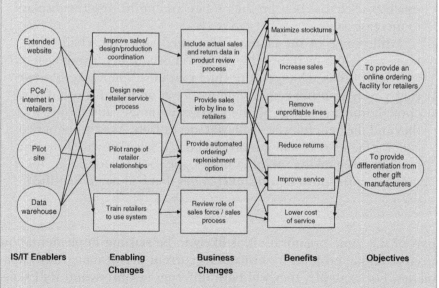

Figure 8.3: Benefits dependency network for a gift manufacturer

(*Continued*)

the number of 'turns' (the rate at which the gifts in a display stand are sold) and reducing 'lost sales' by reducing stockouts. As well as leading to increased sales for the retailer and the manufacturer, the order information could also be used, by both the retailer and manufacturer, to understand which gifts had been selling well and which had not. Unprofitable lines could then be removed from sale more quickly and the number of gifts returned from retailers as unsold could be reduced. Overall, it was expected that the service to retailers would be improved and would be provided at a lower cost.

Business and enabling changes identified included the tasks involved in ensuring that the system met the needs of the retailers and how large a number of them could be trained to use it, plus the new service process to be implemented to support their use. If both the retailers and the manufacturer were to benefit from the additional sales information, then both parties would need to learn how to interpret this information and, in the case of the manufacturer, how to convert the information for use in the product review and new design processes. An important change was the intention that sales staff could move from being effectively 'order takers', to providing real customer service, such as helping retailers select the best product range and improving the displays to increase sales.

While some of the changes identified would be challenging, none was felt to be impossible. However, when identifying owners for each of these changes, the chief executive's name kept recurring. Given his other responsibilities, it was unlikely he would have enough time to manage all the necessary changes and ensure that they and the benefits were achieved successfully. As a consequence, a senior member of staff was promoted to a Sales Director role and, in addition to taking on other duties, she took responsibility for a number of the most significant changes that had been identified.

part of the same organization, is likely to be starting implementation from a unique position in terms of its current performance and capabilities. For example, they will have differing resources and staff skills or be using a particular set of existing systems and they will be operating in different local business or social situations. A benefits plan that identifies the specific and significant benefits and associated changes that can be achieved by each unit, given its current position, should therefore be developed.

This approach was adopted by the Hilti Corporation in implementing global customer service systems and processes (vom Brocke *et al.*, 2011). Hilti manufactures, sells and hires out equipment and tools to the construction industry and operates in over forty countries. Its 'one Hilti' vision was aimed at providing the same high quality service to all customers in all countries. This meant rationalizing and standardizing processes from a diverse base of both existing systems and customs and practices across the units. The stated aim of the programme was to achieve a 'smooth implementation' through 'compromise not confrontation'. Once the standard processes and data had been defined and targets set for overall service performance, each unit was encouraged to develop its own implementation plan to deliver the maximum local benefits, adjusting and customizing some processes to fit the unit's capabilities and customer base. This meant that each unit was keen to take advantage of the more efficient and reliable processes and systems. The implementation was very successful – success being defined by both the extended and improved services offered and increased customer satisfaction.

Variations across the applications portfolio

The applications portfolio enables investments to be considered according to the contribution that they are expected to make to the organization's strategy or operations. As shown in Figure 8.4, key operational and support applications improve the effectiveness of the current business operations. In contrast, investments in strategic and high potential applications are intended to provide advantage through innovation or by differentiating the organization from its competitors.

The degree of knowledge and understanding of the 'why, what and how' – *why* the investment is being made, *what* has to be done to realize all the potential benefits and *how* this can best be achieved – will also vary across the portfolio.

The reasons for both key operational and support investments are likely to be well understood, since they are related to current operations. In the case of support applications, both the 'what is expected from the project' and 'how this will be realized from a combination of organizational changes and IS/IT' are likely to be reasonably obvious. This may require more detailed analysis and consideration of the

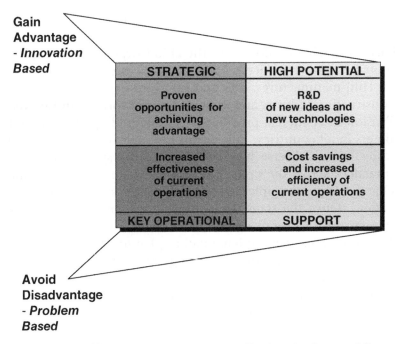

Figure 8.4: Different contributions of applications in the portfolio

feasibility of various options in the case of key operational investments, due to risks that might be incurred if the changes prove too difficult and some benefits are not realized.

Strategic applications, in contrast, are related to new opportunities for the organization and the rationale for an investment may be difficult to state explicitly, at least initially. Again, since strategic investments relate to new activities or new ways of working, the 'what' and the 'how' will be less well understood.

These variations in the extent of existing knowledge and degrees of certainty about the expected benefits and the associated business changes across the portfolio suggest the need for different emphases and approaches when using the tools and frameworks. In particular, the way in which the benefits dependency network is developed will differ, depending on whether the main intention is to remove or reduce business or organizational problems or to achieve a successful innovation. In the context of the business strategy, the approach to be taken should depend on whether the investment is primarily 'ends', 'ways' or 'means' driven. This is considered in more detail in the following sections.

Problem-based: key operational and support investments

Problem-based investments arise when an organization is primarily considering the use of IS/IT to improve performance in order to:

- avoid an existing disadvantage compared with competitors;
- prevent performance deteriorating in the future to a level that would be a disadvantage;
- achieve stated business targets;
- remove constraints that are preventing known opportunities from being taken.

Examples might include: integrating customer data to provide a single point of contact for customer enquiries; implementing an ERP system to remove reconciliation problems between production and finance; providing employee self-service applications to reduce administration and purchasing costs.

The main purpose in constructing a benefits dependency network for problem-based investments is to identify the most cost-effective and lowest risk combination of IT and business changes that will achieve the required improvements, most of which can be expressed as explicit, quantified benefits. The changes will be largely to stop doing unnecessary activities or to carry out essential tasks better: more consistently, accurately, reliably or efficiently, which may include outsourcing some of them.

As shown in Figure 8.5, it is important first to agree the investment objectives, expressed in terms of the performance improvements required to overcome the problems or constraints being faced, and identify the particular benefits expected from achieving the objectives. Ownership and measurement of the benefits should then be determined before considering the changes to ensure that the required 'ends' have been defined accurately.

The possible combinations of business and enabling changes and IT functionality can then be considered together. The preference should be to change business processes and procedures wherever feasible, either to make better use of existing systems or to minimize the costs of customizing software. The IS/IT options should consider the use of existing or off-the-shelf software to minimize the need for new IS/IT development. These approaches will reduce both initial investment costs and risks and ongoing systems maintenance and support costs.

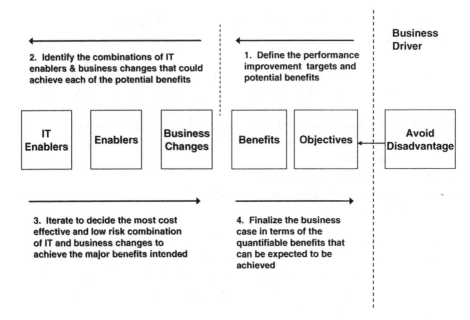

Figure 8.5: Developing an 'ends-driven', problem-based network

The alternative IS/IT and change combinations should then be prioritized based on overall cost effectiveness and least risk, in relation to achieving the highest value set of benefits. It is then advisable to carry out a stakeholder analysis on the preferred option to identify any reasons why implementation could be problematic and, if necessary, revise the business case accordingly.

Innovation-based: strategic and high potential investments

Innovation-based investments occur when an organization is deploying IS/IT to:

- do something new in its market;
- do something in a new way;
- do something it could not do before.

Normally, successful innovation is dependent on a combination of the technology, the organization's technical expertise and its ability to change in order to make effective use of the new technical capabilities. Examples could include: creating an online sales and service channel to reach new customers; enabling customer service updates from mobile devices; utilizing a professional network (e.g. LinkedIn) for marketing; using RFID tags for tracking stock items; allowing customers to do self-billing or deploying sophisticated analytics to automate some operational decision making.

One reason for constructing a benefits dependency network for innovation-based investments is to understand whether a combination of business changes and technology deployment can create a worthwhile advantage and, if so, how that can best be achieved. Such investments will often require extensive customization of available software or the bespoke development of software to meet the new, even unique, requirements. Advantages gained are usually from a combination of doing things better, achieving a performance level that competitors cannot match or doing new things that others cannot easily copy.

These investments are of two different types, both of which are aimed at creating advantage for the organization, but one is essentially 'ways' driven and the second is 'means' driven.

'Ways-driven' investments are more appropriate for strategic applications, where an opportunity exists and the purpose is to identify whether and how the organization can make the necessary business changes and IS/IT investment to gain advantage from the opportunity. As shown in Figure 8.6, this involves a number of stages:

1. The creation of a 'vision statement' that describes the nature of the advantage should lead to a set of initial objectives. Within that overall picture, the possible business benefits should be brainstormed and the likely business changes needed to achieve it should also be identified.
2. The feasibility of making the business changes and risks involved should then be assessed to determine those benefits that are most likely to be achievable and the benefits revised as necessary.
3. Then, the extent to which technology could be used to enable each of the business changes should be appraised and the overall likely cost of the technology needed compared with the estimate of the benefits to determine whether, overall, the investment will be worthwhile. Given that this is an innovation, it is likely that a range of

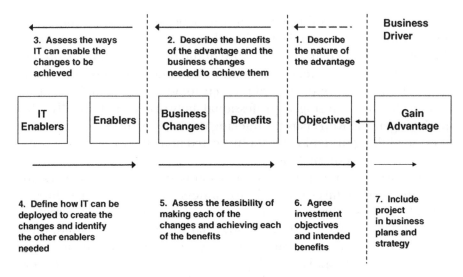

Figure 8.6: Developing a 'ways-driven', innovation-based network

enabling changes will also be required to develop new processes, and even new competences, and redefine responsibilities.

4. Finally, a full assessment of the organization's ability to deliver the combinations of IT and business changes is needed, including a stakeholder analysis to establish the achievable benefits before developing the final business case.

Compared with the problem-based network development, the process is more iterative, since the benefits are difficult to define initially. They also depend on the nature of the changes the organization is willing and able to make plus its ability to develop and deploy new technology. It is likely that the potential benefits will change considerably during these iterations.

'*Means-driven*' investments are appropriate for high potential projects when a business idea for using IS/IT or other new technology appears to offer an opportunity to create advantage for the organization. As high potential projects, many of these evaluations will lead to a decision not to proceed further because it is shown not to work or is financially unfeasible.

As shown in Figure 8.7, although high potential projects should be considered as R&D activities, it is still important to define the business context and drivers in order to spell out why the creation and evalua-

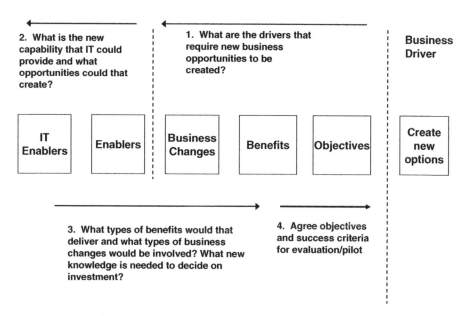

Figure 8.7: Developing a 'means-driven', innovation-based network

tion of new business options is important. This will also provide the rationale for deciding how these R&D projects are prioritized.

The main purpose in creating a benefits dependency network is to identify if there are sufficient potential benefits to justify further investigation.

In the case of new technology, the capabilities of the technology need to be understood in order to establish a proof of concept, including the enabling changes needed to use it effectively. It is then possible to make an initial estimate of the potential business benefits and describe the nature of business changes that will be needed. If the initial estimates of the benefits and scale of changes needed suggest that the project could be worthwhile, a more detailed evaluation could be agreed.

This use of the benefits dependency network is less a formal process than a way of ensuring that all the necessary aspects of the potential innovation are considered and interrelated. It does not include the development of a full business case or benefits plan. Like the 'ways-driven' innovation investments, the use of the benefits dependency network is iterative and it is likely to change significantly as more is understood about the opportunity being considered.

Different application types

Many organizations are implementing similar information systems, often using the same software packages. However, as discussed at the start of this chapter, the particular context of individual organizations will have a significant influence on the nature of the benefits achievable and the changes required when implementing even very similar systems in different organizations. Although generic benefits and changes should not be assumed, some recurring patterns in benefits and changes and interrelationships between these can be observed.

We cannot cover all types of application, but we include here some of those that are currently being deployed by a wide range of organizations. They include applications that can have a significant impact on organizational performance and business strategies and present the greatest challenges in terms of identifying and managing the expected benefits. The applications considered also illustrate many of the issues encountered in using the benefits management approach.

E-commerce and e-business

E-commerce and e-business have become the norm for most organizations, and developments are now managed like more traditional IS/IT projects in terms of the identification and realization of benefits. However, there are some particular issues associated with them because they involve extensive interaction with outside parties.

The terms e-commerce and e-business are often used interchangeably, although:

- e-commerce normally describes the use of IS/IT to perform business transactions and other trading activities with external parties;
- e-business usually refers to the use of IS/IT to improve information communication and use, both within the organization and with external parties.

A characteristic of e-commerce investments is the requirement to involve external stakeholders, typically customers, consumers or suppliers, and so it is important to understand 'what is in it for them'. Not all external stakeholders will perceive the same benefits and some may see no benefits at all, but they may be required to make significant changes in the way they do business with the organization. Implementation of an e-commerce system cannot be mandated to external organizations or individuals, except by threatening to reduce the level of business with them or even exclude them in future; that is, by emphasizing the 'disbenefits' of not cooperating.

Understanding and anticipating the potential reactions, both positive and negative, to an e-commerce investment requires a thorough stakeholder analysis as early as possible in the project. Ideally, representatives from all the various external parties who will be affected should be consulted. This should enable additional actions, including changing the systems' features, that can be undertaken to encourage or facilitate their participation. This may include other actions such as incentive payments or discounts to encourage usage, and/or the provision of a help desk and other support services.

E-commerce developments are also characterized by requiring almost continuous, even overlapping, cycles of application identification and implementation, especially when they serve the consumer market. Rapid changes in many industries and markets, often brought about by e-commerce itself, have necessitated an almost immediate response to innovations by others from organizations in those industries. While the benefits management process could be seen to add additional time to the development process, a benefits focus will tend to reduce the total time and cost of implementation, because it will identify the key benefits expected and the minimum set of changes required to deliver those benefits.

Information management (IM)

Since the majority of information systems capture, organize, store and disseminate information, they are all, to some extent, information management investments. However, the term is usually confined to systems whose primary aim is to provide the information required to improve decision making, acquire new knowledge, analyse performance and plan for the future. An example of a relatively simple IT-based information management investment is described in Box 8.3.

IM projects tend to present a number of particular issues in relation to the identification and realization of benefits. Given the overall need to make better-informed decisions, it is important to start by understanding and defining those decisions that need to be improved and why, who currently makes the decisions, how and when they are made and to review the results. The information required and currently available and how it is analysed and used in the decision-making processes should also be defined and agreed. This applies to both regular

Box 8.3: Information management in clinical trials

A driver for all pharmaceutical companies is the ability to develop new drugs and to bring them to market as quickly as possible. Undertaking clinical trials is a critical stage in new drug development, when clinicians, often dispersed around the world, will be approached by the pharmaceutical company to participate in trials of new drugs. The trials can last for a number of years in order to prove the efficacy of the drug and that it has no adverse side-effects. A major challenge in the trials is the recruitment of suitable patients. For rare medical conditions, or trials that require very large numbers of patients, recruitment may take a considerable time and hence lead to a delay in bringing the final product to market.

A pharmaceutical company decided to develop an online system that would encourage the timely recruitment of patients, by allowing the dispersed clinicians involved in trials to share their progress with others involved, including scientists and medical staff within the pharmaceutical company. Figure 8.8 shows a simplified version of the benefit network that was developed for the system.

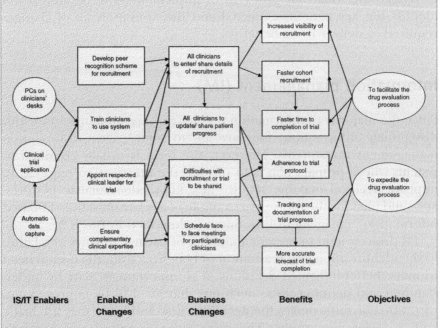

Figure 8.8: Benefits dependency network for a clinical trial application

Rather than rely on a technical solution alone to encourage information sharing between those involved in the trial, the company thought it important to make the participants in the trial feel as if they belonged to a team. A respected clinical leader was appointed to form links among the individual clinicians and finance and time were also set aside to enable the participants to meet each other face to face. Participating clinicians were encouraged to share difficulties in patient recruitment, or issues that they encountered in treating the patients with the new drug with others in the trial. This provided the pharmaceutical company with valuable insights into the progress of the trial and its likely successful completion date.

provision of management information, such as monthly reports, and ad hoc analyses.

'Better decision making' should not be viewed as an end in itself and should never be considered a sufficient description of a benefit: the improvements in business performance the organization is expecting as a result of better analysis and decision making should be clearly articulated. The 'net' benefit will also depend on the costs of collecting and organizing the information – in many cases, senior managers do not understand how much effort is involved in providing ad hoc information which may only be of value for a very short time.

For many IM investments, the full value may not be clearly known until some time after implementation. If staff have not previously had access to appropriate information, it may be hard for them to identify all the benefits that could be realized when it is available. This suggests that these investments should be considered in two phases.

The first, or problem, phase could include accessing new information sources, improving the integrity of the information by implementing stricter content management processes or consolidating data from several sources into one integrated repository or data warehouse. The subsequent innovation phase is then a series of developments, when the new opportunities due to the new information and tools now available are identified and evaluated. The benefits of the first phase could include significant efficiency improvements, whereas the second would require a level of understanding of the decision-making processes described earlier. In general terms, obtaining evidence to prove the benefits of the second phase would tend to be by reviewing a representative sample of decisions, rather than by more systematic measurement.

Identification of the changes to ways of working is as critical to the delivery of benefits from IM projects, if not more so, as other types of application. One change is often to extend and strengthen the analytical skills within the organization. While current analytical and business intelligence software is very powerful, it must be used by people who understand the analysis being undertaken and the meaning of the results, and it is particularly important to understand the limitations of the analytical techniques or reliability of the underlying information. These skills tend to be highly specialized and in short supply in most organizations, as witnessed by the reports of many organizations that have invested in large data warehouses and associated analytical software, but have derived little or no value from them. Indeed, as they fill with vast amounts of data, often of uncertain quality, such data warehouses can often simply add to the costs of information management without providing any significant benefit.

Other important areas that may require changes are the ways the organization presents information and makes decisions, including the timings of decisions and who is involved in making them. For example, by allowing greater information access throughout the organization, it may be appropriate to devolve decisions closer to the point of need. It may also be possible to allocate responsibility for more decisions to individuals, rather than require the agreement of a group of people, because the individual now has all the necessary information available. Instead of simply being able to make decisions more quickly, it may be possible to move to more 'just-in-time' decision making. This contrasts with having to make decisions rapidly, often under pressure, based on incomplete information.

Customer relationship management (CRM) systems

Many organizations in both business-to-consumer markets and business-to-business markets have invested, and continue to invest, considerable sums in customer relationship management (CRM) systems. Studies have shown that, between 2000 and 2005, organizations globally spent $220 billion on CRM software, but up to 75% of those companies failed to achieve the expected benefits (Maklan *et al.*, 2011). Part of the problem is that considerable up-front IT investment is needed, but the benefits depend on making consequent changes in organizational practices and capabilities, which are often underestimated and frequently do not happen. For example, deriving insights about customer behaviour from the information collected usually requires quite sophisticated analytical and statistical skills in order to use the analysis tools provided by the system.

While the specific rationale for these investments varies from one organization to another, the general intention is to understand their customers or clients better and then build enduring relationships with them (Knox *et al.*, 2003), which are, in turn, expected to increase revenues and reduce the costs associated with customer attrition and acquisition. CRM systems have also been deployed by not-for-profit organizations, including local authorities and the police, to improve the service they provide to their users and the value for money provided to the source of their funding.

One characteristic of CRM systems is the considerable time taken after implementation for many of the significant benefits to be realized. Many CRM systems have been sold with vendors' promises of rapid improvements to organizational performance. However, studies show that it may take up to five years or more for the major benefits to be realized (Peppard and Ward, 2005). For example, in 2002, the Britannia Building Society in the UK won an award for the best CRM implementation in the financial services sector, but had begun its CRM initiative in 1995. Similarly, one particular life assurance company was recently voted by a countrywide survey of brokers, who are their main channel to market, the 'best company to deal with'. However, this accolade was three years after the implementation of the company's CRM system.

'New technology is not transformational on its own . . . appropriate use requires considerable complementary investment in people, processes, culture and support . . . some or all of these things are usually missing.' *iSociety (2003)*

The nature of the benefits from CRM is shown schematically in the return on investment (ROI) curve shown in Figure 8.9. It can be seen that operational benefits, such as process efficiencies and cost savings, can be expected to emerge relatively quickly after implementation. However, the benefits that result from improved customer relationships depend on building new marketing capabilities based on knowledge gleaned from customers and are therefore likely to take years, rather than months, to realize. Recent research even suggests that the new capabilities should be developed

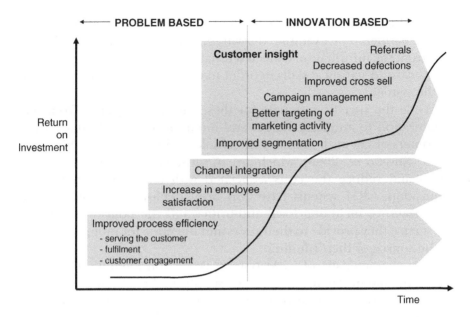

Figure 8.9: Return on investment curve for CRM systems (after Peppard and Ward, 2005)

in advance of the CRM implementation if the investment is to be successful (Maklan *et al.*, 2011).

The long-term nature of many of the benefits from CRM systems has implications with regard to setting the measures for benefits and how their achievement will be assessed. Since it is not feasible to delay the review of a project for several years, the review stage must recognize that some benefits will not, as yet, have been achieved. Instead, the review should focus on the shorter-term operational benefits. If there have been difficulties in realizing these, this suggests that action may be required to ensure the longer-term benefits will still be achieved. In addition, it may be possible to design measures for the longer-term benefits which, while not confirming their full realization, indicate that the organization is on track to obtain them in the future.

When building the business case, it is useful to do an initial stakeholder analysis to identify both the range of perceptions customers may have of the changes and the benefits different types of customer could expect. This may produce a number of benefit streams, requiring different changes to be made to address the needs of different customer segments. In turn, this may help phase the implementation to gain some quick wins by delivering benefits to some customers without major changes.

Other issues that are particularly pertinent in CRM deployments are related to the critical role of frontline staff, both to the collection of valid and accurate customer information and to the effective use of that information. In many organizations, staff members are accustomed to focusing on the products or services sold, but are less comfortable focusing on the customer, whose needs may not precisely match the organization's products or preferred ways of doing business. Hence, the areas where staff are able to use their discretion or must follow the prescribed processes need to be defined clearly. This also implies that it is important to understand the views these frontline staff have of the system and ways of working and 'what is in it for them'. Due to the central role they will play in enabling the benefits to be realized and sustained, the stakeholder analysis must identify actions that will address their issues and concerns.

Another issue regarding the use of CRM systems is the perceived link between information and power in organizations. Individuals often believe that sharing their information with others reduces their personal value and, hence, power or influence within the organization. The development of new performance measurement or incentive schemes which recognize and reward team or organizational, rather than individual, achievements may be needed.

Enterprise resource planning (ERP) systems

Enterprise resource planning (ERP) provides an integrated suite of systems that coordinate operational and management processes across a broad range of internal business activities, including procurement, accounting, finance and human resources. Many organizations, in a wide range of industries, have invested in, or are currently implementing, ERP suites and associated business changes, such as Shared Service Centres. ERP deployments tend to focus primarily on improving the performance of internal processes and operations, often by rationalizing and integrating the core business systems,

> '. . . project failures come from such things as not having new workflow processes, not adapting the structure of the organization to the new ways of working, not revising incentives and keeping the old cultural practices in place, even when they impede the new ways of working . . .' Gibson (2003)

processes and information sources used in operational and managerial decision making. As a consequence, the quality and reliability of the data in the ERP system are critical to achieving the majority of the benefits.

One common issue is that, too often, ERP investments can be viewed, by both the business managers and IS staff, as primarily software replacement projects, which may lead to reluctance from business staff to participate fully, leaving the IS staff to lead the project. Unfortunately, it usually transpires later that the IS staff only know how the systems in the business operate, rather than how business is actually done. The lack of involvement of business staff means that business changes necessary to utilize the new systems effectively are overlooked. Even when business managers and staff are involved, they often ask for the system to be configured or amended to reflect current business practices. If such requests are met, this can result in both increased initial investment and ongoing support and maintenance costs. This is also likely to reduce the benefits realized, since it reduces consideration of new ways of working, and all too frequently the old ways of working remain in place despite having incurred the significant cost and disruption associated with introducing new technology.

For example, a major global pharmaceutical company invested £11 million in an ERP and supply chain management system to replace 17 different legacy systems in different business units and functions within the organization. Due to this emphasis on standardization and systems replacement, the project was viewed almost solely as '*a technology replacement project, with little change to the underlying business*'. This resulted in the planning stage of the project being characterized by a clear belief that the project and its impact on the organization were well understood. Problems began to emerge when it became apparent that successful implementation and operation would require greater changes to the way units and functions operated and interacted than had been anticipated. These groups were traditionally highly autonomous and were not willing to have changes to the way they worked mandated by the project team. In particular, it became clear that: '*We needed to work according to processes – however, the organization is predominantly organized along unit and functional lines. Process ownership and governance were problems that surfaced and needed to be resolved.*' Concerned about the challenge to their traditional functional control, many of the managers began to look after their own and their function's interests. At the end of the implementation stage, although the system was operational, significant problems remained and few benefits had been delivered.

The implications of these common characteristics of ERP deployments for effective benefits realization emphasize the importance of the choice of business project sponsor and business project manager. As discussed in Chapter 7, for projects with significant degrees of business change, the individuals in both roles should be experienced senior managers drawn from the business. Given that most ERP deployments will affect a large number of functions within the organization, it is important that they can garner respect and cooperation right across the organization and are not seen to represent certain interest groups alone.

All functions that will be significantly affected by the ERP deployment should be involved in the development of a benefits plan: both in identifying those benefits that they might expect to receive and the changes they will be involved in or affected by. Some functions may already have effective processes and access to appropriate information, while others may not. Therefore, some groups will be less willing to change, but may have to, while others will see it as an opportunity to upgrade to better systems and technology. A comprehensive stakeholder analysis can help to ensure that actions are put in place early in the implementation to address the range of different starting points and perceptions.

A two-stage model of enterprise systems deployments

Our own research (Ward et al., 2005) has led to a model that can be used to guide the implementation of ERP and other enterprise-wide systems. The two-stage model shown in Figure 8.10 is based on how those organizations in our study that had implemented an ES successfully addressed the complex set of issues they encountered. The model draws upon the work of Markus and Tanis (2000), but many others have also proposed or observed a staged approach, albeit with a varying number of stages.

Implementation is effectively broken into two phases. The first phase is consistent with the problem-based investments discussed earlier in this chapter. This phase of the implementation aims to overcome known problems or constraints in the organization, producing a new baseline, where the existing problems have been removed. This accepts the logic that it is difficult to operationalize a new vision when surrounded by current problems.

Equally, it allows for the fact that different stakeholder groups will be at different stages of development in terms of the capabilities of

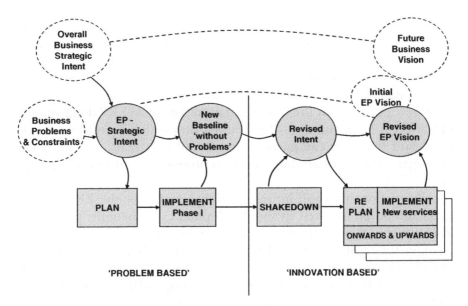

Figure 8.10: The two-stage model of ES implementation

existing systems. Those with excellent existing systems will have a different perspective on the need for, and nature of, the changes required compared with those with poor systems, who have much to gain simply by replacement. The compromise usually errs on the side of bringing the weaker areas up to the new baseline and deferring the riskier and more innovative changes.

Following any ES implementation there is some form of shakedown phase, which may involve resolving serious problems if business performance has been adversely affected, or merely tuning the system and business processes to achieve the expected performance levels. Any implementation should anticipate and plan for this stage, ensuring resources and procedures are in place to deal with the consequences of implementation. Once the baseline benefits have been delivered, the organization needs to define a revised intent for the ES in terms of future business change (and further ES investment if necessary) to deliver new business options that will be available following systems and process integration or as a result of having common systems across the business units.

New iterations of planning and implementation normally follow, often in smaller, incremental steps, focused on specific business activities or processes. The approach to this so-called onwards and upwards stage is consistent with use of benefits management for innovation-based investments, as described earlier in this chapter. It is often best planned and executed in discrete steps if business risks are to be avoided and it is important that the knowledge gained during the first, large-scale implementation is retained and transferred to this second phase.

Infrastructure investments

Infrastructure, such as new network capacity, processing capability, data storage or operating and general utility software, can often be one of the most difficult areas of IT investment to justify in terms of business benefits. In many cases it is equally difficult to measure the actual benefits realized after implementation. It can be argued that some aspects of IT infrastructure are required just to be in business and should be justified in the same way as other essentials, such as office space. This would normally mean on a cost-per-employee basis. However, this is not appropriate when major new infrastructure investments or upgrades are being considered.

New infrastructure may be required for one or more application being planned by the organization, but frequently the benefits arising from these are insufficient to justify the significant investment involved. It is also often the case that many other existing or future applications will use the same infrastructure. Hence, the argument for infrastructure investments often needs to be based on unknown benefits from, as yet unspecified, future use, making it difficult to justify the costs involved.

A suggested approach to justification is based on the various ways in which a particular type of infrastructure can contribute to improvements in organizational and individual performance or create new business options. Figure 8.11 suggests five different ways in which this contribution can occur.

Any specific investment is likely to produce benefits in a number of these dimensions, each of which should be examined in order to build a combined business case.

1. **Reduce current costs:** newer technologies often incur lower costs in terms of support and maintenance than older versions, hence new infrastructure can often be, at least partly, justified by a reduction in IT operating costs. Such savings are most likely to arise in relation

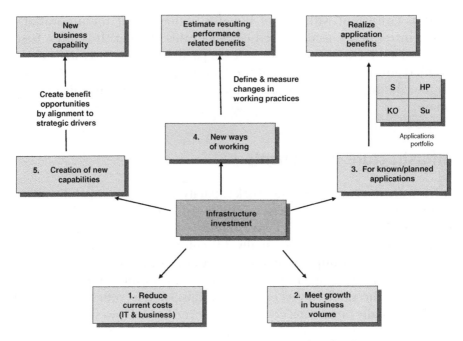

Figure 8.11: Infrastructure investment justification

to the running costs of extensively used support or key operational applications and personal productivity and communications tools. There may also be business cost savings, especially by providing mobile communication and application or information access.

Included in this category is also the forced or burning platform need to replace a technology that is, or is becoming, obsolete and will no longer be supported or further developed by the vendor. As with any technology investments that involve supporting existing applications, it is prudent to question whether all those applications are still essential to the business. If they cannot be discontinued, alternatives which will result in different benefits and costs should be considered, for example:

(i) transferring the applications to another existing technology already in use in the business or a new technology consistent with the IT strategy and policies;

(ii) modifying, replacing or redeveloping the applications to take advantage of new, lower-cost technology platforms;

(iii) reducing the functionality of the applications to the essentials before transferring them to another technology.

2. **Meet growth in business volume:** infrastructure investments may be needed to meet the growth in the volume of business transactions, both internally and externally. However, it needs to be clear whether the increased volume is related to real business growth that leads to increased revenue or higher service levels, rather than merely increased internal activity. Much of the increased network and storage capacity required by organizations is simply due to poor practice in the management of emails, intranet content and documents, rather than growth in volume or value of business being conducted.

   Additional infrastructure may also be required to accommodate a changing mix of transactions, for example, customers switching to online ordering from the call centre, or to meet changing business practices or customer and employee expectations. In some markets, customers now expect just-in-time deliveries from suppliers in order to avoid holding stock, resulting in more single-line ordering rather than consolidating purchases, leading to an increased volume of transactions for the supplier but no additional revenue.

3. **For known or planned applications:** as already discussed, infrastructure costs can be justified, in part, based on the benefits delivered by known future applications that will use the infrastructure, and the relevant proportion of the costs should be included in the business justification for those application investments. Normally, more than one application will make use of any significant infrastructure investment, therefore explicit links should be identified between the planned infrastructure and each of the applications in the portfolio, both being developed and currently in operation, that will use the new infrastructure.

4. **Emergent and planned new ways of working:** although many changes to business processes and working practices are associated with specific applications, increasingly, improvements in the ways of working can result from people using the tools and facilities provided by the infrastructure without major application investment. Some of the changes can be identified by analysing working practices while others evolve over time as individuals and groups find new or better ways of carrying out their tasks and roles.

   These emergent new ways of working should be considered as pilots, which will be reviewed after a certain time to determine whether they could be adopted beneficially elsewhere. When a new type of infrastructure is introduced, it may be possible to identify potential benefits by seeing what has happened in other organizations that have already adopted the technology. This may also yield insights into the types of change that are needed to take full advantage of the capabilities provided as well as enabling the organization to avoid believing that the technology will provide certain benefits when others have failed to realize them.

5. **Creation of new capabilities:** in some cases, IT infrastructure investment is essential for building a new capability required for the future business strategy to be achieved or for a particular strategic initiative. For example, a multinational energy company stated that one of its strategic intentions was 'to become location independent', thereby enabling its technical and professional staff to perform their jobs wherever in the world they happened to be. This was subsequently used as the main justification for a major investment in network capacity, mobile devices and high functionality portable workstations.

In the UK, a requirement to move to electronic access and delivery of services to citizens has led many local authorities to justify major infrastructure investments as an integral part of delivering e-government services. It has also been recognized by a number of such authorities that the deployment of improved IT infrastructure will, over the long term, reduce the need for more traditional types of infrastructure, such as offices and depots. As the infrastructure to enable online access and mobile working by staff is implemented, savings in the capital and operating costs of existing physical sites are being used to balance the IT costs incurred.

Non-IT projects

The headline quoted from the *Guardian* is one example of many non-IT projects that have also failed to deliver the expected benefits or, worse still, were undertaken with no clear idea of what the benefits would be and how they could be obtained. Non-IT project failure rates are no different from IT projects, confirming IS/IT research findings that managing changes to achieve benefits is the core problem rather than the IT. As this

> 'BBC spent £2bn on developments* with no clear idea of benefits, says watchdog.' *The Guardian (26th February 2010)*
> (* The £2bn was spent on three major building projects.)

suggests, the benefits management process and tools can be, and have been, applied successfully to many projects involving change that have little or no IT content.

Non-IT projects that the process has been applied to include:

- corporate restructuring and reorganization, including the centralizing of functions into 'onshore' and 'offshore' shared services;
- extending the business into new markets and the development of new products and services;
- restructuring service delivery in local authorities;
- evaluation of alternative options for office relocation or refurbishment;
- the development of a new postgraduate marketing strategy for a higher education institution;
- integration and rationalization of business processes and performance management following a merger;
- ensuring the potential patient and quality of care benefits of a new hospital were achieved by optimum use of the new accommodation and relocation of clinical departments;
- adoption of the benefits management approach throughout an organization – which was described in more detail in Chapter 7.

Each of the stages of the process and the tools can be applied as described in earlier chapters. The one exception will be that the left-hand column in the benefits dependency network which identifies the required IS/IT may be empty or include other types of enabling facilities, such as buildings.

For all the projects listed above, using the key elements of the benefits management process resulted in improved implementation and increased benefits. In particular, linking of investment objectives to the strategic drivers, the identification, measurement and quantification of benefits and understanding new working practices, processes and roles that are needed to deliver the benefits, are relevant to almost any project, not just those involving IT.

Different IS/IT supply arrangements

How an organization provisions its IS/IT will also have an impact on the way it plans for and manages the realization of benefits. An organization has two basic options when considering the provision of IS/IT:

to provide systems and technology using in-house staff or to buy products and services in from external suppliers. The expanding range of uses of IS/IT by organizations requires increased expertise to implement and support, causing many organizations to either outsource some of their existing IS/IT resources or increase their reliance on external suppliers. This trend is reinforced by a need to reduce costs, share risks, increase flexibility and also, often, by a shortage of relevant skills.

However, effective IS/IT exploitation is dependent on the way an organization integrates the use of the technology with its other capabilities and this requires knowledge and skills within the organization, either in a dedicated IS/IT group or within other business functions. The discussion of the use of the benefits management approach so far has assumed that the majority of the expertise and resources needed to implement the systems and changes is available in-house or can be obtained as and when required from external sources. If an organization relies on outside parties to provide much of its IS/IT capability, there are particular implications for the management of IS/IT projects and hence the use of the benefits management approach.

External supply: outsourcing

Bendor-Samuel (2000) describes a popular view of outsourcing when he describes it as an exchange between buyer and provider, in which the buyer exchanges control of a process or activity in return for the ability to define the results. Keen to ensure the performance of their outsourcing providers, many organizations put in place tightly specified service-level agreements. In some cases, buyers have even sought to make the outsourcing provider responsible for business benefits. However, the achievement of business benefits is seldom dependent on the deployment and operation of IS or IT alone, but requires changes to working practices within the organization for which an outside provider cannot be made responsible, and hence they cannot be made responsible for the delivery of many of the benefits. As shown in Figure 8.12, although an outsource provider can be made responsible for the development and operation of the IS and IT enablers and some of the related enabling changes, responsibility for the majority of the enabling changes and the business changes remains firmly with the management of the purchasing organization.

As also shown in Figure 8.12, use of an outsource supplier will create the need for additional business changes: for example, the need to

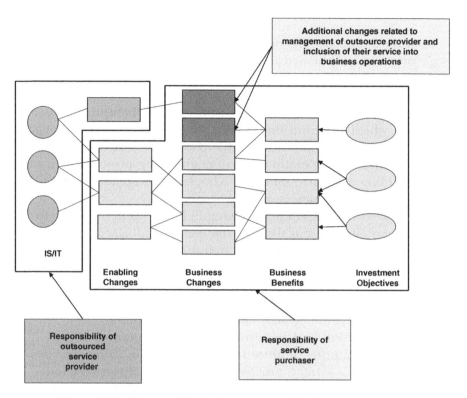

Figure 8.12: Responsibilities in outsourced IS/IT arrangements

manage the contractual relationship with the provider, monitoring the level of service delivered and the inclusion of the services provided into the ongoing operations of the organization. Mechanisms and responsibilities for the management of the relationship should be expressly identified. While it may be tempting to view the management of the contract as the responsibility of the IS/IT group, the criticality of their service to the operations of the business suggests that one or more business managers should have a significant input to that relationship management process.

In the case of the outsourcing of entire processes, it may be that the number of business changes to be undertaken internally is reduced, since whole sets of activities will be provided by the third party. However, once again business changes related to the management of those services will be needed, for example to ensure that improvements in the outsourced process are aligned with the other internal operations. As an increased range of activities is outsourced, it may become difficult

Box 8.4: Challenges of outsourcing IT in the public sector

In order to improve the delivery of public services in the UK, the government has pursued a strategy of partnerships with the private sector: *public–private partnerships* (PPPs). One form of PPP is the *private finance initiative* (PFI) in which private sector organizations take on the responsibility for constructing and operating a public service, which the government undertakes to purchase on a long-term basis. While many of the initiatives to date have been for the construction and operation of civil engineering projects, such as the building or refurbishment of schools and hospitals, a number of them are to provide large IT projects.

The key objectives in undertaking PFI projects in the IT sector have been described as to *'effect risk transfer and impose commercial discipline'*. However, despite the definition by the public sector client of what is required from the private sector partners in such initiatives, a study by the Treasury itself (HM Treasury, 2003) found that such projects had *'not delivered the step-change in perform-ance the Government originally intended and still requires'*.

In 2011 the Public Administration Select Committee of the UK House of Commons produced a report entitled *Government and IT – 'a recipe for rip-offs': time for a new approach*, which concluded that 'the lack if IT skills in government and over-reliance on con-tracting out is a fundamental problem'. As a result, the 'govern-ment's overall record in developing and implementing new IT systems is appalling'.

Key factors identified as giving rise to this poor performance included:

- the fast pace of change in the IT sector, which makes it difficult for the public sector to effectively define the outputs it requires from a long-term contract;
- the high level of integration of IT into other business systems of the client, which make it difficult to clearly delineate areas of responsibility of the client and the provider;
- IT projects have a much shorter life than other types of project and often require significant asset refresh, which makes it difficult to define and enforce long-term service needs.

To overcome these and other problems, the committee recom-mended that the government needs to retain or reacquire the skills and knowledge needed to understand how IT can transform and improve its services and not rely on suppliers' capabilities.

to clearly differentiate areas of responsibility of the supplier and the service purchaser. While attempts should be made to clarify responsibilities from the start in a contract of engagement, it is not possible to cover every eventuality, particularly in long-term relationships. Blurred boundaries should therefore be recognized and ways of dealing with resulting issues developed and included in the necessary changes or enablers.

These issues are not unique to the public sector. They are commonly encountered in all IT outsourcing and underline the fact that the realization of benefits from IT cannot be passed to a third party. The supplier can deliver and manage the new technology, but the client has to have the capability to identify how it will contribute to business improvement and manage the associated organizational changes needed. The client organization must also retain or develop skills and working practices within its own staff to manage the relationship with the outsourcer to ensure the services provided continue to be aligned with the organization's goals.

Summary

This chapter has explored the implications of context on the realization of benefits from IS/IT projects and how the benefits management approach can be adapted to suit different situations. Since, in most contexts, the achievement of substantial benefits will require changes to roles, responsibilities, processes and working practices, the actual changes required to make effective use of a new system will vary between organizations. They will depend on particular attributes of the organization, including their current operations, structure and the skills and motivations of their managers and staff. Equally, what is viewed as a benefit will differ between organizations depending on their current performance and the drivers shaping their future strategies.

The importance of context precludes specifying or prescribing a generic set of benefits for a certain application type or for a particular type of organization. While we have presented a number of examples of the tools and frameworks in this chapter, it should be stressed that these are to illustrate their use and they cannot be taken as templates for actual projects. Not only would this ignore the particular situation of an organization, it would also prevent the sense of shared ownership among the project team and benefit and change owners that results from generating their own benefits plan together.

That benefits depend on context also warns against the silver bullet approach to system deployment, in which IS/IT functionality or features promised by vendors are assumed to be benefits that will actually be realized by an organization. Even if the features and functionality are directly relevant to addressing the business's strategic drivers, the organization must ensure that it understands the business changes needed to translate that functionality into a business benefit and then be willing and able to make such changes.

The next chapter goes beyond single projects and considers how the use of the benefits management process can provide additional value when applied to multiple projects, both within a programme and for the whole investment portfolio. Use of the process enables organizations to combine individual project benefits into a coherent benefits plan that recognizes the benefit and change dependencies between projects and also identifies when several projects are claiming the same benefits.

Chapter 9

From projects to programmes to portfolios

So far we have discussed IS/IT investments as discrete projects, which has been the traditional way of managing them. However, as many organizations embark on much larger scale change initiatives, often impacting the entire organization, the term *programme* has become more widely used to refer to a set of interlinked projects. In these complex initiatives it is not possible to foresee all the potential benefits or define all the changes at the start of the programme. Rather, investment objectives and benefits will evolve as the organization learns what can, and cannot, be achieved. Also, business circumstances may change during the extended time involved in completing the full implementation of the systems and business changes, requiring a reappraisal of the benefits that can be realized. The nature of large-scale IT-enabled change programmes and the applicability of the benefits management approach in that context are considered in this chapter.

Organizations often adopt a programme management approach when there is a range of applications that require inherently different types of change to be managed during implementation, with varying degrees of certainty of realizing the benefits. For example, a programme may involve significant automation of clerical activities to release 'back office' resources and reduce systems and information duplication (support) and, at the same time, implement a data warehouse to replace its existing legacy reporting systems (key operational) *and* enable the introduction of a new approach to performance management (strategic or high potential). While the overall benefits to be realized depend on all three being successful, each could be managed separately, in parallel, in terms of the business changes needed.

Large organizations are likely to be undertaking many projects and programmes simultaneously, putting pressure on resources and funds and requiring a means of prioritizing and balancing competing demands. *Portfolio management* approaches, including the applications portfolio introduced in Chapter 2, are an effective means of understanding the complete picture of current and planned activity and ensuring that this is appropriate and achievable. The latter part of the chapter considers how using the benefits management approach can be included in governance processes and thereby increase the value derived from an entire portfolio of IS/IT projects.

Defining programmes

There are many definitions of the term programme, most of which are intended to differentiate a programme from a big project. In many cases the word programme is used to ensure that appropriate senior management attention is paid to the investment – attention they would fail to give to a mere project. However, Williams and Parr (2004) suggest that there are two essential differences: *programmes* create new organizational capabilities *and* change the existing organizational capabilities in completing the changes successfully. That implies that not only are some of the final benefits difficult to forecast, but also that some of the changes will not, directly, produce performance improvements, merely the capability to achieve them through further changes in the future. *Projects*, in contrast, normally deploy existing capabilities to achieve definable benefits.

The International Centre for Programme Management (ICPM) at Cranfield School of Management has used this distinction in its definitions:

Project: A pre-defined scope of work delivered using existing capabilities to achieve agreed outputs in accordance with an authorized business case.

Programme: A dynamic collection of related projects and activities that, in combination, achieve agreed organizational objectives and emergent outcomes, including the creation of new capabilities.

Portfolio: A set of related and unrelated projects and programmes that compete for an organization's resources and funds.

As considerable evidence shows, many project risks are directly related to the scale and duration of a project and so breaking them into smaller, more manageable tasks – effectively a programme of interrelated projects – can help reduce risk. It can also enable some benefits to be realized earlier, an increasingly important factor in today's uncertain and changeable business environment, when investment priorities have to be reassessed frequently. In concept, programmes allow an organization to adjust its use of resources to match changing priorities and emergent opportunities. This implies that programmes are used to bring about major changes over extended periods, whereas projects focus on achieving specific deliverables in as short a timescale as possible.

Based on an analysis of 20 major IT-enabled change programmes in a range of different industries, a number of characteristics distinguished those that succeeded in gaining most of the benefits from others that were less successful:

- Organizations should manage programmes as orchestrated, continuous incremental sets of changes and change projects – co-evolving and co-existing with business as usual priorities.
- Most programmes involve at least two distinct and different phases – first to create a new capability and second to exploit it. In most of the cases studied, the capability was created but was not always exploited, hence the benefits achieved were often fewer than those originally envisaged.
- Having a clear vision of the intended future business and organizational models and then allowing compromises and trade-offs in the detail of how they are implemented, is more likely to achieve stakeholder commitment than imposition.
- Effective management of the change content and benefits delivery is more important than the efficiency of the process. The process should reflect not only the changes required but the organization's values, experience, capabilities and culture.
- Successful programmes tend to address the organizational, people and capability aspects of the transformations first, then the process and IT aspects. The less successful try to do the reverse.

These lessons are not really surprising, since most are instances of good benefits management practices, but here applied to complex programmes as well as the component projects.

Facing increased global competition, many large multinational organizations are undertaking extensive changes to the way in which traditional business functions are performed, where they are performed and by whom. The purpose is usually twofold: to dramatically reduce overhead costs and to become more capable of responding globally to changing business and economic conditions. Common features of these initiatives are establishing shared service centres for largely administrative tasks, enabling employees or even trading partners self-service access to some applications and, to support these changes, rationalizing and standardizing the business processes and the underlying IT infrastructure and systems. These are complex initiatives involving many interdependent changes, which tend to succeed when managed as a programme of related activities rather than as predominantly an IT project. We have witnessed many examples where such initiatives became largely IT led and failed to deliver the business changes that produced most of the benefits. Examples of success and disappointment are described briefly in Box 9.1.

Planned and emergent programmes

There appear to be two different types of programme, which we term *planned* and *emergent*.

- **Planned:** those that are defined as a programme at the outset – as a set of related projects and other activities that all need to be undertaken to achieve the objectives of the required change. This also includes programmes resulting from an appreciation that a large project needs to be broken down into smaller components due to changes that have emerged since it was initiated.
- **Emergent:** programmes that result from the realization that existing or planned projects are interdependent and need to be managed as a coherent set to avoid the failure of one of them putting the others at risk. This may also occur when a number of projects require changes in the same area of the business at the same time or over a short period. The focus of the programme is then on scheduling the related projects, particularly in coordinating the business changes needed so that organizational risk and stress are minimized.

Programme dependency networks

The interrelationships between the underlying projects in a programme can be defined explicitly in terms of a programme dependency network. The development of a programme network will be slightly different for planned and emergent programmes.

Box 9.1: Comparing two IT-enabled transformation programmes

Two major global organizations, Vodafone (Kresak *et al.*, 2011) and an insurance company, known here as Lukas (Giordano *et al.*, 2011), both embarked on similar IT-enabled business transformation programmes involving: standardizing on a common suite of back-office systems and restructuring support functions in shared service centres in a single location. The software used was the same but the results were different due to the approach taken to realizing the benefits.

At Vodafone, the expected financial and performance benefits were defined in detail and linked specifically to the changes expected to deliver them, whether they were process standardization, systems rationalization or restructuring into shared services. In defining the programme, it was clear that creating the new shared service organization was necessary first to enable the simplified, common processes to be agreed and the new systems to be put in place. The new units were established and staff transferred or recruited to resource them as the new systems were rolled out across the different countries and local departments were closed down. Benefits achieved were assessed as each country was transferred into the new arrangement and, overall, a very significant number of expected benefits was realized.

At Lukas, the transformation was seen as primarily an IT programme, which would deliver IT cost savings plus business benefits from the consolidation of several support units into a centre of excellence in one location. The programme was driven initially by IT, who attempted to get business support for rationalizing and redesigning the existing processes into a standard set. There was little business enthusiasm for this, since there were no obvious benefits to the units which were expected to cooperate, rather, the benefits were seen as corporate benefits. As a result, the process-mapping project, which was the first phase of the programme, became protracted, partly due to inadequate business resources being deployed on it and partly due to the complexity involved in accommodating the huge variety of practices in the different units. The programme was eventually abandoned after 18 months. Four years later, the transformation was re-initiated by Finance in a programme that took into account the mistakes of the first attempt. The new programme is ongoing at the time of writing.

Planned programmes

The development of a network for a planned programme is shown in Figure 9.1. This shows the simplified case of a programme that has been broken into three component projects: A, B and C. The business drivers form the basis for the definition and agreement of a set of investment objectives for the overall programme, which, in turn, are split up to become the objectives for the component projects.

As shown in the case of projects A and B, it may be helpful to agree additional investment objectives at the project level, in order to ensure that the project has sufficient definition and focus. The benefits that could be expected if each of the projects achieved their objectives should then be identified, compared to avoid any double-counting and consolidated into the overall programme benefits. The agreed set of objectives and benefits can then be used to assess or reassess the best way to divide the necessary activities into a set of manageable projects. For each of these, a full benefits dependency network should be developed and interdependencies amongst the component projects highlighted by means of linkages between the individual project networks.

Typically, there are four ways in which individual projects can be interdependent. These are exemplified with regard to a programme to improve both the efficiency and quality of service provided by the field service engineers of a major utility company. This programme was divided into a number of component projects that addressed all parts of the service cycle:

1. **Benefits of earlier projects can be enablers of later projects.** For example, in the utility company, efficiency improvements in the administrative operation of the field service division allowed a reduction in the number of staff needed in the back office. This was expressed as a benefit in the 'back office administration project'. Rather than being released, these staff were transferred to the customer service division where they were retrained in order to provide improved and extended services. The requirement for additional customer service staff had been recognized as a necessary enabling change in the 'customer service transformation project'.
2. **Some benefits of earlier projects are new or improved organizational capabilities required for later projects.** In the case of the utility company, it wished to offer a premium service to customers. However, it was not possible until the organization could provide faster response times to service requests. The ability to improve response

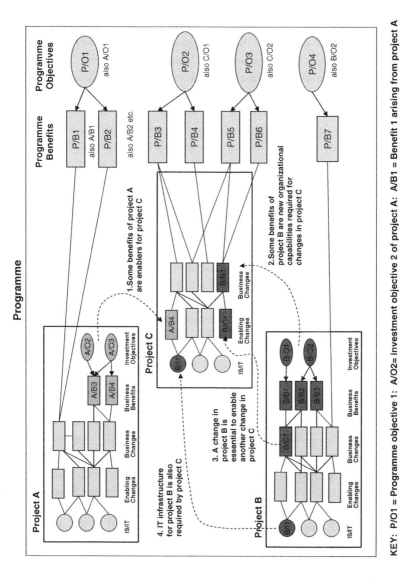

Figure 9.1: Programme dependency network for a planned programme

times relied on improved service engineer productivity, which was a benefit expected when the 'field engineer mobile working' project enabled engineers to be dispatched based on real-time activity data.

3. **A change in one project is required to enable a change in a later project.** For example, in order to reduce the time taken for field engineers to service equipment, it was necessary for them to have complete and up-to-date information about the equipment, such as components and circuit diagrams when on the customer's premises. Online access to this information relied on the changes in an earlier project that identified, compiled and indexed the most up-to-date versions of product information.

4. **IS/IT developed in an earlier project is a prerequisite for later projects.** A new broadband mobile working infrastructure was required as part of the 'field engineer mobility' project aimed at improving service engineer productivity. This network was also key to reducing customer complaints, since it allowed information generated in the field to be passed back to the service centre immediately. Most complaints experienced by the utility were due to engineering and maintenance work being carried out on the network. The ability to provide accurate and timely information about the work, such as the duration and likely interruptions to supply, allowed customer concerns to be dealt with effectively.

Having developed benefits dependency networks for the individual projects, it may be necessary to iterate back to the programme objectives and benefits, and the division between individual projects, to ensure that, in combination, these address the drivers and appear achievable. A business case should be developed for each of the projects within the programme, since this will clarify the nature of the benefits expected and the costs associated with these, as well as for the entire programme. It may be that some of the projects cannot be justified as standalone investments. However, their criticality to the realization of the programme benefit should be recognized explicitly. Although it is the projects that deliver the benefits, it is the programme that orchestrates the projects' implementation activities to ensure that they cumulatively produce all the benefits envisaged.

Emergent programmes

For programmes that were not planned from the outset, but have arisen from the recognition that projects being planned or undertaken are interdependent, a programme-level dependency network can also be developed. This will look similar to that shown in Figure 9.1, although development of the network will involve combining the individual project-level networks. In addition to identifying the project interdependencies, the programme network should be used to bring together all of the benefits expected from the individual projects and their investment objectives. This can result in either finding duplicated benefits or identifying additional benefits from the combination of changes.

This consolidated view is useful in identifying benefits that are expected, or claimed, by more than one project and then whether the expected benefits can be cumulative. The transformation programme of a large retailer in the UK, discussed in Chapter 7, provides an example of benefits identified in separate projects that can be cumulative in nature. The regular customer satisfaction surveys undertaken by the retailer are a key performance indicator and any project that could produce improvements in this was likely to be well received. Many projects within the programme had the potential to improve customer satisfaction, such as reducing queuing times at tills and improving the on-shelf availability of stock, hence, an increase in customer satisfaction ratings was identified as a benefit. In this case, the benefits from the improvements are likely to be cumulative and so can be counted in more than one project.

In other cases, benefits cannot be cumulative. For example, when accumulated benefits would result in an unfeasible outcome, such as lower than zero stock holding, the project that can most easily give rise to the benefit, based on the changes involved should be identified. The benefit, and any associated changes, should then be removed from both the benefits dependency networks and the business cases of the other projects in the programme. If the benefit that has been claimed more than once is significant, it may be necessary to reappraise the business cases of those projects from which it has been removed.

Bringing together the benefits and investment objectives of individual projects can also highlight when there are contradictions. For example, in the case of a major organization that was undertaking an improvement programme within its customer call centre, on examining the benefits from individual projects, it was found that one project claimed the benefit of 'shortening call durations', while another claimed to 'lengthen call durations to allow greater cross-selling'. In cases such as this, the organization must reappraise what it is trying to achieve and remove the benefits that are no longer relevant from the individual projects, together with their associated changes.

Finally, a consolidated programme network will also show when the realization of a benefit is reliant on the successful completion of more than one project. Such instances can result in 'double-counting' of the benefit or alternatively not including the benefit in any of the project networks or business cases. An approach to address the issues relating to consolidating benefits across individual projects is to establish a 'register' of all the intended programme benefits. As the benefits of each project are identified, the register should be updated to specify which project will deliver 'how much' of each benefit, based on the changes that each project will bring about. The register should also be updated with the benefits realized as the projects are completed.

The management of programme benefits

In addition to developing a programme-level network, it is important to explicitly define the management structure and responsibilities for the programme. Such a structure is shown schematically in Figure 9.2.

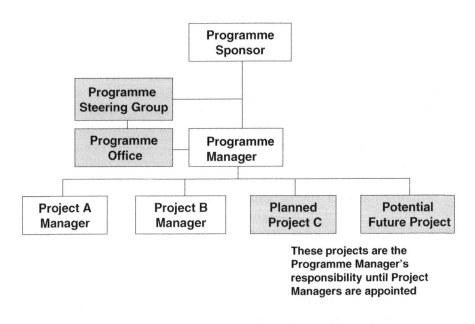

(adapted from OGC Guidelines – Managing Successful Programmes)

Figure 9.2: Outline structure for programme management

The roles as shown are variants on the roles of project sponsor and business project manager described in Chapter 7, however, given the greater scope and uncertainties inherent in programmes, there are some essential differences. First, executive sponsorship relates to the overall programme and a programme manager, or director, should be appointed, as well as business project managers for each of the projects. The skills and abilities required to be a programme manager include, but go beyond, those of a good project manager. He or she will require what Partington *et al.* (2005) describe as 'higher order conceptions and competences'. These enable a programme manager to cope with the ambiguities and conflicts that inevitably arise in large programmes and know when it is necessary to be directive, achieve consensus or reconcile conflict among stakeholders.

While project managers can usually rely on adherence to a project management methodology to judge how well the project is progressing, a programme manager has to be aware of the broader organizational context within which all of the projects have to be accomplished. It is also likely that the programme manager will need to be very senior, in order to have sufficient credibility and authority to gain the respect of the project managers.

Second, since almost all programmes will involve changes in many parts of the organization, many of which cannot be defined at the outset, the sponsor and programme manager will need to consult and be advised by a range of other senior managers from the areas involved. This is described here as a 'programme steering group', which should be involved in all the investment and priority-setting decisions that have to be made as the programme evolves. As stated earlier, some of the projects will not be justified as standalone investments, and the steering group will need to assess the combined business cases and how they deliver the objectives of the programme.

As the programme evolves, more will be known about the later projects. This implies that the membership of the steering group will also need to evolve over time as the emphasis of the programme changes, especially as development activities reduce and implementation gathers momentum.

In most cases, the programme manager, sponsor and steering group will also need the support of a Programme Office to collect, collate and interpret all the relevant information across the projects. This might be accomplished by an existing organizational Project Management Office (PMO), as discussed in Chapter 7, but for large programmes a dedicated Programme Office is often necessary. It would normally be the job of the Programme Office or PMO to maintain the benefit register discussed earlier and also to ensure that all the benefits are accounted for once, and once only, in all project business cases.

Managing the IS/IT project investment portfolio

In the benefits management surveys mentioned earlier in the book (Ward *et al.*, 2007), we also asked how satisfied organizations were with the way they managed the overall portfolio of IS/IT projects. The majority of the organizations surveyed (90%) carried out some form of portfolio management, but 60% of these stated that they were not satisfied with how well it was done. The levels of satisfaction with different aspects of portfolio management are shown in Table 9.1.

When deciding on new investments:

- All the organizations in the survey take into account *desirability factors* – positive arguments for the investment, including return on investment and strategic alignment.
- Only a minority include *feasibility factors* – affecting whether the project is likely to succeed and the effects of adding an additional project to the plans, including investment size, risks, using shared resources and project interdependencies.

The more successful organizations (levels 3 and 4 in the maturity analysis in Chapter 7) do take into account feasibility factors, whereas the less successful tend only to consider desirability factors.

Table 9.1: Levels of satisfaction with portfolio management practices

	Stated rationale for PPM	Not satisfied with the current approach
Strategic alignment of projects	90%	41%
Preventing resource over-commitment	88%	42%
Priority setting	81%	42%
Value maximization	70%	69%
Balancing investment risks	38%	49%

Governance and portfolio management

Portfolio management is an integral component of governance, since making the wrong investments or not realizing the business value from the investments made can seriously impact both organizational performance and the achievement of future strategy. Table 9.1 suggests that organizations find that this is not an easy task when they are making many different types of IT investments, delivering a range of benefits and involving varying levels of business risk.

> 'Successful IT portfolio management techniques change the conversation from technical to strategic considerations.' *Weill and Aral (2006)*

Effective governance is required to ensure that the organization does not waste its funds and resources on investments that do not adequately contribute to the business. It also has to ensure that, in the worst case, the organization does not incur disadvantages or become uncompetitive due to lack of investment in key operational and support systems and essential infrastructure. Therefore, it must not only be reactive, vetting and approving investments as they arise, but also proactive in ensuring that the overall portfolio of current and planned investments supports the strategic priorities of the business.

Most organizations realize that making the right decisions requires both accurate and reliable information about each of the investments and also collective agreement at a senior management level that the mix of investments is using organizational resources in the most appropriate ways. This complexity means that rarely, if ever, can the decisions involved be delegated to one individual and normally some form of investment board or steering committee is set up to ensure that the specific investments made, in combination, contribute effectively to achieving the organization's strategy. The term 'investment board' is used throughout the rest of this discussion to mean a group of senior managers charged with deciding on the contents of the IS/IT investment portfolio and therefore, by implication, responsible for priority setting and defining the appropriate level of overall IS/IT spend on new investments.

The basic terms of reference for the group can be considered as ensuring that:

- There is an information systems strategy that expresses the areas where investment will have the most beneficial contribution to business strategy.
- The organization has, or can acquire or develop, the required IS/IT resources and capabilities to deliver the critical components of the IS strategy in the timescale needed.
- All projects that require significant resources or funds are approved based on comprehensive and rigorous business cases supported by adequate evidence that the benefits plans are deliverable.
- When contention for resources occurs, as it inevitably will, decisions to allocate or reallocate funds and resources are based on achieving the highest level of overall business benefit possible from the resources available. This may, from time to time, mean removing resources from existing projects or even cancelling some, because their contribution is insufficient compared with new opportunities available.
- All investments are reviewed after implementation, so that the benefits achieved from the overall investment plan can be assessed and that lessons learned are taken up by other projects to improve the quality of benefits plans and, as a consequence, the overall value realized.

The threshold level for requiring the investment board to approve expenditure will vary from organization to organization and setting it at a low level will not only increase the work of the board, but also involve it in considering projects that demean its role. It should also be recognized that whatever level is set will encourage large numbers of investments to be estimated to cost just below the threshold! Therefore, the board should also review the overall IS/IT budgets from time to time.

Where projects are a part of a major programme, some of the responsibilities of the investment board can be delegated to the programme board, providing it is adopting the same rigorous approach to investment management. However, it needs to retain its oversight role, since new or emergent opportunities may provide a better return than existing programmes.

Equally, the governance of many smaller investments, especially support applications, can be delegated to line managers who have to justify them financially within an allocated budget. Similarly, the approval of high potential funds can be made within a budget reserved for R&D activities. All the investment board needs to know is whether the resources absorbed by these investments are preventing more significant investments from proceeding.

Setting priorities

Not only do all investments have to be assessed on their individual merits, they need to be compared with alternative investments available, including existing ongoing projects and emergent opportunities. To do this, the board must establish rules by which it will determine the priorities and also make those rules and the reasons for its decisions known. It will also need to have a full set of information available when making approvals to prevent investments being considered in isolation. This is often provided by a Project Management Office (PMO), which both vets the proposals to check their validity before submission to the board and provides the additional information required to ensure any issues of relevance to a decision are not overlooked.

The development of an investment board by a major telecommunications company is described in Box 9.2.

This example implies that a governance process which insists on the rigorous use of a benefits management approach makes the task of

---

Box 9.2: Priority setting at a major telco

A major telecommunications company established an investment board to oversee its IS/IT projects, which totalled over £250 m per annum and the majority of which were components of strategic change programmes. The programme directors were required to submit regular reviews of the overall business cases for their programmes in order to obtain continuing funding. In addition, each business case and benefits plan was peer reviewed by another senior manager, not associated with the project, who advised the board on the rigour used to build the business case and change plan. This was in addition to the work of the PMO, whose remit was to vet the evidence supporting the claimed benefits. As a result, the board received high quality input to its decision making and the whole organization had increased confidence in the decisions it made.

The board was equally demanding regarding the submission of post-implementation benefits review reports. Imposing stringent disciplines and cross-checks meant that very few weak business cases or reviews were ever put forward to the board.

managing the investment portfolio somewhat easier, since the projects that cannot provide adequate evidence of benefits do not get approval. However, there are some additional techniques that can assist this process further.

The applications portfolio for classifying IS/IT projects according to their expected contribution to the organization is a valuable technique for informing the investment board of the implications of choices between alternative projects. All current projects and programmes being put forward for approval should be presented to the board with a full business case and benefits plan. Other, more emergent ideas for investment, which are likely to be in the high potential quadrant, cannot be the subject of such detailed assessment but still require a reasoned argument explaining why they should be considered.

A simplified example in Figure 9.3 includes both individual projects, some of which are interdependent, and programmes that contain a number of projects. The two programmes, customer relationship

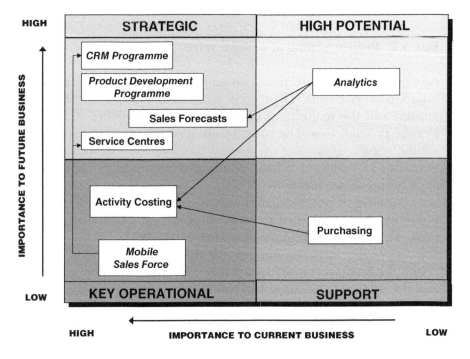

Key: Italics = projects and programmes underway   normal = planned projects

Figure 9.3: Example of an applications investment portfolio

management and new product development, were instigated at executive level to directly address a number of strategic drivers, while the projects were initiated through the IS planning process. Projects and programmes that are underway are shown in italics. These require an update of the business cases at regular intervals when the investment board reviews the overall plan or if priorities need to be reassessed. The other projects shown require decisions on whether to approve funding for the project to proceed or defer a decision until a later date, due to the need to reserve funds for other projects.

In some organizations, funds are not always the constraining factor; it is the availability of critical resources, people or skills. Scarcity in any of these may affect the timing of investments. Some projects will be in competition for the same resources whereas others will not and could go ahead sooner even if they promised less net benefit. The portfolio view does not provide rules for such decisions, but allows the context within which a particular decision is made to be understood, such that funds and resources are not committed prematurely to low-value projects.

Another variant on the approach includes the consideration of the relative value of projects and the level of risk involved (Jeffrey and Leliveld, 2004). This matrix is shown in Figure 9.4, together with the most likely locations for the different application portfolio categories.

For strategic projects, the decision to be made is whether it is a priority investment, with high certainty of benefit delivery, or if commissioning an R&D evaluation is needed to confirm the value. Many key operational investments are also likely to produce significant benefits, but some may be able to be deferred in order to use funds on more urgent or higher return options. While some support investments are likely to provide a significant financial return at low risk, many will be able to be postponed, if strategic or key operational investments require resources or funding first, since efficiency benefits will still be available at a future date. Having undertaken an R&D or pilot project for a high potential investment, it should become clear whether the organization could expect significant value or if they should not invest.

Managing the investment portfolio is not merely about the approval of funding and setting priorities, it includes ensuring that the range and pattern of investments reflects the business priorities. It also involves assessing whether the overall plan is the best way of using the resources, over time, to achieve the maximum set of intended benefits. This requires an understanding of the dependencies between projects and the relative risks involved. To increase the overall level of benefits

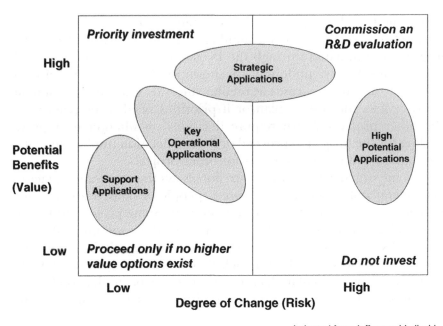

(adapted from Jeffrey and Leliveld,

Figure 9.4: A portfolio approach to funding decisions

realized, the portfolio of investments should be balanced carefully between high-value but high-risk, and lower-value projects, where the certainty of benefit delivery is higher. It would, of course, be ideal for all investments to be high-value, low-risk, but this is rarely, if ever, the case.

Links to drivers

More detailed information about the investments and their relevance to particular business drivers is also required in order to assess the relative priorities of investments in the same segment of the portfolio. The relationship between the investments and the drivers should be understood clearly, in case the drivers change and the investment plan has to be revised to realign the IS/IT contribution to the changing business priorities.

Table 9.2 shows such information for the example portfolio shown in Figure 9.3 (in Figure 9.3, the projects and programmes in italics are

Table 9.2: Linking projects and programmes with business drivers

Drivers/projects and programmes	Cost reduction	Customer service	Safety legislation	Sales growth	Staff retention	New product development	Costs, dependency and comments
CRM programme							Cost £1.2m
Project A	**High**			*Low*			90% done
Project B	Med	**High**					50% done
Project C	*Low*	Med		**High**			Project A
Project D		**High**		Med			Projects B, C and 3
Prod. development programme							Cost £800k
Project A			**High**	Med		*Low*	80% done
Project B				**High**		**High**	Project A
Project C			Med	*Low*		**High**	Projects A and B
Project 1: Sales forecasts (strategic)				**High**		Med	Cost £600k, Project 6
Project 2: Service centres (strategic)	**High**	**High**		Med			Cost £750k, Project 3
Project 3: Mobile sales force (key operational)	Med	Med	Med	**High**		Med	Cost £400k, 70% done
Project 4: Activity costing (key operational)	**High**			Med		Med	Cost £250k, Projects 5 and 6
Project 5: Purchasing (support)	Med		*Low*				Cost £150k
Project 6: Analytics (high potential)	?			?		?	Cost £25k, Pilot for Projects 1 and 4

already underway, whereas the others have yet to start). This table includes the strategic drivers, the contribution of the projects to each driver (high, medium or low), progress to date and the estimated overall costs of the investment. Additional information such as project start and expected end dates could also be shown. For the two major programmes, the contribution of each of the projects is shown, since, although it may be a high priority now, some of the later elements or phases of the programme may become less important if the business imperatives change.

The links between investments and drivers can also be presented in the form of a high-level network, as shown in Figure 9.5.

Presenting the portfolio of investments in a high-level network highlights critical dependencies and the degree to which the business drivers are being addressed by the investment plan. For example, as shown in Figure 9.5, although the purchasing project does not contribute major benefits, it is an enabler of the activity costing project. Before deciding on funding it, the degree to which the benefits of the activity

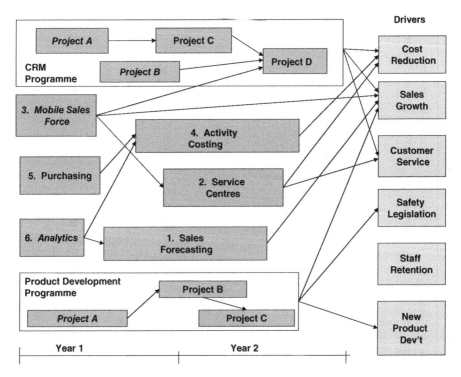

Figure 9.5: The investment plan dependencies

costing project would be reduced if the purchasing project was deferred or cancelled should be considered. The mobile sales force project, in addition to providing significant direct benefits, is an enabler of two others, including part of the CRM programme. Ensuring that it is adequately resourced to enable its timely and successful completion should be a high priority, even if other projects have to be deferred.

In this example the investment board should be concerned that although a number of investments address five of the drivers, no investments are underway or planned to address the remaining driver: *staff retention*. By definition, a business driver implies that it is an issue that the organization must address. The board should consider whether any change programmes or IS/IT projects could be made to improve the organization's performance in respect of, in this case, improving staff retention. Alternatively, the organization's executive should revisit the rationale they used to determine that staff retention was actually an important business issue.

Benefits management lite

Although the investment board can only accurately assess a project when the full business case has been developed, not all decisions can be made on that basis. The timings of business problems or opportunities that require investment are unpredictable and organizations must be able to respond quickly and coherently to new choices as they arise. In many organizations it is these emergent opportunities that cause repeated disruption to existing plans, resulting in funding and resourcing uncertainties and frequently changing priorities.

It is possible that new options would be better potential investments than those already in progress. To be fully effective, the portfolio management approach should also allow new options to be included, even though they may not have been fully evaluated.

To overcome this problem, a number of organizations have introduced a simpler, cut down variant on the first stages of the benefits management process, which allows a rapid appraisal of new options. This is perhaps best described as *benefits management lite*. It could be argued that all new options and ideas could be considered high potential projects to be tested and evaluated through an R&D approach. However, many will not be particularly innovative and will not, therefore, justify in-depth exploration. Those that genuinely have the potential to deliver strategic advantage need to be identified as early as possible and an R&D phase commissioned as a priority. If there is contention for particular resources or a need for extra R&D funding, this new opportunity should be compared with other current high potential projects to determine whether it should take priority.

The remaining emergent investments need a quick, but incisive, evaluation to determine whether the benefits available are likely to be worth the costs and risks, particularly when compared to existing investments. The purpose is not to make a decision about the new investment, but to decide whether to delay decisions about better-formulated projects until a comparable business case can be developed. It would not be appropriate, based on this simplified evaluation, to stop already approved projects from proceeding.

Figure 9.6 describes the essentials of this light-touch approach, for both technology-based opportunities (in italics) and business-based opportunities. It contains all the components of the benefits dependency network, but only requires a summary of the main benefits and changes, sufficient to determine its portfolio positioning. This allows

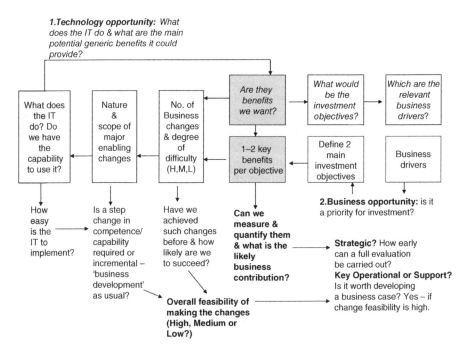

Figure 9.6: Benefits management lite to assess potential investments

it to be compared with other alternative investments of the same type. If it is a new technology opportunity, the first stage is to identify the potential benefits it offers in relation to the business drivers. If they are significant, the second step is to assess the organization's capability to deploy the technology in the short term and the extent of the business changes needed to achieve the potential benefits. If it is a business-based idea, it should have been derived from the drivers and the purpose of the assessment is to define the main benefits that could be realized, the extent of the changes and if the necessary technology is already available or can easily be acquired and deployed.

In both cases, the resulting argument for considering the investment further is based on the contribution and relevance of the potential benefits to the business drivers and the estimated feasibility of achieving them (high, medium or low). The assessment of the ability to accomplish the changes should be based on the organization's previous experience of achieving similar changes successfully. This appraisal will only be rigorous enough to commission the work needed to produce a full business case or decide not to pursue the investment further.

Project portfolio management in practice

In 2010 we carried out a research project, funded by the Chartered Institute of Management Accountants (CIMA), to explore the use of Project Portfolio Management (PPM) by organizations during the prevailing difficult economic conditions. During economic downturns uncertainty increases and organizations have fewer resources to invest in new business projects and programmes. This makes investment selection more difficult and more critical. Some projects may be important in achieving cost savings, sustaining revenue or improving aspects of performance on which the survival of the organization may depend. So it becomes more important than ever for organizations to be able to identify and prioritize the projects that will deliver maximum benefits to the organization. The findings from that research are outlined in Box 9.3 and are discussed in detail in the published research report (Daniel *et al.*, 2011).

Summary

Organizations of all types are increasingly undertaking interrelated projects and large-scale programmes of change. As described in this

Box 9.3: Project portfolio management in practice – findings from research

For the purposes of the research, PPM was defined as 'managing a diverse range of projects and programmes to achieve the maximum organizational value within resource and funding constraints', where 'value' implies not only financial value but also includes delivering a range of benefits which are relevant to the organization's chosen strategy. We carried out five case studies on different organizations of different sizes in a range of business sectors: News and Media, Professional Services, Insurance, Pharmaceuticals and Business and Technology Services (B&TS). All the firms had either introduced or changed their approach to PPM since 2008 with the purpose of increasing the value from project investments and avoiding wasting increasingly constrained resources. The main findings from the study were:

1. All five organizations stated that identifying and selecting the 'right' projects was at the heart of their rationale for PPM. 'Right' meant both contributing to the business strategy *and* being feasible to achieve successfully.
2. All the organizations included multiple criteria in their appraisal of projects and, importantly, this now included a balance of both *desirability* (strategic alignment, ROI, IRR, forecast benefits) and *feasibility* (resource availability, business risks). In the past, the organizations only tended to consider desirability criteria – was it worth doing? This may partly explain the level of project failure all the firms said they had experienced previously.
3. Previous research has shown that most organizations identify and manage risks within projects, but few carry out risk analysis at the level of the portfolio. The organizations studied recognized the benefits of being able to address risk both within projects and across the portfolio.

    For example, the insurance firm identified when there was a risk to the success of projects due to other projects impacting the same part of the organization at the same time. They could then postpone or even cancel particular projects to avoid disruption from too many changes to the relevant business areas and hence reduce the risk of both project failure and business performance problems.

4. Organizations often find it difficult to stop projects once they have been started. All five organizations explained that, prior to introducing the new PPM processes they had rarely cancelled approved projects, even when they were no longer worthwhile. The media firm described how bringing projects together in the portfolio allowed it to identify when projects were claiming the same benefits. They could therefore avoid authorizing projects that would not deliver additional benefits.

A number of themes stood out across the case studies, which demonstrate the value of PPM and offer some guidance to other organizations:

> 'The ultimate test of effective PPM is killing poor projects and explaining why.' *CIO of the media company*

- All the organizations believed that PPM improved their decision making about which projects to undertake and which to postpone or not pursue. They also believed that their approach ensured that resources were not wasted on projects that did not contribute to the strategic objectives of the organization or were unlikely to succeed.
- All the organizations would prefer to use their organizational strategy to identify projects. This requires the strategy to be sufficiently specific to allow necessary projects to be identified, which is difficult to achieve in uncertain times, as the strategy needs to be adapted frequently in response to changing conditions.
- Whilst strategic alignment is given as the main criterion for project identification, prioritization and scheduling are based on resource availability.
- All the organizations said that the introduction of PPM had led to better accountability and control of the projects themselves – fewer over-runs on time and cost or delays due to resource or funding issues.
- The organizations described how PPM increased transparency – making visible which projects are being undertaken and what

(*Continued*)

resources have been committed. However, they recognized that it was challenging to decide what proportion of projects to include in the portfolio.

- PPM is effective in improving investment decisions and project performance, but only if it is supported by comprehensive, enforced governance processes, rigorous investment cases and good control and reporting of project progress and achievements.

chapter, the benefits management tools and frameworks enable organizations to understand the interdependencies between multiple projects and the implications for benefit delivery and achieving the programme objectives. This is important as there is a risk that important benefits may fall between projects, depend on the successful delivery of earlier benefits or be duplicated by different projects. In large programmes it can be difficult to specify all the final benefits expected with much certainty, and the benefits plan will need to be revised as more becomes known about the achievable benefits.

Given the significant number of projects and programmes in most organizations, governance processes must be robust and sustained consistently over time. As well as regularly monitoring progress, a key element of governance is making appropriate investment decisions. Statistics continue to show that the majority of IS/IT projects fail to deliver the expected benefits. While much of this is due to poor implementation, poor investment selection also plays a part. However, such decisions have to be made with the best available knowledge about alternative uses of resources and funds. It is therefore important that management is presented with adequate information about the choices in a consistent way so that such comparisons can be made. Benefits management, coupled with the use of a portfolio management approach, can allow such consistency to be achieved across diverse projects and programmes.

The final chapter broadens the application of benefits management and considers the process of strategy development and implementation as potentially a process of identification and delivery of benefits to the organization and its stakeholders. How the use of the benefits management frameworks and tools can help is exemplified and the insights such an approach can offer are discussed. The chapter also considers the application of benefits management to newer areas of IT, such as mobile technologies and green computing.

Chapter 10

Creating a better future

In this chapter the key characteristics of the benefits management approach are summarized and further evidence of the improved outcomes resulting from the use of the approach is described, including a comparison of two projects in one organization. The first project did not take a benefits management approach and produced very few benefits; the second project, which did use the benefits management process, not only delivered all the expected business benefits, but also changed the relationship between the business managers involved and the IT function, to the benefit of all future projects. From being thought of previously as a high-cost/low-value unit, the IT function became viewed as a strategic capability that could significantly enhance the company's competitive position.

Investments in IS/IT projects and other change programmes are ways of improving organizational performance and creating new strategic options and capabilities. If an organization adopts a benefits management approach to managing its complete investment portfolio, it is effectively using it to manage the implementation of significant components of its business strategy. As a result, some organizations have seen the value of using the same frameworks, tools and techniques as a way of helping the formulation and improving the implementation of organizational strategies. Extending the use of the benefits management approach to strategy formulation and implementation is discussed in this chapter.

To conclude the book, we turn our attention to the future. We consider the future of IS and IT within organizations, with particular regard to envisaged developments, the nature of the potential benefits and the implications for their realization. Speculating on the future is always a hazardous business, so to reduce the inherent risks we have based the discussions on the views of many researchers and experts in the field.

The continuing challenge of IS/IT projects

Traditionally, attempts to increase the value derived from IS/IT investments have focused on improving the management of defining, developing or acquiring and implementing technology and the changes needed to utilize it effectively. Existing methodologies reflect established best practices and enable activities such as systems development and project management to be managed effectively, but they do not directly address many of the organizational issues that arise in most IS/IT projects.

To address these challenges, an organization needs to develop competences that enable it to identify how and when to use IS/IT to improve its performance and then deliver those improvements. The nature of those competences was described by Mata *et al.* (1995), who found that many issues related to IT, such as technology, access to capital and technical IT skills, could not provide sustained competitive advantage. However, they did find that the capability of managers to conceive of, develop and exploit IT applications in a way that supported or enhanced the activities of their business were skills that took time to develop and could provide a source of sustained competitive advantage. Developing these skills depended on the ability of IT managers and other functional managers to work together to understand the particular context of the organization and use this combined knowledge to develop appropriate new systems. Having a coherent and effective approach to managing the benefits of its investments can be considered a critical competence for an organization.

Characteristics of the benefits management approach

The characteristics of the benefits management approach, as incorporated in the process and the tools presented in this book, are summarized below. These characteristics, which can be considered the key success factors for identifying and delivering benefits, are:

- Ensuring that the links between IS/IT investments and business strategic priorities are explicitly stated and understood.

- A clear understanding that benefits only occur from active involvement of business managers in defining and owning those benefits and carrying out the changes that deliver them.
- Business cases have to be realistic, reflecting the ability of the organization to realize, as well as identify, the benefits.
- Not all investments will be able to be justified financially. However, the ability to explicitly measure the benefits is essential to their delivery.
- The business case should be based on evidence that shows how the value of each benefit was derived.
- When the investment involves significant innovation, it may be necessary to pilot the new ways of working and prove the technology, in order to be confident that the benefits can actually be achieved.
- Achieving benefits requires the sustained commitment of business resources and extends beyond the delivery of the new systems and technology.
- Reviewing the benefits that are, and are not, realized from each investment is essential if an organization is to increase the value it obtains from all of its IS/IT investments.
- The 'softer' benefits that accrue to individual stakeholders are often important prerequisites for the achievement of the 'harder' organizational or business benefits. Understanding, attending to and overtly addressing the interests and perceptions of stakeholders are essential aspects of the change management and benefits realization activities.
- Implementations should be phased, if possible, to deliver some benefits as early as possible – the 'quick wins' – and sometimes these are benefits that require business changes rather than major technology implementation.

We know, from our work with a wide range of organizations that they appreciate the relevance of these points. Many have subsequently changed how they plan, justify and manage investments in IS/IT based on the benefits management approach.

The value of the process

Our own experience, corroborated by independent research, has shown that the adoption of a benefits management approach results in projects that are more successful than those carried out without such

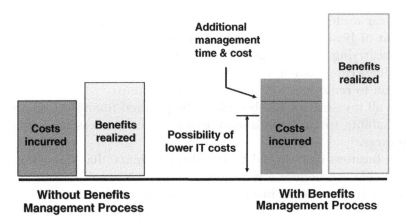

Figure 10.1: The value of benefits management

an approach. In making this assessment, our measure of success is that used by DeLone and McLean (2003); that is, the net benefits realized. Figure 10.1 was derived from actual investments undertaken in a major pharmaceutical company. They analysed a number of IS/IT investments to which the benefits management approach had been applied and compared these to earlier investments to which it had not.

The numbers have been removed from this comparison, due to sensitivity around the large sums that are often involved in investments in this sector. However, the comparison clearly shows that the benefits management approach resulted in greater benefits. The comparison only included the benefits to which a financial value could be attributed, but there was also a concomitant increase in the non-financial benefits realized.

It can be seen that use of the benefits management process can increase the costs of some investments. The additional cost involved is that of management time: the time spent by business managers and IS/IT colleagues working together to develop a coherent and agreed benefits plan, monitoring progress against that plan and finally reviewing the outcomes of the project. However, this additional management time produces a proportionally greater increase in the net benefits actually realized.

Although an additional management cost may be incurred, this can often result in the reduction of other costs, particularly IT costs, as shown in Figure 10.1. This can arise for three reasons:

- The development of a robust benefits plan early in the investment cycle identifies projects that do not yield sufficient benefits and these can be stopped before significant sums are spent.
- The logic of the right-to-left working of the benefits dependency network is to ensure that all activities in the project are driven by business need. As discussed in Chapter 4, this results in identification of the IT 'sufficient to do the job' and so can avoid the commonly encountered problem of organizations developing or buying additional IS/IT functionality that has no real business value. This not only increases the cost but also often slows down implementation, thereby deferring the realization of some of the available benefits. Although there is no rigorous research to support the statistic, many observers have suggested that organizations often use less than 20% of the features or functions of software they purchase.
- In some cases, adopting this approach enables organizations to appreciate that they can realize the benefits they want, simply by making changes to working practices in order to use existing IS or IT better, rather than needing to invest in additional hardware or software.

A brief case history of the implementation of an enterprise-wide system within one organization is given in Box 10.1. The implementation occurred in two phases – the first did not make use of the benefits management approach while the second phase did.

Using benefits management to formulate and implement strategy

Probably the simplest of the many definitions of business strategy is that of Porter (1980): '*An integrated set of actions aimed at increasing the long-term well-being and strength of the enterprise*'. In order to achieve this, the enterprise must satisfy the requirements of a wide range of stakeholder groups, including those who fund the enterprise and those who work in it. Therefore, a possible equivalent definition could be: '*An integrated set of actions aimed at providing benefits over the long term to enterprise stakeholders*'. This perspective is particularly relevant for public sector, mutually owned and not-for-profit organizations, but can also be appropriate for commercial corporations.

If this view is taken, then each of the organization's strategic objectives should result in the provision of benefits to one or more groups

Box 10.1: Implementing enterprise systems at Ctel

Ctel provides systems and hardware for broadband IP networks for voice and data communications. Sales to large organizations are made directly to customers, while sales to smaller companies are made through resellers. The company also provides equipment and software to original equipment manufacturers (OEMs) for inclusion in their own networking solutions. Ctel has operations in over 70 countries, divided into two regions: Europe, the Middle East and Africa (EMEA) and North America.

Ctel's implementation of an enterprise system (ES) occurred in two phases, the first of which did not adopt a benefits management approach and the second of which did. By the time of completion, the first phase of the project was four times over budget and had taken twice as long as expected. It was also recognized that the project resulted predominantly in the delivery of a technical solution, with little benefit to the business. In contrast, the second phase of the investment realized the expected benefits and, importantly, involved business staff in a positive way that left them well disposed to use of the system and participation in future IS and IT projects.

Phase 1: Project Genesis: a global ERP implementation

The executive management of the EMEA region tasked a project team with evaluating options for implementing an ERP system.

This team recommended the adoption of software being used successfully within a recently acquired semiconductor business. When staff in Ctel's headquarters in North America learned of this project, several senior managers argued that the benefits of improved business integration through ERP would be even greater if Ctel deployed the same software organization-wide. Accepting this argument without a careful consideration of the expected benefits, the board approved a single, global implementation.

A complex project management structure, reflecting the regional and business unit structure, was created with the project management role being distributed across four separate project managers. Each project manager was given responsibility for implementation in specific business units, with a requirement to cooperate on technical matters. This was described by the EMEA project manager as encouraging a '*premature focus on technical issues*', rather than clearly evaluating the business benefits that might be expected and the changes to organizational processes and working practices that would be needed to realize them. Without a clear understanding of the benefits that they might expect, the business managers were reluctant to commit the resources that were needed for implementation. Instead they preferred to protect their own interests, which concerned maintaining the smooth running of their respective units.

Cooperation was eventually gained from the managers and their staff, however, the limited consultation was regarded as a sign of a technology-centred approach to implementation that neglected the impact on core business processes and working practices: '*to many of those in the business, it felt like it was being done to them, rather than they were involved or part of it.*' After much delay and considerable overspend, the software was implemented and went live without significant problems. Few stakeholder groups believed that they had benefited from the ERP implementation, as was observed: '*it's our old business on a new system.*'

Phase 2: Service management implementation in EMEA

Phase 2 involved the deployment of further modules in the EMEA After-sales Service Division. The approach witnessed during this phase was significantly different from that of phase 1. While the

(*Continued*)

geographic scope and the number of business activities involved were less than in phase 1, the modules implemented affected the most complex parts of the business and the version of the software installed had not, at that time, been installed in Europe by any other organization.

Unlike the first phase, phase 2 commenced with the EMEA senior management establishing a vision of why and how the service organization had to change, and how this could be achieved by implementing the new modules. There was an explicit statement of the intended benefits and an understanding that these would result from a combination of organizational, process and system changes.

As the project moved to the implementation stage, the project team presented the business case at workshops where stakeholder groups were extensively involved in discussing how the changes would be implemented and benefits realized. This stage, which lasted for over half the duration of phase 2, included developing a system prototype for demonstration to key business users and gaining their feedback about how implementation could be refined. Once technical and business changes were agreed, responsibility for achieving them was explicitly assigned to cross-functional teams, involving both field engineers and central service management staff, who committed to cooperate with each other to deliver them.

Also in contrast to phase 1, phase 2 was managed by a single senior business manager who had access to sufficient financial and other resources. As the changeover to the new system approached, key stakeholders were becoming concerned about the details of implementation and changes within their own areas. The project manager was able to discuss the implications with each stakeholder group and provide extra resources, where needed, to effect the necessary changes, thus avoiding any deterioration in services to customers.

A formal post-implementation review of the project gave a detailed account of the benefits achieved, both from a financial perspective and according to the views of key stakeholders. The project had been delivered on time and on budget, but, more importantly, almost all the intended benefits were achieved.

of stakeholders, such as its shareholders or its customers. In many ways this is similar to the concept of the balanced scorecard (BSC), which shows how a combination of objectives that meet the expectations of a number of stakeholders, if achieved, results in improved overall performance (Kaplan and Norton, 2001). In essence, the BSC suggests that investment in innovation leads to better products and services, which, in turn, capture more customer value through better processes. In combination, these produce more revenues at lower cost and therefore greater profits. However, there are more stakeholders than just customers and investors who can influence the outcome of the strategy, and they will be more willing to support the organization's actions if they, too, are beneficiaries of the strategy. Most notable are the employees, but modern organizations are also dependent on how well they satisfy the expectations of other interested parties. Typically, enterprise stakeholders include:

- Shareholders and other investors, such as partners or members in the case of mutual societies.
- Customers and consumers who benefit from the use of the products and services.
- Suppliers, distributors and other trading partners, who benefit from the income they receive by doing business with the organization.
- Employees who benefit not only financially but also from the skills they acquire, career development, job satisfaction and an enjoyable working environment.
- Government, which benefits directly from the tax revenues raised, but also from the overall improvements in economic and social welfare created by the organization.
- Regulators who ensure industry standards are complied with, to the benefit of society.
- The communities in which the organization operates benefit from the economic activity it generates and also from, in many cases, the provision of local amenities and sponsorship of social developments.
- Even competitors benefit, albeit indirectly, from the success of one another, due to the continuing improvements in standards of product and service quality. Having a competitor with a poor reputation or, worse, one that breaches the law, is detrimental to others, since it can tarnish the industry image and create fears and uncertainties in customers.

This is not meant to be a comprehensive list, but it is intended to show that there is a wide range of potential beneficiaries from an organization's activities. Also, few of these categories of stakeholders can be treated as homogeneous groups and most will have to be divided into segments or subgroups that reflect their different relationships with the enterprise and the benefits they are seeking from that relationship. Segmentation is commonly applied to customers, but can also be applied with useful effect to other stakeholder groups such as suppliers and employees.

Incorporating benefits management into strategic thinking

Figure 10.2 depicts how the benefits management approach can be applied to business strategy. Following an analysis of the business drivers, using a combination of techniques such as PEST, competitive forces and competence analysis, the organization establishes strategic

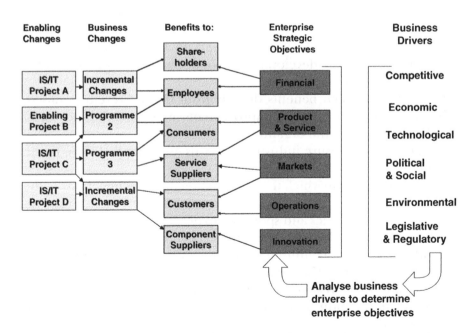

Figure 10.2: Business strategy described as a high-level benefits network

objectives for the future. These can then be expressed as the benefits that particular stakeholders will receive if and when the objectives are achieved. These benefits will be produced by both incremental improvements resulting from specific projects and/or step changes resulting from major programmes. The IS/IT projects may be either standalone, in the sense that they deliver a specific set of benefits to certain stakeholders, or they may be components of larger change programmes, as shown in the figure.

Once the strategy has been expressed as intended benefits to groups of stakeholders, the organization can define the types of projects or change programmes needed to achieve sets or combinations of those benefits. This is, of course, a complex task, but it does maintain a focus on benefits from the formulation of the strategy through to the scoping of projects, such that all project and programme activities will be related back through the network to intended benefits and, hence, the business objectives. This, in turn, means that projects should not have to search for benefits to justify themselves; instead they will be commissioned to realize subsets of the range of benefits that the organization wants to deliver. The feasibility and costs must also be determined, in order to decide whether the benefits can be justified or to decide between investment options. Of course, once this is done, the decision may be not to proceed, in which case the enterprise's strategic objectives will have to be revised.

This approach should also enable a more coordinated and structured approach to the ownership of benefits from the senior executives, who own the overall benefits that derive from the strategic objectives, and the managers, who are responsible for realizing subsets of those benefits from the programmes and projects. Equally, all staff involved in managing change and benefits realization will understand the contribution they are making to the organization's strategy. It also enables a problem described in Chapter 9 to be addressed more easily. In a complex multi-project, multi-programme environment, benefits can either be double-counted or not counted at all; that is, they are assumed to be the result of another project. This emphasis on strategic benefits management should enable a structured cascade from the top down, making it easier to align benefits to the most appropriate investment and avoid benefits 'falling down the cracks' between them.

As strategies evolve or drivers change, it should be possible, through the 'master network', to identify those existing investments that have increased or decreased priority or are even no longer required. Also, additional projects that address emergent needs not already covered can be defined. This does not imply that all strategies and the resulting activities should only be devised and managed top down, since that has been shown to be inadequate for modern organizations. Inevitably, many investments will be initiated in response to operational issues. Having a network of all the strategic initiatives and other projects will enable an organization to reconcile and coordinate changes resulting from both top-down and bottom-up initiatives.

The ways in which benefits management tools and techniques can be included in the strategic planning process can be summarized as follows:

- The organization should carry out a regular strategic analysis to understand and interpret its business drivers and establish or revise its medium- and longer-term objectives.
- Each objective should be interpreted in terms of the benefits that it could produce for different organizational stakeholders and how these benefits could be measured through key performance indicators (KPIs).
- By assessing the nature and mix of these objectives across the stakeholder groups, the range of changes required to deliver them can be identified and described.
- These changes can be analysed, synthesized and structured to enable programmes and projects to be designed and configured to achieve particular subsets of the benefits. It may be that some benefits are not feasible and the strategy as originally intended cannot be realized and needs revision.
- A high-level map of the projects and initiatives can show the dependencies among projects. Detailed benefits dependency networks and plans for each component should be developed.
- Business cases should be developed for each project and programme. A consolidation of these individual cases will therefore represent the business case for the implementation of the overall organizational strategy. The investment board, as described in Chapter 9, will then be able to assess more comprehensively the overall contribution of each case submitted for funding, based on its role in achieving the organization's strategy.
- The benefits management process should be used to guide implementation and review in each individual project and programme in order to ensure that the benefits of each are delivered.

Examples of benefits-driven strategies

This approach to strategy formulation and implementation has been adopted, at least in part, by a number of organizations that were already using the benefits management process for all major projects. An example is described in Box 10.2. The organization was faced with significant changes in its industry and used the benefits management techniques to help in developing a business strategy to address the new situation. In this case, using this approach made it possible to develop a long-term plan for the major IT infrastructure changes needed to support the new strategy. This benefits view of strategy can therefore help in the difficult task of justifying infrastructure investments discussed in Chapter 8.

Box 10.2: Benefits management use in business strategy formulation

Following its successful introduction on the services project at Ctel, as described in Box 10.1, it was used on all subsequent IS/IT projects and a number of change programmes.

Due to major changes in the industry and also a restructuring of the company in order to concentrate on its core products and services, the executive recognized the need to overhaul the business strategy. In particular, the company's R&D group had developed a new product range that would open up new markets, but would require the development of new ways of selling to customers and providing after-sales support. The new products would also cannibalize existing products and the organization realized it would have to manage the transition away from the old product set effectively.

Based on thorough market research and industry forecasts, the executive established a clear understanding of the drivers and agreed an initial set of objectives to be achieved in phases over two to three years. The benefits that could be expected to be achieved, by all the relevant stakeholders, over that period were identified and, where possible, ratified by discussions with key stakeholders. An initial priority was set to introduce the new products and services to existing customers first in order to prevent losing them to competitors.

(Continued)

This framed the main objectives of the first change programme, and five other programmes were also defined. Each programme was broken into projects, many of which were to create the new competences and capabilities to enable the new services, including a number of IS/IT application and infrastructure projects. Once all the projects and programmes had been defined in terms of the changes they would involve and measurable benefits they should deliver, the whole strategy was reappraised to determine whether there were alternative ways that could either realize the benefits earlier or achieve more ambitious targets overall. This reappraisal resulted in reducing the programmes to five and consolidating a number of the change activities and IT projects. It was agreed that to increase the flexibility of bringing about the changes, it would be advisable to implement all the major changes to the IT infrastructure as early as possible, so that it did not become a constraint to amending the priorities or sequence of the change programmes and associated projects.

Early development of the IT infrastructure proved to be a wise move because it soon became apparent that the initial plans for the programmes were constrained by the skills and resources available. The plans had to be revised to avoid some parts slipping back unacceptably. The strategy itself also had to be revised as economic conditions deteriorated and fewer customers than expected were willing to invest in new systems. As a result, the company was forced to focus on the cost-reduction components of the strategy, including the programme to rationalize its after-sales service by using more outside contractors. Fortunately, the benefits already realized from the field service system, described earlier, meant that the transition to external service provision was achieved without any customer service problems.

Future trends in IS/IT and their implications for benefits management

In this final section of the book, we consider some of the expected future trends in IS and IT. Many developments and changes in IS/IT functionality, capability and use are being forecast. It is therefore not possible for us to be exhaustive and we have concentrated our attention on those issues that appear to be most significant and that have particular implications for the realization of benefits from investments. Rather than turn to a single source for our view of the future, we have blended together the views of other academics and commentators. Our consideration of the future is consistent with the concerns of most managers and their organizations, i.e. the short to medium term, which we have taken to mean the next one to five years.

Mobile working

In 2010 the number of mobile Internet subscribers exceeded fixed Internet subscribers (Townson, 2011). This growth has been fuelled by the falling prices of mobile devices and their increasing functionality and also by improved data transmission rates. The growth of mobile devices in business is following a trend referred to as IT consumerization, where new IT becomes popular in the consumer market and is then adopted for business use. This, in turn, is leading some organizations to adopt a use-your-own-device policy, where employees are supported to use their own mobile devices for work applications.

While many types of employees, such as sales representatives and field engineers, have always worked away from a fixed location, many organizations are now considering this approach for a much wider range of their employees. Some organizations may adopt mobile working in order to allow staff to work from home, with the aim of providing a better 'work/life balance'. Others, with multiple locations, may use mobile working as a way of improving collaboration among their staff by enabling individuals to work at different sites as the need arises.

Mobile working appears to offer many advantages to both organizations and individuals, for example:

- productivity can be increased by reducing the time taken up by commuting or travelling between sites;
- staff can enter data or update records while in the field, providing a more accurate and even a real-time picture of organizational performance;
- access to complete and up-to-date information means that mobile staff are better able to meet the needs of customers or clients, thus increasing satisfaction.

However, organizations and individuals are also beginning to identify issues and challenges. Individuals find that, once provided with the ability to be connected to the organization *at any time*, the organization expects them to be connected *all of the time*. Work and home life can begin to blur. Many individuals enjoy coming to work in order to interact with others. Without such contact, they can begin to feel isolated, which may, in turn, reduce their loyalty to the organization.

One challenge organizations currently face when considering mobile working is being able to demonstrate an acceptable return on the investment, since it is difficult to identify the achievable benefits and ascribe a realistic financial value to them. We have earlier emphasized the importance of understanding the organizational context in which the IT-enabled changes are being introduced. The functionality offered by mobile technologies cannot simply be adopted by an organization as the expected benefits, since generic benefits do not exist. Rather, such functionality should be carefully considered in the particular context of the organization, its staff and their current ways of working. Reduced commuting is likely to be a benefit, but how this benefit is realized and by whom will vary. If the individual works for longer, then the organization benefits from the additional productivity. However, if the individual does not use the time saved for work, the organization may still benefit by having a less tired and more effective member of staff, but it is unlikely to be able to place a direct financial value on this.

> 'By enabling a field sales force to understand its performance vs. quota at all times of the day and wherever they were located . . . they outperformed their competitors.' *Townson (2011)*

The difficulty many organizations are currently experiencing in developing a robust business case for mobile working can be understood by appreciating that such projects should be considered high potential investments in most organizations: they may provide considerable advantage in the future, but as yet not enough is known. As discussed earlier in the book, high potential projects are unlikely to provide certainty about financial benefits until more work is undertaken to provide sufficient evidence. This exploratory approach to benefit identification is consistent with an iterative approach to development – in which high-level requirements are identified and prototypes developed for testing – that is appropriate for emerging and rapidly developing fields such as mobile applications.

Greater support for collaboration

The activities being carried out by organizations are becoming ever more complex. This increase in complexity and scale usually requires the organization to draw on a greater range of skills and involve more staff. As teams become bigger and more diverse, it is less likely that they will be able to be co-located or meet face to face regularly. Mobile working will further exacerbate this, with individuals preferring to work where it suits them, rather than being tied to a team location. Organizations are therefore seeking to use IS and IT to support collaborative working within and between dispersed, 'virtual' teams.

Griffith *et al.* (2003) considered the use of IS to support virtual teams. They found that while it could offer support for this way of working, it could also act as a *jealous mistress*, capturing the tacit expertise of individuals without offering them the opportunity to replace this. We would suggest that for IS and IT to support collaborative working successfully, it should offer benefits at three distinct levels: to the individual, to teams and to the organization. When developing a benefits plan, changes to working practices may need to be designed to ensure that benefits at all three levels are realized and balanced. For instance, although mobile technologies can allow all team working to be carried out remotely, saving the organization travelling expenses, it may be necessary to fund staff to have face-to-face meetings with colleagues and even longer periods of working together. This may be essential to developing the personal trust, which is often required to gain the individual- and team-level benefits that depend on sharing knowledge and ensuring that tasks are allocated appropriately and equitably.

Continued technology push

Technology and system vendors will continue to develop new products and enhance existing ones and try to convince organizations that they must invest in these new products either to keep up with competitors or to gain advantage. While some increases in product functionality or new products are of real benefit, others are of only marginal value and will only add to the considerable amount of functionality that is already not used in most applications. However, even if organizations are aware that they will get little benefit from upgraded functionality, they are often required to migrate to such versions as vendors limit or even stop their support for earlier versions.

Many organizations wanting to avoid the control of powerful software vendors have opted for open source solutions. Interestingly, in their study of the use of open source software (OSS) in a large-scale deployment in a hospital in the Republic of Ireland, Fitzgerald and

Kenny (2003) found that users became more interested and involved in the deployment when they learnt that it was OSS and were also more accepting of the limitations of the system than they were for systems from large vendors.

In applying the ideas within the benefits management process to the issue of technology push, it is useful to remember how the benefits dependency network was constructed starting with the investment objectives, which define the business need or demand. The network is developed from this, ending with an identification of 'technology that is sufficient to do the job'. This approach will help prevent investment in new systems and technology simply because they are available or because other organizations are investing in them. Rather, it will ensure that an organization understands how it can expect to realize benefits from the IS and IT it has identified as being useful.

Cost containment and demonstration of value

A perennial concern for senior managers in all types of organization is the continued increase in the sums spent on IS and IT. Despite the falling cost of processing power, data transmission and storage, organizations are spending ever-greater sums on IS/IT and this trend is expected to continue in the future. The growth in expenditure is, in part, due to the fact that organizations are using IT to carry out a greater range of organizational activities, but it is also fuelled by the continued sales push from technology vendors, as discussed previously.

This concern for value realized becomes particularly intense in difficult economic times, such as those following the global financial crisis of 2008. At such times, funding for new projects will be restricted and managers must be sure that they are investing in the 'right' projects; that is, those that are going to deliver their strategic objectives. The benefits management process can help with ensuring the alignment with strategic objectives, by explicitly demonstrating how the project investment objectives address the drivers acting on the organization.

At such times, managers will also want to leverage the most value they can from investments that have already been made. This places emphasis on the last two stages of the benefits management process: the review of the benefits realized and the identification of further benefits. As described earlier, one objective of the review is to establish those expected benefits that have not been realized, so that actions can then be put in place to recover them, where this is feasible. The identification of further benefits should also be given greater emphasis, particularly since it is often possible to identify new benefits that do not require additional investment in IS/IT but can be realized from changes in working practices or processes.

Continued growth in outsourcing and off-shoring

Many organizations are turning to outsourcing and off-shoring as a route to reduce costs and increase flexibility. It is expected that this trend will continue.

The increased value of outsourcing and off-shoring is expected to reflect not only increased volumes of work transferred to third parties, but also an increase in the complexity of the work. Figure 10.3 depicts an evolution of outsourced activities. Outsourcing typically commences with the transfer of routine activities, such as data entry and the operation of call centres. As organizations become more familiar with this way of operating, they are increasingly prepared to transfer more highly skilled and value-adding work. However, questions remain

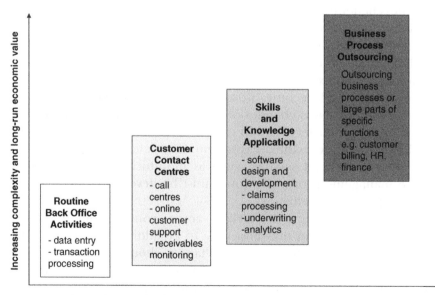

Figure 10.3: The evolution of outsourcing

as to the impact of the transfer of increasingly skilled and knowledge-based activities on the future innovative potential of the 'sending' organizations.

While outsourcing and off-shoring have many parallels, outsourcing refers to the transfer of activities to a third party organization. In contrast, in addition to describing the transfer of work to third parties overseas, off-shoring can also be used to describe the transfer of work to the overseas operations *within* an organization. In these cases the organization may be willing to transfer activities beyond those shown in Figure 10.3, including the transfer of research and new product development.

An example is provided by GE. At its John F. Welch Technology Centre in a suburb of Bangalore there are 1800 scientists and engineers undertaking research and development activities for all divisions of the organization. They are developing new products for GE and have helped to contribute to the 1000 patents filed by the Indian units of such firms at the US Patent Office over the last few years (Rai, 2003).

Chapter 8 considered a number of issues relating to the realization of benefits when adopting outsourcing of either IS/IT or entire business processes. The most fundamental and important of these is that the provider or supplier cannot be made responsible for the delivery of business benefits. Their traditional contribution is to provide IT and IS enablers or other enablers that function to the specified service level. They may also provide other enabling changes, such as the provision of a help desk or of training for staff. As organizations outsource increasingly complex and open-ended activities, such as entire business processes, these will become business as usual and hence should be represented as business changes on a dependency network. However, contracting for such services will not be sufficient to ensure business benefits are delivered to the organization. Competences in the management of such external services, such as monitoring of performance and the management of exceptions, must be developed and become ongoing operational activities.

Additional challenges of working across considerable distances, time zones and cultures may also have to be addressed. Specific enabling changes or ongoing business changes should be identified to address these and other issues that may arise and these should be included in the benefits plan. Hence, outsourcing may not reduce the competences required by an organization, rather, it might shift their nature from the traditional operations of the organization to the management of distributed and remote activities.

In their book *Gurus, Hired Guns and Warm Bodies,* Kunda and Barley (2005) note a tension that results from the use of hired staff to undertake increasingly complex work. They observe that the outsourcing and contracting market tends to turn staff, even those with particular experience and expertise, into commodities that can be purchased as and when required. Furthermore, the organization's employees often wish to see clear demarcations between such temporary staff and themselves, for example in the provision of office space or the latest equipment. However, to address the business issue being tackled, it is usually necessary for the hired staff to become highly involved and operate as part of the team. Enabling changes or ongoing business changes should be identified to address these competing forces, if the 'hired guns' are to contribute effectively without disaffecting existing employees.

Green computing

Many organizations wish to improve their environmental credentials (Siegel, 2009). This may be driven from a belief that it is the correct and responsible thing to do, or because they believe that it makes good business sense, lowering costs and attracting certain customer segments. Green computing refers to the design, manufacture, use and disposal of IS/IT in ways that minimize the impact on the environment (Kurp, 2008), and this is now part of many organizations' environmental strategies. These can include a wide range of activities, such as purchasing energy-efficient equipment, designing data storage centres that minimize the use of power and ensuring that obsolete equipment is responsibly recycled (Sayeed and Gill, 2010). It also includes investing in new applications that monitor, and sometimes control, the use of energy and emissions of environmentally harmful materials

Some benefits from green IT initiatives may be straightforward. For example, improvements in data centre layout and cooling may produce direct energy savings when considered over a number of years (Hemminger *et al.*, 2010). These energy savings can be calculated, allowing for business or activity growth, and a financial value produced.

Other green initiatives provide interesting challenges in identifying and managing the associated benefits, many of which are likely to be hard to measure, quantify or provide a financial valuation. Hence, whilst there may be an overall reduction in environmental impact, this can be difficult to express in terms of benefits to the organization. Whilst this may not be a problem for some organizations, others will find it difficult to secure investment funding, especially in tough economic times, if they cannot demonstrate benefits to the organization in addition to the general societal benefits.

Reports suggest that the greatest environmental impact from PCs arises from their manufacture. Hence, it is likely to be better for the environment to upgrade existing PCs, rather than buy new ones. However, in large organizations the costs of upgrading thousands of PCs are likely to be very high – both in terms of the new components and the labour costs involved. As suggested above, it may be thought that a well-publicized environmental policy will attract certain customer segments. Hence, the environmental benefit of upgrading PCs rather than buying new ones would contribute to attracting such customers. This may well be correct, but to be consistent with the approach to measuring benefits outlined in Chapter 5, evidence needs to be found to substantiate benefits such as increased customer numbers or increased sales. Other benefits that may accrue to the organization may be difficult to measure and hence should be considered *observable benefits*, such as greater motivation by IT staff since they are working in a department that is promoting socially responsible values (Jenkin *et al.*, 2011).

> 'Benefits that may arise from Environmental Social Responsibility include enhanced product differentiation, reputation/image enhancement, and improved relations with workers, customers, suppliers, government, and the community.' *Siegel (2009)*

Cloud computing

Cloud computing refers to the on-demand availability of IT hardware and software, such as applications, data storage, networking and processing (Armbrust *et al.*, 2010; Kushida *et al.*, 2011). These are provided via a Web browser over the Internet, or via Internet protocols in the case of private clouds, and allow access by a wide range of devices wherever such connections can be established.

The interest in cloud computing arises from the ability of organizations to access a range of applications and increased storage and processing capacity, without having to invest in and maintain the relevant hardware and software. Instead, the applications and capacity are provided by third party service providers and can be accessed on a subscription or pay-per-use basis (Creeger, 2009). It is suggested that such a service or utility approach to IT will lower the cost for individual organizations, allowing them to pay only for what they use. The main IT providers are making many of their infrastructure and application products available as cloud services. The ability to use a range of devices and to access the cloud from most locations is expected to allow individual users to be able to access the information and applications that they need to do their jobs wherever they are and regardless of which device they are using; that is, the systems are expected to become device- and location-independent (Marston *et al.*, 2011).

The ideas behind virtualization and cloud computing have been around for some time, but it is now feasible to operate major applications and data storage via the cloud, largely due to increased data download rates. Whilst the cloud promises certain benefits in theory, it is not yet clear that these will arise in practice. For example, the providers of cloud services claim that it will lower costs for organizations. However, this will depend on the pricing levels and structures adopted by the service providers (Durkee, 2010). Equally, the providers claim that the cloud offers organizations greater resilience, but again, this will depend on how the providers invest in and configure their hardware and software.

Whilst the claims made about cloud computing sound persuasive, organizations should be aware that this is still an emerging area and investments should therefore be considered high potential opportunities until there is clear evidence of the benefits and some of the apparent risks, such as information security, have been overcome. Given the early adoption stage of these technologies, organizations that do not feel comfortable being at the 'bleeding edge' of technology should adopt a fast follower approach. This could involve joining cross-industry groups to stay aware of technology developments and their implications and only investing when there is a better understanding of the long-term consequences of adoption and use plus demonstrated benefits.

Agility from IS/IT

Traditionally, IS/IT has been used mainly to improve organizational performance through its ability to increase the productivity of existing processes or create new, more effective and efficient processes. Hence, the focus has been largely on increasing organizational productivity.

Improved productivity, as typified by just-in-time manufacturing practices, suggests highly standardized approaches with the minimum of redundancy. However, in increasingly changeable and unpredictable business environments, organizations also need to be able to adapt quickly and effectively to changing business conditions – to become more 'agile'.

Agility can apply at two levels: the ability to respond accurately and quickly to changes in levels of activity, such as changes in demand, and the ability to use the resources it has available to create new business options in anticipation of changes in the business environment. In contrast to high productivity, high levels of agility imply the need for flexible approaches and also spare capacity, to be able to respond rapidly to changing demands. It also suggests the empowerment of staff in terms of being able both to recognize and respond to changing conditions.

This raises a number of issues and challenges for IS/IT investments and their management in the future, if they are to provide benefits across the spectrum of organizational productivity *and* organizational agility. It has already been suggested earlier in the chapter that the benefits realized by individuals and teams are important in making staff accept and use new systems and undertake the required changes. Such individual- and team-level benefits are therefore at least as important as organizational-level benefits. Identifying, measuring and realizing these benefits will require a different focus of attention, moving away from processes to the way people work individually and collectively. Organizational performance improvements will derive from both productivity gains and the flexibility of individuals to carry out a wider range of tasks. It would seem that, in the future, more attention should be paid to the overall mix of work an individual does, in order to understand how he or she can be more effective in performing all those activities.

In addition to allowing staff to work in ways that suit them, two other aspects of IS/IT investment become more significant when considering agility. The first is that resource flexibility, at both the individual and organizational level, requires an extensive and standard infrastructure, so that people can carry out all the tasks required without constraints or a long learning curve whenever they change roles or move jobs. This implies that an increasing proportion of IT investments will be infrastructural, either to create new capabilities or sustain performance. As previously discussed, the justification of infrastructure investments is an enduring problem, which requires some new ways of thinking now that it is integral to how almost every organization conducts its business.

The second implied challenge is that the move towards more dynamic capabilities requires extensive knowledge sharing and reuse across the organization. This includes the knowledge that has been captured in the form of proprietary information and also ensuring individuals can and do collaborate to share their personal knowledge. As with infrastructure investments, it is difficult to identify and then put in place specific actions to realize the benefits that result from investments in information resources and related retrieval and analysis tools. Again, unless there is greater understanding of how staff use information and make decisions, individually and collectively, it will be increasingly difficult for organizations to make information management investments that actually support the creation of new capabilities. Worse still, as suggested by the research by Griffith *et al.* (2003), inappropriate deployments of IS/IT with the intention of improving the use of organizational knowledge can actually produce the opposite effect.

A final word or two

The benefits management approach was developed to enable organizations to increase the business value realized from specific IS/IT investments. However, it can be, and is being, used to assess how well organizations are employing their IS/IT assets and to increase the benefits they can leverage from them, as well as to formulate, manage and implement strategic change programmes. It can even help formulate and implement business strategies themselves. Overall, this enables organizations to stop focusing on the *cost of ownership* of IT and start to understand the *value of ownership,* by first considering the potential benefits it can obtain from investments, rather than searching for sufficient benefits to justify the costs involved. Having a coherent and comprehensive approach to identifying and realizing the benefits of each of the IS/IT investments it makes is essential to understanding the value that IS/IT contributes to the organization.

However, this cannot happen unless that approach enables business managers and IT specialists to work together in new ways, to share their knowledge in order to identify the best ways to combine IS/IT implementation with business changes. This will ensure the maximum benefits are delivered and, importantly, it will allow the organization to learn from what it has and has not achieved.

The benefits management process, tools and techniques described in this book have been adopted by many organizations, because they provide a comprehensive, yet common sense, approach that business managers and IT specialists can easily understand, learn and use together.

It has also been said many times, by both groups, that working in this way, when compared with more traditional approaches to managing IS/IT investments, is also more *enjoyable*!

Glossary

Benefit owner   An individual who will take responsibility for ensuring that a particular benefit will be achieved. This usually involves ensuring that the relevant business and enabling changes progress according to plan.

Benefit streams   A set of related benefits and their associated business and enabling changes and enabling IS/IT.

Benefits management   The process of organizing and managing such that the potential benefits arising from the use of IS/IT are actually realized.

Business benefit   An advantage on behalf of a particular stakeholder or group of stakeholders.

Business changes   The new ways of working that are required to ensure that the desired benefits are realized.

Business and organizational drivers   Issues which executive and senior managers agree mean the organization needs to change – and the timescale for those changes. Drivers can be both external and internal but are specific to the context in which the organization operates.

Change owner   An individual or group who will ensure that an identified business or enabling change is achieved successfully.

Enabling changes   Changes that are prerequisites for achieving the business changes or that are essential to bring the system into effective operation within the organization.

Enabling IS/IT   The information systems and technology required to support the realization of the identified benefits and to allow the necessary changes to be undertaken.

Financial benefit   By applying a cost/price or other valid financial formula to a quantifiable benefit, a financial value can be calculated.

Investment objectives   A set of statements that describe what the organization is seeking to achieve from the investment. They should be a description of what the situation should be on completion of the investment.

Measurable benefit   This aspect of performance is currently being measured or an appropriate measure could be implemented. But it is currently not possible to estimate by how much performance will improve when the changes are completed.

Observable benefit   By use of agreed criteria, specific individuals/ groups will decide, based on their experience or judgement, to what extent the benefit has been realized.

Projects, programmes and portfolios

Project: A pre-defined scope of work delivered using existing capabilities to achieve agreed outputs in accordance with an authorized business case.

Programme: A dynamic collection of related projects and activities that, in combination, achieve agreed organizational objectives and emergent outcomes, including the creation of new capabilities.

Portfolio: A set of related and unrelated projects and programmes that compete for an organization's resources and funds.

Quantifiable benefit   Sufficient evidence exists to forecast how much improvement/benefit should result from the changes.

Stakeholder(s)   An individual or group of people who will benefit from the investment or are either directly involved in making or are affected by the changes needed to realize the benefits.

Why, what and how of a potential investment   *Why* is the investment being made – why does the organization need to change and how critical to its future is the successful management of the changes? *What* types of benefit is the organization expecting to achieve by making the changes – to reduce costs, improve operational performance, gain new customers, create a new capability, etc.? *How* can a combination of IT and business changes deliver those benefits at an acceptable level of risk?

References

Alshawi, S., Irani, Z. and Baldwin, L. (2003) 'Benchmarking information technology investment and benefits extraction', *Benchmarking: An International Journal*, **10**(4): 414–423.

Applegate, L. M. (1993) *Frito-Lay Inc. Strategic transition (A)*, Harvard Business School Case Study, Boston, MA.

Armbrust, M., Fox, A., Griffith, R., Joseph, A., Katz, R, Konwinski, A., Lee, G., Patterson, D., Rabkin, A., Stoica, I. and Zaharia, M. (2010) 'A view of cloud computing', *Communications of the ACM*, **53**(4): 50–58.

Avison, D. and Fitzgerald, G. (2002) *Information Systems Development: Methodologies, Techniques and Tools*, 3rd edition, London: Pearson Education.

Ballantine, J. and Stray, S. (1998) 'Financial appraisal and the IS/IT investment decision making process', *Journal of Information Technology*, **13**(1): 3–14.

Balogun, J. and Hope Hailey, V. (2004) *Exploring Strategic Change*, 2nd edition, Harlow: Pearson Education.

Bancroft, N. H., Seip, H. and Sprengel, A. (1998) *Implementing SAP R/3 – How to Introduce a Large System into a Large Organisation*, 2nd edition, Greenwich, CT: Manning Publications.

Barney, J. B. (1991) 'Firm resources and sustained competitive advantage', *Journal of Management*, **17**(1): 99–120.

Bell, S. and Wood-Harper, T. (1998) *Rapid Information Systems Development: Systems Analysis and Systems Design in an Imperfect World*, Maidenhead: McGraw-Hill Education.

Bendor-Samuel, P. (2000) *Turning Lead into Gold: The Demystification of Outsourcing*, Provo, UT: Executive Excellence Publishing.

Benjamin, R. I. and Levinson, E. (1993) 'A framework for managing IT-enabled change', *Sloan Management Review*, **34**(4): 23–33.

Brynjolfsson, E. and Hitt, L. M. (2000) 'Beyond computation: Information technology, organisational transformation and business performance', *Journal of Economic Perspectives*, **14**(2): 33–48.

Carr, N. (2003) 'IT doesn't matter', *Harvard Business Review*, **81**(5): 41–49.

Chang, L. and Powell, P. (1998) 'Towards a framework for business process re-engineering in small and medium-sized enterprises', *Information Systems Journal*, **8**(3): 199–215.

Checkland, P. and Holwell, S. (1998) *Information, Systems and Information Systems: Making Sense of the Field*, Chichester: John Wiley & Sons, Ltd.

Checkland, P. and Scholes, J. (1999) *Soft Systems Methodology in Action*, Chichester: John Wiley & Sons, Ltd.

Collis, D. J. and Montgomery, C. A. (1995) 'Competing on resources: strategy in the 1990s', *Harvard Business Review*, **73**(4): 118–128.

Cragg, P., Caldeira, M. and Ward, J. (2011) 'Organisational information systems competences for small and medium-sized enterprises', *Information and Management*, **48**: 353–363.

Creeger, M. (2009) 'CTO Roundtable: Cloud Computing', *Communications of the ACM*, **52**(8): 50–56.

Dai, C. X. Y. and Wells, W. G. (2004) 'An exploration of project management office features and their relationship to project performance', *International Journal of Project Management*, **22**(7): 523–532.

Daniel, E., Ward, J. and Franken, A. (2011) *Project portfolio Management in Turbulent Times*, CIMA Research Executive Summary Series, **7**(2): 51–52.

Davenport, T. H. (2000) *Mission Critical: Realizing the Promise of Enterprise Systems*, Boston, MA: Harvard Business School Press.

DeLone, W. H. and McLean, E. R. (2003) 'The DeLone and McLean model of information systems success: A ten year update', *Journal of Management Information Systems*, **19**(4): 9–30.

Dhillon, G. S., Caldeira, M. and Wenger, M. R. (2011) 'Intentionality and power interplay in IS implementation: the case of an asset management firm', *Journal of Strategic Information Systems*, **20**(4): 438–448.

Dobson, M. S. (2003) *Streetwise Project Management*, Avon, MA: Adams Media Corporation.

Doherty, N. F. and King, M. (2001) 'An investigation of the factors affecting the successful treatment of organisational issues in systems development projects', *European Journal of Information Systems*, **10**(3): 147–160.

Doran, G. T. (1981) 'There is a S.M.A.R.T. way to write management goals and objectives', *Management Review*, November.

do Valle, J. A., Silvia, W. and Soares, C. A. P. (2008) 'Project management office (PMO) – principles in practice', *ACEE International Transactions*, **PM.07**: 1–9.

Durkee, D. (2010) 'Why cloud computing will never be free', *Communications of the ACM*, **53**(5): 62–69.

Earl, M. J. (1989) *Management Strategies for Information Technology*, Englewood Cliffs, NJ: Prentice Hall.

Earl, M. J. (1992) 'Putting IT in its place: A polemic for the nineties', *Journal of Information Technology*, **7**(1): 100–108.

Eisenhardt, K. M. and Martin, J. A. (2000) 'Dynamic capabilities: What are they?' *Strategic Management Journal*, **21**(10–11): 1105–1121.

Farbey, B., Land, F. and Targett, D. (1993) *IT Investment: A Study of Methods and Practice*, Oxford: Butterworth-Heinemann.

Fitzgerald, B. and Kenny, T. (2003) 'Open source software in the trenches: Lessons from a large scale implementation', *Proceedings of 24th International Conference on Information Systems (ICIS)*, Seattle, December.

Galliers, R. D. and Leidner, D. E. (2003) *Strategic Information Management: Challenges and Strategies in Managing Information Systems*, Oxford: Butterworth-Heinemann.

Gates, W. (1999) *Business @ the Speed of Thought*, Harmondsworth: Penguin.

Gibson, C. F. (2003) 'IT-enabled business change: An approach to understanding and managing risk', *MIS Quarterly Executive*, **2**(2): 104–115.

Giordano, G., Lamy, A. and Janasz, T. (2011) 'Financial integration at a global insurance company', *Business Transformation Journal*, issue **1**: 52–59.

Grant, R. M. (1996) 'Toward a knowledge-based theory of the firm', *Strategic Management Journal*, **17**(2): 109–122.

Gregor, S., Martin, M., Fernandez, W., Stern, S. and Vitale, M. (2006) 'The transformational dimension in the realization of business value from information technology', *Journal of Strategic Information Systems*, **15**(3): 249–270.

Griffith, T. L., Sawyer, J. E. and Neale, M. A. (2003) 'Virtualness and knowledge in teams: Managing the love triangle of organisations, individuals and information technology', *MIS Quarterly*, **27**(2): 265–287.

Hares, J. and Royle, D. (1994) *Measuring the Value of Information Technology*, Chichester: John Wiley & Sons, Ltd.

Helfat, C. E. and Peteraf, M. A. (2009) 'Understanding dynamic capabilities: progress along a developmental path', *Organization*, **7**(10): 91–102.

Hemminger, C., Rogers, D. and Guster, D. (2010) 'Planning and managing the data center to green computing', *International Journal of Business Research*, **10**(4): 105–113.

Hill, C. and Jones, G. (1998) *Strategic Management. An Integrated Approach*, Boston, MA: Houghton Mifflin.

HM Treasury (2003) *PFI: Meeting the Investment Challenge*, London: The Stationery Office.

House of Commons, Public Administration Select Committee (2011) *Government and IT – a recipe for rip-offs: time for a new approach'*. London: The Stationery Office.

iSociety (2003) *Getting By, Not Getting On*, London: Work Foundation.

Jeffrey, M. and Leliveld, I. (2004) 'Best practices in IT portfolio management', *Sloan Management Review*, **45**(3): 40–50.

Jenkin, T., McShane, L. and Webster, J. (2011) 'Green information technologies and systems: Employees' perceptions of organizational practices', *Business & Society*, **50**(2): 266–314.

Johnson, G. and Scholes, K. (1999) *Exploring Corporate Strategy*, 5th edition, London: Prentice Hall.

Johnson, K. and Misic, M. (1999) 'Benchmarking: A tool for web site evaluation and improvement', *Internet Research*, **9**(5): 383.

Jordan, E. and Silcock, L. (2005) *Beating IT Risks*, Chichester: John Wiley & Sons, Ltd.

Jurison, J. (1996) 'Toward more effective management of information technology benefits', *Journal of Strategic Information Systems*, **5**(4): 263–274.

Kalakota, R. and Whinston, A. (1997) *Electronic Commerce: A Manager's Guide*, Reading, MA: Addison Wesley.

Kaplan, R. S. and Norton, D. P. (2001) *The Strategy-Focused Organisation: How Balanced-Scorecard Companies Thrive in the New Business Environment*, Boston, MA: Harvard Business School Press.

Knox, S., Maklan, S., Payne, A., Peppard, J. and Ryals, L. (2003) *Customer Relationship Management: Marketplace Perspectives*, Oxford: Butterworth-Heinemann.

Kohli, R. and Devaraj, S. (2004) 'Realizing the business value of information technology investments: An organisational process', *MIS Quarterly Executive*, **3**(1): 53–68.

Kresak, M., Corvington, L., Wiegel, F., Wokurka, G. and Williamson, P. (2011) 'Vodafone answers call to transformation', *Business Transformation Journal*, issue 2: 54–67.

Kumar, K., Van Dissel, H. G. and Bielli, P. (1998) 'The merchant of Prato – revisited: Toward a third rationality of information systems', *MIS Quarterly*, **22**(2): 199–226.

Kunda, G. and Barley, S. (2005) *Gurus, Hired Guns and Warm Bodies: Itinerant Experts in a Knowledge Economy*, Princeton, NJ: Princeton University Press.

Kurp, P. (2008) 'Green computing', *Communications of the ACM*, **51**(10): 11–13.

Kushida, K., Murray, J. and Zysman, J. (2011) 'Diffusing the cloud: Cloud computing and implications for public policy', *Journal of Industry, Competition & Trade*, **11**(3): 209–237.

Maklan, S., Knox, S. and Peppard, J. (2011) 'Why CRM fails – and how to fix it', *Sloan Management Review*, **52**(4): 77–85.

Markus, M. L. (2004) 'Technochange management: Using IT to drive organisational change', *Journal of Information Technology*, **19**(1): 4–20.

Markus, M. L. and Benjamin, R. I. (1997) 'The magic bullet theory of IT-enabled transformation', *Sloan Management Review*, **38**(2): 55–68.

Markus, M. L. and Tanis, C. (2000) 'The enterprise system experience – from adoption to success', in R.W. Zmud (ed.) *Framing the Domains of IT Research: Glimpsing the Future through the Past*, Cincinnati, OH: Pinnaflex Educational Resources.

Markus, M. L., Axline, S., Petrie, D. and Tanis, C. (2000) 'Learning from adopters' experiences with ERP: Problems encountered and success achieved', *Journal of Information Technology*, **14**(4): 245–265.

Marston, S., Li, Z., Bandyopadhyay, S., Zhang, J. and Ghalsasi, A. (2011) 'Cloud computing – The business perspective', *Decision Support Systems*, **51**(1): 176–189.

Mata, F. J., Fuerst, W. L. and Barney, J. B. (1995) 'Information technology and sustained competitive advantage: A resource based analysis', *MIS Quarterly*, **19**(4): 487–505.

McManus, J. and Wood-Harper, T. (2002) *Information Systems Project Management: Methods, Tools and Techniques*, London: Prentice Hall.

Melville, N., Kraemer, K. and Gurbaxani, V. (2004) 'Information technology and organizational performance: An integrative model of business value', *MIS Quarterly*, **28**(4): 283–322.

Mumford, E. (2003) *Redesigning Human Systems*, Hershey, PA: Idea Group Inc.

National Audit Office (2006) *Delivering Successful IT-enabled Business Change*, London: The Stationery Office.

Nelson, R. (2005) 'Project retrospectives: evaluating project success, failure and everything in between', *MIS Quarterly Executive*, **4**(3): 361–372.

Nelson, R. (2007) 'IT project management: infamous failures, classic mistakes and best practices', *MIS Quarterly Executive*, **6**(2): 67–78.

OGC, Office of Government Commerce (2002) *Management of Risk: Guidance for Practitioners*, London: The Stationery Office.

OGC, Office of Government Commerce (2003) *Managing Successful Programmes*, London: The Stationery Office.

OGC, Office of Government Commerce (2004) *Project Initiation Guidelines*, www.ogc.gov.uk.

OGC, Office of Government Commerce (2007) *Managing Successful Programmes*, London: The Stationery Office.

OGC, Office of Government Commerce (2009) *Managing Successful Projects with PRINCE2*, London: The Stationery Office.

Partington, D., Pellegrinelli, S. and Young, M. (2005) 'Attributes of programme management competence: An interpretive study', *International Journal of Project Management*, **23**(2): 87–95.

Peppard, J. and Ward, J. M. (2005) 'Unlocking sustained business value from IT investments: Balancing problem-based and innovation-based implementations', *California Management Review*, **48**(1): 52–70.

Peters, T. and Waterman, R. (1980) *In Search of Excellence*, New York: HarperCollins.

Pettigrew, A. and Whipp, R. (1991) *Managing Change for Corporate Success*, Oxford: Blackwell.

Pollard, C. E. and Hayne, S. C. (1998) 'The changing face of information systems issues in small firms', *International Small Business Journal*, **16**(3): 70–87.

Porter, M. (1980) *Competitive Strategy: Techniques for Analysing Industries and Competitors*, New York: Free Press.

Porter, M. (1985) *Competitive Advantage: Creating and Sustaining Superior Performance*, New York: Free Press.

Pullan, P. and Murray-Webster, R. (2011) *Facilitating Risk Management*, Aldershot, UK: Gower Publishing Limited.

Rai, S. (2003) 'From India, genius on the cheap', *International Herald Tribune*, 15 December: 12.

Remenyi, D., Sherwood-Smith, M. and White, T. (1997) *Achieving Maximum Value from Information Systems*, Chichester: John Wiley & Sons, Ltd.

Renkema, T. (2000) *The IT Value Quest: How to Capture the Business Value of IT-Based Infrastructure*, Chichester: John Wiley & Sons, Ltd.

Ross, J. W. and Beath, C. M. (2002) 'Beyond the business case: New approaches to IT investment', *MIT Sloan Management Review*, **43**(2): 51–59.

Sayeed, L. and Gill, S. (2010) 'An exploratory study on organisational adjustments due to Green IT', *International Journal of Management & Enterprise Development*, **9**(3): 233–250.

Siegel, D. S. (2009) 'Green Management Matters Only If It Yields More Green: An Economic/Strategic Perspective', *Academy of Management Perspectives*, **23**(3): 5–16.

Simon, R. (1995) 'Control in an age of empowerment', *Harvard Business Review*, **73**(2): 80–88.

Stabell, C. B. and Fjeldstad, O. D. (1998) 'Configuring value for competitive advantage: On chains, shops and networks', *Strategic Management Journal*, **19**(5): 413–437.

Strathern, M. (1997) 'Improving ratings: audit in the British university system', *European Review*, **5**, 305–321.

Swanson, E. B. and Ramiller, N. C. (1997) 'The organising vision in information systems innovation', *Organisation Science*, **8**(5): 458–474.

Teece, D. J., Pisano, G. and Shuen, A. (1997) 'Dynamic capabilities and strategic management', *Strategic Management Journal*, **18**(7): 509–533.

Thorp, J. (2003) *The Information Paradox*, Whitby, Ontario: McGraw-Hill Ryerson.

Townson, S. (2011) 'The World is going mobile', *360: The Business Transformation Journal*, **2**: 7–17.

Treacy, M. and Wiersma, F. (1993) 'Customer intimacy and other value disciplines', *Harvard Business Review*, **71**(1): 84–93.

Upton, D. M. and Staats, B. R. (2008) 'Radically simple IT', *Harvard Business Review*, March: 118–124.

Ury, W. L., Brett, J. M. and Goldberg, S. B. (1993) *Getting Disputes Resolved*, San Francisco: Jossey-Bass.

Venkatraman, N., Henderson, J. C. and Oldach, S. (1993) 'Continuous strategic alignment: Exploiting information technology capabilities for competitive success', *European Management Journal*, **11**(2): 139–149.

vom Brocke, J., Petry, M. and Schmiedel, T. (2011) 'How Hilti masters transformation', *360: The Business Transformation Journal*, **1**(1): 38–47.

Walsham, G. (1993) *Interpreting Information Systems in Organisations*, Chichester: John Wiley & Sons, Ltd.

Ward, J. M. and Daniel, E. M. (2008) 'Creating solid business cases from start to finish', *Cutter Benchmark Review*, **8**(2): 5–13.

Ward, J. M. and Elvin, R. (1999) 'A new framework for managing IT-enabled business change', *Information Systems Journal*, **9**(2): 197–221.

Ward, J. M. and Griffiths, P. (1996) *Strategic Planning for Information Systems*, 2nd edition, Chichester: John Wiley & Sons, Ltd.

Ward, J. M. and Peppard, J. (2002) *Strategic Planning for Information Systems*, 3rd edition, Chichester: John Wiley & Sons, Ltd.

Ward, J. M., Daniel, E. M. and Peppard, J. (2008) 'Building better business cases for IT investments', *MIS Quarterly Executive*, **7**(1): 1–14.

Ward J., De Hertogh, S. and Viaene, S. (2007) 'Managing the benefits from IS/IT investments: an empirical investigation into current practice', *Proceedings of the 40th Hawaii International Conference on Systems Science*, Hawaii, January.

Ward, J. M., Hemingway, C. J. and Daniel, E. M. (2005) 'A framework for addressing the organisational issues of enterprise systems implementation', *Journal of Strategic Information Systems*, **14**(2): 97–119.

Weill, P. and Aral, S. (2006) 'Generating premium returns on your IT investments', *Sloan Management Review*, **47**(2): 39–48.

Williams, D. and Parr, T. (2004) *Enterprise Programme Management*, Basingstoke: Palgrave Macmillan.

Index

Printed and bound by CPI Group (UK) Ltd, Croydon, CR0 4YY

16/04/2025

14658500-0005